To:

Grandma

From:

♡ Bois

Date:

3/15/20

365 Devotions for
a Thankful Heart

ZONDERVAN

365 Devotions for a Thankful Heart

Copyright © 2018 by Zondervan

Requests for information should be addressed to:

Zondervan, *3900 Sparks Dr. SE, Grand Rapids, Michigan 49546*

ISBN 978-0-310-08964-3

Printed in China

18 19 20 21 22   TIMS   10 9 8 7 6 5 4 3 2 1

JANUARY

Awakening Gratitude

Oh come, let us worship and bow down; let us kneel before the LORD our Maker.

—Psalm 95:6

A quick step to a thankful heart is to spend a few minutes worshiping God. Open your Bible and read aloud a favorite psalm, Philippians 2, or any favorite passage. Sing a classic hymn. Thank God for evidence of His presence.

Another idea: in your journal, share your reaction to Brother Lawrence's thoughts on worship:

- "To worship God in truth is to recognize Him for being who He is, and to recognize ourselves for what we are."
- "To worship God in truth is further to admit that we are entirely contrary to Him, and that He is willing to make us like Himself if we desire it."
- "We must worship him . . . by a humble and true adoration of spirit in the depth and center of our souls."

Brother Lawrence, a seventeenth-century monk, was the author of *The Practice of the Presence of God*, in which these and other thoughts about worship are found. The book's very title seems synonymous with the psalmist's call to worship the King. And spending time in worship awakens gratitude in our hearts.

Father, You alone are worthy of worship—and I praise You for helping me know that joyful truth!

At Work Behind the Scenes

A man's heart plans his way, but the LORD directs his steps.

—Proverbs 16:9

Have you ever had to make a decision and then watched the situation turn out better than you'd hoped? Consider a couple of examples:

- The worship leader needed a substitute singer—in half an hour. He wasn't sure why Haley came to mind, but he was confident she was the one he should call. Haley had just been turned down for the lead in the school musical, and now she was the worship leader's first choice!
- The temp agency sent many possible hires to the human resources department. One of them, Brenda, had been interviewing at various businesses and sensed God telling her to accept the first offer that came. Before he interviewed people for the position, the decision maker in HR had prayed for guidance, and he was the first to offer Brenda a job. Now another believer brings God's light and grace to that company.

When we realize that the Lord has worked behind the scenes, let's be quick to thank Him. Hindsight offers many reasons to grow in gratitude!

I am grateful, Lord, for the hope-and peace-giving truth that You are at work in my life!

3

God's Rhythm

"The seventh day is the Sabbath of the LORD your God. In it you shall do no work."

—Exodus 20:10

Are you someone one who reads the instructions before you start assembling the bike or the bookcase? Paying attention to what manufacturers have to say about what they've made is a good thing.

In the command to rest from Exodus, the fourth of the Ten Commandments, we see a basic rhythm God wove into His creation: six days of work followed by a day of rest. How could we regret setting apart that one day to rest and let God reorient, redirect, recharge, and refresh us? After all, when we do so, we are living according to the Manufacturer's specifications.

Sometimes, though, a manufacturer doesn't address every situation that might arise. Many of us have learned, for instance, that turning off our computers or smartphones for a few minutes and then restarting them can override a glitch, and we're good to go!

But you and I are far more complex than any computer or smartphone. Let's be thankful that God knows how important it is for us to turn off, to slow down, to rest so He can reset us for use again in His kingdom work. God has given us the instructions; all we have to do is follow them!

Thank You, Lord, for wanting to bless me with rest. Please give me the discipline to choose Your rhythm for my life.

Whistle While You Work

I know that there is nothing better for people than to be happy and
to do good while they live. That each of them may eat and drink, and
find satisfaction in all their toil—this is the gift of God.
—Ecclesiastes 3:12–13 NIV

𝒥 f you have watched Disney's classic film *Snow White and the Seven Dwarfs*, you probably know the song "Whistle While You Work." Even if you've never heard it, the song's title is self-explanatory, and the lyrics flesh out its idea of choosing joy even while performing mundane tasks.

Snow White made it look simple, but this mind-set takes effort. It is all too easy to grumble and complain while working, whether you're sweeping up your child's Cheerios for the millionth time, sitting through a long meeting, studying for a big exam, or working long hours to finish a project. But when we gripe, we often find feelings of negativity following us for the rest of the day. If we decide to adopt a positive attitude or choose to figuratively whistle while working, we'll find life much more enjoyable.

Consider whistling through work today, in whatever form is helpful to you. Listen to your favorite song to start your day. Savor your coffee during a tough drive to the office. Remind yourself of the good that's coming from your work, whether it's a clean and peaceful home, a paycheck to feed your family, or a step closer to your degree. Don't grumble; whistle!

Father, please remind me to choose a lighthearted response to the
mundane tasks of the day.

The Author and Sustainer of Life

God, who made the world and everything in it . . . gives to all life, breath, and all things.

—Acts 17:24–25

Aren't you glad that God did not create the world and walk away, as some people believe? Deists, for instance, don't question God's existence, and they give Him total credit for creation. But they don't believe God is involved in His creation. God is, so to speak, the clockmaker who wound the clock and left the room.

What a sharp contrast to the biblical truth that God is not only the Author but the Sustainer of life. Job's "friend" Elihu acknowledged that "the breath of the Almighty gives me life" (Job 33:4). A psalmist recognized God's power over life and death: "You take away their breath, they die and return to their dust" (Psalm 104:29). And the Levites in Nehemiah's day praised God for maintaining life: "You alone are the LORD; You have made heaven, the heaven of heavens, with all their host, the earth and everything on it, the seas and all that is in them, and You preserve them all" (Nehemiah 9:6).

Let's thank God for giving us the air we need to breathe and the food we need to survive, for keeping our hearts beating and our lungs filling with air. Most of all, let's thank Him for loving His creation enough to be involved rather than walking away.

Thank You for being intensely interested in Your creation, in my life. Teach me to live with an awareness of Your faithful involvement.

Called—and Empowered

"Go, and I will . . . teach you what you shall say."

—Exodus 4:12

Any parent, anyone interviewing for a job, any teacher, any pastor, perhaps anyone on this planet can thank God that when He calls us to do something, He empowers us to do it.

Though Moses protested, "I am not eloquent . . . I am slow of speech and slow of tongue" (Exodus 4:10), in today's verse we see God specifically promising that He will help Moses and tell him what to say to Pharaoh.

God's power is available to us, but receiving it requires faith. We must open ourselves to receive His promises. God gave Moses a specific promise for a specific situation, but rather than responding in faith, Moses said to God, "O my Lord, please send by the hand of whomever else You may send" (v. 13).

God granted Moses' request and bestowed his brother, Aaron, with the ability, strength, and words to speak to Pharaoh. We miss out if, like Moses, we ask God to find someone else to do what He has called us to do. We are blessed when we, like Aaron, yield ourselves to God's plan, open ourselves to His power, and experience His using us in His kingdom work.

Thank You, Lord, for assigning certain tasks and roles to me. When I hesitate to obey, help me rally my courage to forge ahead.

Knowing, Loving, Trusting

Be still, and know that I am God.

—Psalm 46:10

Sometimes revisiting a familiar truth can help us be thankful throughout the day. In Psalm 46, for instance, God calls us to stillness for a specific reason: to know Him. What are we to know about our God? British theologian and pastor John Gill said this:

> "Know"; own and acknowledge that he is God, a sovereign Being that does whatsoever he pleases; that he is unchangeable in his nature, purposes, promises, and covenant; that he is omnipotent, able to help them and deliver them at the last extremity; that he is omniscient, knows their persons, cases, and troubles, and how and where to hide them till the storm is over; that he is the all wise God, and does all things after the counsel of his own will, and makes all things work together for good to them; and that he is faithful to his word and promise, and will not suffer them to be overpressed and bore down with troubles.

The more we know about God, the more readily we can trust Him and love Him. When we revisit the truth that stillness can help us know our God, we can be thankful for His accessibility in our silence before Him.

Lord, help me pursue greater knowledge of You so that I may love You better.

 8

A Tone of Thanksgiving

I love the LORD, because He has heard my voice and my supplications.
Because He has inclined His ear to me, therefore I will call upon
Him as long as I live.

—Psalm 116:1–2

Take another look at these two verses from Psalm 116. Though not one key word about gratitude—*thanks, thankfulness, grateful*—appears here, the tone of thanksgiving is unmistakable.

The proclamation "I love" implies gratitude and communicates joy. The writer celebrates the reason for this love: "Because He has heard my voice and my supplications." The vow to "call upon Him as long as I live" also reflects this speaker's thankfulness for the way God hears and answers.

Even without the word *thanks*, these verses communicate gratitude. Do our lives do the same? Put differently, what do the ways we carry ourselves, speak, and communicate using facial expressions and body language suggest about our attitude toward life? Is it clear we're grateful people?

Consider what retooling your attitude might need. Of course the "tone" of our lives alone cannot sufficiently express our gratitude to God or to the people in our world. But when our actions indicate a thankful heart, the words we speak ring truer. Let's express our thanks to God in every way we can.

Lord, show me how I can make a tone of thanksgiving unmistakable
in my life.

Our Infinite God

Oh, the depth of the riches both of the wisdom and knowledge of God! How unsearchable are His judgments and His ways past finding out!

—Romans 11:33

The saying "The bigger, the better" is not always true. We don't necessarily need a larger house, and a more robust dinner may not be healthy. A longer to-do list? No, thank you! An increased mortgage? That's going the wrong direction. But a big God—a God far greater than the very limited version we tend to carry around in our heads and hearts—would indeed be better.

We can thank our all-encompassing God, for instance, that His wisdom far surpasses ours. We can be grateful that His ways aren't our ways, that His thoughts aren't our thoughts, that His judgments are righteous beyond our understanding, and even that His decisions can be puzzling and His timing perplexing.

If we human beings—with our limited brainpower—could fully understand the whys and hows of God's ways, thoughts, judgments, decisions, and timing, our God would be pretty limited. Isn't that an unsettling thought? Aren't you glad to know you will never (this side of heaven) completely grasp your infinite God in all His glory, power, wisdom, and truth?

Bigger isn't always better—unless it's the God of heaven we're talking about!

Thank You, Lord, for being beyond what my reason can fathom.

New Life

Anyone who belongs to Christ is a new person. The past is forgotten, and everything is new.

—2 Corinthians 5:17 CEV

Each season has its own unique sort of beauty. Spring offers warmer days and bright, blooming flowers. Summer is lush with green and alive with birds and animals. Fall shines with its rich colors of gold and red and russet. And winter . . . yes, it has its beauty with glimmering snowfalls and crystal-clear days. Yet so much of winter seems cold and even lifeless. Trees bared of their leaves stretch bony fingers up to the sky, seeking the rare rays of the winter sun's warmth.

But as you gaze out your window, consider those trees from another perspective: those trees with their bare branches are actually a beautiful promise from God. They remind us that winter doesn't last forever, that spring is not only coming but is, in fact, actively on its way. Deep inside the hearts of those winter trees, new life is stirring, and before too long it will bloom forth.

There are days when you may feel a bit like those cold trees of winter. When you do, reach up to God, who is never stingy with the warmth of His love. Let Him stir new life within you during this winter season, and watch Him make you bloom in beauty.

Lord, when the days are cold, thank You for the warmth of Your love and the new life in Christ You have given to me.

Living for the Eternal

I also count all things loss for the excellence of the knowledge of Christ Jesus my Lord.

—Philippians 3:8

The world offers much that we can enjoy, much that makes us feel valuable, and much that offers status according to the society's value system. Let's be thankful for the option of freeing ourselves from this temporal mind-set.

The apostle Paul wrote that he was "circumcised the eighth day, of the stock of Israel, of the tribe of Benjamin, a Hebrew of the Hebrews; concerning the law, a Pharisee; concerning zeal, persecuting the church; concerning the righteousness which is in the law, blameless" (Philippians 3:5–6). Paul had worked hard to be considered righteous according to Mosaic law, and he had indeed gained a place of honor among fellow Jews. Yet as Philippians 3:8 attests, he no longer valued those things the world around him valued.

Encouraged by Paul's example, what can you let go of in order to more fully be God's person? Are you still looking for status from worldly endeavors? Set your mind on eternal things, release yourself from the world's pressure to conform, and find your freedom in Christ. Then, like Paul, be thankful you have counted "all things loss."

Lord, thank You for this reminder, this wake-up call. Help me live for the eternal. Help me live for You.

Where Is Your Focus?

Surely you have granted him unending blessings and made him glad with the joy of your presence.

—Psalm 21:6 NIV

Your car won't start. The weather forecast calls for sleet on your wedding day. Your spouse lost his job. You overslept, beginning your day with frenzy. You can think of many other difficult circumstances, right? What is your reaction when everything seems to be going wrong?

Almost everyone focuses on the problem: the old car, the less-than-ideal wedding weather, financial stress, time constraints. Another reaction is harder to pull off but pays more in dividends: focus on what you *do* have. You have friends who will drive you to work or a good public transportation system. You're marrying the love of your life—regardless of rain or shine. Your spouse is healthy, and he can look for more work. Your day doesn't need to be dictated by its beginning; it can still have a good ending. Do you see how focusing on what you have, rather than what you lack, can change your perspective?

When things aren't going your way, or when you feel overwhelmed by life's hardships, look at the blessings all around you. When everything seems to be going wrong, recognize the many, many things that are going right.

Father, so much of my life is good and whole and wonderful. Thank You for all of it.

Strength for a Failing Heart

My flesh and my heart fail; but God is the strength of my heart and my portion forever.

—Psalm 73:26

The Bible doesn't hide the pain of life on earth. In these verses the speaker's despair is obvious. Whenever our flesh and our hearts fail, when darkness falls and storms rage in our lives—those times when we realize, *Where else can I turn but to God?*—we may find the writer of Psalm 73, Asaph, to be a welcome companion.

Asaph knew he would find no real relief from his suffering in this world. He might not even have found someone who understood or a compassionate friend to sit with him in his pain. But despite his exhaustion Asaph could say, "God is the strength of my heart and my portion forever." Look at what he went on to say: "It is good for me to draw near to God; I have put my trust in the Lord GOD, that I may declare all Your works" (v. 28).

We can thank God for Asaph's example, and that God's Word recognizes the strain of life on earth. When our hearts break, we do well to move closer to God and "put [our] trust in the Lord," just as this fellow believer did.

Thank You, my trustworthy God, for always being there, offering me strength and comfort whenever I draw near.

The Lifter of Your Head

You, O LORD, are a shield for me, my glory and the One who lifts up my head.

—Psalm 3:3

You've probably heard the expression "Keep your chin up!" Someone in your life may have spoken these words to you in a time of trouble or discouragement. One of the earliest uses of this phrase appears to have been in the Warren, Pennsylvania, newspaper called the *Evening Democrat*. In October 1900, the following wisdom was offered under the title "Epigrams Upon the Health-giving Qualities of Mirth": "Keep your chin up. Don't take your troubles to bed with you. Hang them on a chair with your trousers or drop them in a glass of water with your teeth."

As simple as this advice sounds, being optimistic in a difficult situation is a tough assignment. Just ask King David, who wrote Psalm 3. For him the idea of keeping his chin up was heartbreakingly difficult. At the time he wrote these words, he was fleeing from his son Absalom, who desperately wanted David dead so he could sit on the throne. "Keep your chin up" would have sounded trite to David, although it was true that looking up to God was the best course of action. And God helped lift David's head above his fears and doubts.

Remember that you can keep your chin up. Our gracious God is "the One who lifts up [our heads]."

I am grateful, Lord God, that You are indeed the lifter of my head when I need hope.

Settling for Mud Pies

Now to Him who is able to do exceedingly abundantly above all that we ask or think, according to the power that works in us, to Him be glory in the church by Christ Jesus.

—Ephesians 3:20–21

Sometimes our thankfulness fades when we look at what other people have. Have you ever felt envious, maybe even short-changed? At those times we can be grateful that God has so much more for us than even what our neighbor may be enjoying.

In *The Weight of Glory*, C. S. Lewis wrote: "We are half-hearted creatures, fooling about with drink and sex and ambition when infinite joy is offered us, like an ignorant child who wants to go on making mud pies in a slum because he cannot imagine what is meant by the offer of a holiday at the sea."

When we struggle to give thanks, maybe we are trying to muster up gratitude for mud pies when He gives us the opportunity to thank Him for vacations at the beach.

Yes, we can thank God for many concrete blessings and for the various ways He clearly provides, protects, and answers prayers. But how often do we offer thanks because He gives us patience, helps us see people with His eyes of compassion, or grants us hope though circumstances are difficult?

May God open our eyes to all He grants to those He loves.

I am grateful, Lord, for the blessings You bestow. Your gifts are always the best.

Begin Again

The LORD is the one who goes ahead of you; He will be with you. He will not fail you or forsake you.

—Deuteronomy 31:8 NASB

At the beginning of each year, many people resolve to make life changes. After the clock strikes midnight, New Year's resolutions are under way. These resolutions take many forms: exercise more, eat less ice cream, run a marathon, prioritize rest, get out of debt, cross something off the bucket list, spend more time with family.

At first you're focused, excited, and determined. But then someone brings donuts to the meeting, work demands more of your time, extra money goes toward a new roof—and what was once a seemingly achievable goal becomes more of a fantasy. After a couple of weeks, your enthusiasm begins to fizzle, and by February you decide to try again next year.

Isn't it wonderful to know that God never gives up on us? Even when we slip and stumble and make mistakes, and even if we wonder if we'll ever change, He cheers us on. He gives us a new beginning any time we need it. In His eyes, every moment is January 1st! Remember that when you rise in the morning: there's a fresh start with each day.

God, thank You for every time You offer me a January 1. I may need one today!

Protection 24/7

The LORD is my rock and my fortress and my deliverer; the God of my strength, in whom I will trust.

—2 Samuel 22:2–3

The surf was high but intermittent, and the occasionally crashing waves kept few people out of the water. In fact one of those beachgoers was thanking God for providing the beautiful day and inviting surf.

The wave that landed Ellen on her head was about six feet high as it broke. She got herself out of the water and joined her friends. Ellen mentioned that her back was sore. Fortunately one of her cohorts was an experienced EMT.

Because of the seriousness of back injuries, the friend insisted on calling an ambulance. Although she assured everyone, "I'll be okay," Ellen was transported—lights and sirens—to the local emergency room.

There the young woman learned that when she landed on her head, an injury had occurred in the upper part of her spinal column. Any such injury puts the spinal cord at risk. "It's a good thing you came in today," the ER doctor said. "With the wrong movement, you could have been paralyzed if you'd waited."

Thank God: when we hesitate to check out sudden pains caused by harsh waters, He is available to save us from life-altering injury to our bodies or souls.

Thank You, Lord, for protecting us from the near misses we are aware of as well as those we aren't.

Not Yours to Carry

Cast all your anxiety on him because he cares for you.

—1 Peter 5:7 NIV

Our human nature makes us urgently want to control our lives and prompts us to worry about things beyond our control. Some of us worry more than others, but the tendency is widespread enough that God speaks to it: "Cast all your anxiety on [Me]." How do you picture the act of casting?

The apostle Peter was not talking about the graceful, gentle motion of a fly fisherman casting his line. Peter was talking about a more forceful act. Consider this story of a young woman camping in the desert. The day of dirt-biking with her friends had been fun but exhausting. Kate was preparing for the most relaxing time of the day: s'mores and talking by the campfire. The kindling had ignited the teepee of wood pieces. It was time to add a log to the fire. Keeping her eye on the young flames, Kate reached to the pile of wood, picked up a piece, glanced at it to confirm its size—then flung it as far away as she could. A furry, eight-legged little body startled her, and Kate knew instantly she wanted the tarantula nowhere near her.

That is the kind of casting Peter was talking about in today's verse. Rather than trying to take control, we are to throw—with force and intentionality—the burden of anxiety to Him who cares for us. Thanks be to God!

I am grateful for Your willingness, almighty God, to take away all the worry that weighs me down.

19

God's Hidden Hand

Who knows whether you have come to the kingdom for such a time as this?

—Esther 4:14

When has exactly the right person been exactly where you needed her at exactly the perfect time? The Old Testament offers a powerful example.

Beautiful Esther had been welcomed into the king's palace and made queen. As her uncle Mordecai's words reveal, he believed Esther was in power at this particular time because her own people, the Jews, faced genocide. When Mordecai told Esther about the scheduled slaughter of the Jews—and reminded her that she would not be exempt—he asked her to approach the king to "plead before him for her people" (Esther 4:8). Approaching the king when he hadn't called for her could cost Esther her life, yet with the support of her people, Esther did what Mordecai asked.

The story involves drama and suspense, feasts, sabotage, a sleepless king, God's Word, a gallows, and finally mercy and justice. God's choreography is very clear even though the book never refers to God Himself, and through Esther God saves the Jews.

God is always at work caring for us, always sending the right person when you need her.

Faithful God, I am grateful for Your mastery over the events of my life, for the ways You align everything for Your glory.

Called by Name

"Fear not, for I have redeemed you; I have called you by your name; you are Mine."

—Isaiah 43:1

How often during a typical day do you hear your name? Maybe you hear *Mom* or *Mrs. _____*. Maybe you hear *Sweetie* or *Honey*. But how often does someone actually say your name? Sometimes when we're fearful—or we're lost, lonely, empty, heartbroken, or uncertain about the future—hearing our names reminds us that someone is thinking about us and cares.

In Isaiah 43:1 we read that God Himself calls each of us by name. That personal connection is rich enough, but He also states, "You are Mine." Those three simple words—that immeasurably profound truth—offer a lifelong reason to give thanks to our gracious God.

Sometimes He sends someone to come alongside, to remind us that we are not invisible or forgotten, and to say our name. We can thank God for sending this person to remind us that He sees us, that He also calls us by name, and that He claims us as His.

Thank You, Lord, for making me Yours, for calling me by name to be part of Your forever family.

All Too Human

He raised up for them David as king, to whom also He gave testimony and said, "I have found David the son of Jesse, a man after My own heart, who will do all My will."

—Acts 13:22

We want all our brothers and sisters in Christ to live according to God's way. So when we see people of God stumble and fall, we feel grieved. Yet we can humbly thank God for warning us through the examples of His chosen ones who stray.

In the story of David, we see that "a man after [God's] own heart" can make grievously sinful decisions. A person serving God can wander from the narrow path of righteousness. And even a person responsible for leading fellow believers can make a decision guided by the flesh, not the Spirit.

King David, though a man once deeply committed to his God, is a tragic example of how this happens. The seemingly insignificant choice to stay home rather than go out to battle started David down a path that resulted in adultery, lies, and murder (2 Samuel 11). God knew David would make sinful choices just as He knows we will. Yet God still chose David to rule on the throne of Israel, and God still chooses us to one day reign with Him (2 Timothy 2:12).

Whenever we stray, we are rightfully humbled and grateful that, like David, we can return to God's path.

I am grateful that You use David's example to teach me to—in Your strength—do what I know is right.

Faithful God, Faithless Us

The LORD your God, He is God, the faithful God who keeps
covenant and mercy for a thousand generations with those who love
Him and keep His commandments.

—Deuteronomy 7:9

We human beings are such a mixed bag! We can be thankful that God doesn't give up on us. Think about Abram. God said, "Go from your country . . . to the land I will show you" (Genesis 12:1 NIV)—and Abram did! God gave him no itinerary, map, GPS, or cell phone, and He hadn't made any hotel reservations. God said, "Go!" and Abram went. What faith!

But Abram hadn't gone far before he made a poor choice. In Genesis 12—the same chapter that tells of Abram's obedience—he lied to Pharaoh's officials, saying that his wife, Sarai, was his sister. Later Abram lied again in a similar situation, and King Abimelech called him on it: "You have done deeds to me that ought not to be done" (Genesis 20:9). Both times Abram protected his own neck. He didn't want a foreign king killing him in order to make Sarai first a widow and then a bride. Apparently doubting God's ability or willingness to protect his life, Abram lied about Sarai twice.

We see in Abram and in ourselves a crazy combination of faithful and fickle, trusting and doubting, obedient and rebellious. Thank God He always stays faithful to us!

Thank You, Lord, that Your faithfulness to me is not dependent on
my faithfulness to You. Please grow my faithfulness!

Seeing Past Our Stumbling

"You are Peter, and on this rock I will build My church."

—Matthew 16:18

A ren't you glad God cares more about the big picture than He does the snapshots of our daily stumblings?

Consider what picture of Peter these snapshots give:

- "Peter . . . walked on the water to go to Jesus. But when he saw that the wind was boisterous, he was afraid; and beginning to sink he cried out, saying, 'Lord, save me!'" (Matthew 14:29–30).
- "Simon Peter, having a sword, drew it and struck the high priest's servant, and cut off his right ear" (John 18:10).
- "Peter said, 'Man, I do not know what you are saying!' Immediately, while he was still speaking, the rooster crowed" (Luke 22:60).

Fast-forward about six weeks and hear the once-timid denier speak to an audience of Jews: "Repent, and let every one of you be baptized in the name of Jesus Christ for the remission of sins; and you shall receive the gift of the Holy Spirit" (Acts 2:38).

We can be grateful that God keeps in mind the big picture, not just snapshots of moments in our lives, and uses us—despite our faltering faith—in His kingdom work just as He used Peter.

Thank You, Lord, for seeing beyond my slipups. Use me as You will.

Blessed Belief

My Lord and my God!

—John 20:28

Have you ever had a nickname you just couldn't shake? That was certainly the case for a certain apostle, better known—poor guy—as Doubting Thomas. We can thank God for the example of Thomas because of the special words Jesus spoke to him.

Since people two thousand years ago, like people today, tended to die and stay dead, Thomas was more than a little skeptical when his fellow disciples excitedly told him they had seen the resurrected Lord. Thomas was willing to believe only on the conditions he outlined: he wanted to see and touch the physical body of his Teacher and Friend. Eight days later Jesus obliged.

In his account, the apostle John was careful to mention that "Jesus came, *the doors being shut*, and stood in the midst" (John 20:26, emphasis added). We don't read that Thomas actually placed his hand into Jesus' pierced side or the nail prints on His hands, only that Jesus invited him to. And we read Thomas's words of awe and worship: "My Lord and my God!" That's when Jesus spoke words to Thomas that are for us today: "Thomas, because you have seen Me, you have believed. Blessed are those who have not seen and yet have believed" (v. 29).

Whatever nicknames you've picked up through your life, Jesus calls you *blessed*. Give thanks for that fact today.

Thank You for giving me the faith and will to believe even though I have not seen You.

The Grace of Forgiveness

In Him we have redemption through His blood, the forgiveness of sins, according to the riches of His grace.

—Ephesians 1:7

How many of us, overcome with emotion, find our tongues out of control? Aren't you grateful that God forgives us when we misspeak? Against the backdrop of Job's horrific losses and pain, we see well-intentioned words misapplied and the damage they do.

Job heard many untruths spoken by his three friends as they tried to explain Job's unparalleled suffering. God Himself addressed those who made harmful and inaccurate statements: "My wrath is aroused against you . . . for you have not spoken of Me what is right" (Job 42:7). He instructed the friends to make an offering, "and My servant Job shall pray for you. For I will accept him, lest I deal with you according to your folly" (v. 8).

Job's friends began the story with accusations of his wrong-doing; they ended in repentance for their wrongdoing. When we also lose control of what we're saying, let's thank God for loving us with unlimited forgiveness.

Thank You, Lord, for Your grace, for loving me despite words I shouldn't say and attitudes I shouldn't harbor.

Check Motives

Righteousness guards the person of integrity.

—Proverbs 13:16 NIV

Have you ever seen a conversation take on a life of its own? In the garden of Eden, we see a conversation end up exactly where the enemy wanted—and not at all where Eve expected.

Satan baited the hook at the very start: "Has God indeed said . . . ?" (Genesis 3:1). That word *indeed* invited her to question if not her memory, then God Himself. Eve bit that baited hook: she responded with an exaggeration of God's command ("nor shall you touch it") and a mention of the consequence: "lest you die" (v. 3).

The serpent reassured her, "You will not surely die" and by implication suggested that an insecure God didn't want competition with Adam and Eve and their forbidden knowledge. With "You will be like God" ringing in her ears, Eve "took of its fruit and ate" and, in a sense, died (vv. 4–6). That death was separation from God, an end to the unblemished relationship with the Creator she and Adam had enjoyed.

When a conversation wanders into unexpected territory, we need to check motives. Does someone have an agenda? Why? And does your response reveal your trust in God? Let's thank God for revealing the enemy's subtly deceitful ways and the high cost of not recognizing his strategy.

Lord God, please give me awareness and discernment that I may recognize the enemy's wiles and avoid sin.

God in the Ups and Downs

Suddenly an angel touched him, and said to him, "Arise and eat."

—1 Kings 19:5

"What goes up must come down" may be just as true in the emotional/spiritual world as it is in the physical. But we can thank God that He is with us as He was with Elijah.

Elijah had just enjoyed a colossal "up": he witnessed God's spectacular victory over Baal. The prophet had challenged the 450 prophets of Baal to a showdown: Whose deity would set a sacrifice on fire? Baal failed to appear, but God showed up in a big way. In the evening, "the fire of the LORD fell and consumed the burnt sacrifice, and the wood and the stones and the dust, and it licked up the water that was in the trench" (1 Kings 18:38). The priests of Baal were executed—then came Elijah's "down": wicked Queen Jezebel wanted the prophet dead.

Elijah fled. In the wilderness, he succumbed to exhaustion and discouragement. He asked God to let him die. But God sent an angel to provide food and water, and Elijah rested.

Often after an enormous spiritual "high," we experience a startling "low." Since God is present in both the ups and downs, we can call out to Him for aid. God may not send an angel, but we can be thankful for the example here: eat, drink, rest, repeat.

Thank You, Lord, for reminding me that the down times are just the other side of the ups, and You'll see me through both.

Being Like Mary *and* Martha

Mary . . . sat at Jesus' feet and heard His word.

—Luke 10:39

Whether or not the dinner guests had been expected, the meal still had to be prepared. Martha was on it! But as she did the meal prep, she grew increasingly frustrated with her sister, Mary, who was no help at all. When Martha asked Jesus to tell Mary to help her, Jesus spoke truth in love: "You are worried and troubled about many things. But one thing is needed, and Mary has chosen that good part" (Luke 10:41–42).

Jesus undoubtedly appreciated Martha's efforts, but He didn't want her to miss the "one thing" that mattered most: learning from Him. Pastor and commentator Matthew Henry (1662–1714) said that perhaps the "much serving" suggests elaborate efforts when a simpler preparation would have sufficed—and would have allowed Martha also to sit at Jesus' feet.

Mary had chosen to be with Christ. Henry wrote, "She chose the better business, and the better happiness, and took a better way of *honouring* Christ and of *pleasing* him, by receiving his word into her heart, than Martha did by providing for his entertainment in her house." After all, Jesus would prefer a "zealous disciple" to a "fine housekeeper"!

Let's not let meal preparation—or anything else—keep us from choosing "the good part," which is time with the Lord.

Lord, thank You for helping me balance the good of Martha (meeting real-life demands) with the good of Mary (being with You).

The Greatness of God

Lord, our Lord, how majestic is your name in all the earth!
—Psalm 8:9 NIV

We see in the world around us the creativity, the majesty, and the greatness of God. Despite this evidence throughout the past and continuing to today, many live for themselves rather than for God and—not surprisingly—lack an attitude of thanksgiving. That truly is the sin nature of human beings: until our rebirth as followers of Jesus, we do not glorify God as God or thank Him for His many gifts. Pastor and writer John Piper explained why: "It detracts from our own glory, and all people by nature love their own glory more than the glory of God."

Even after we name Jesus our Lord, we can still struggle to be completely free of that self-regard. John Piper continued: "At the root of all ingratitude is the love of one's own greatness. For genuine gratitude admits that we are beneficiaries of an unearned bequest. We are cripples leaning on the cross-shaped crutch of Jesus Christ. We are paralytics living minute by minute in the iron lung of God's mercy."

So, by extension, the root of gratitude is the love of God's immeasurable greatness and the acceptance of "the cross-shaped crutch of Jesus Christ." May we remember to live for God, not ourselves, and love His holiness rather than our "greatness."

My gratitude for Your mercy is beyond measure and description.
Thank You, my good and great Lord.

He's a Good Father

*See how very much our Father loves us, for he calls us his children,
and that is what we are!*

—1 John 3:1 NLT

𝑰f you asked one hundred people what the word *father* means to
them personally, you'd likely receive a vast array of answers.
For some, it conjures feelings of being protected, loved, and
deeply cared for. Others feel pain, sadness, or other difficult
emotions. Think about it for a minute: What thoughts or feelings come to mind when you hear the word *father*?

Whether or not you grew up with a positive father experience, here is an encouraging truth for you: the Lord loves you
the way a *good father* loves his children. What is a skilled father
like? He is patient, kind, and tender. He is generous, keeps his
promises, listens, and delights in you. He does not fail you.

If you have any negative association with your earthly father,
talk with a trusted friend or counselor, and hold the truth of
God as your Father in your heart. Ponder its meaning. Take a
few minutes to think of all the attributes a good father has, then
give thanks, because God is even better than that. What a reason
to rejoice.

*My Father, make me aware of all the ways You parent me lovingly.
Thank You for being faithful where others have failed.*

Temporary Success

Whom have I in heaven but You? And there is none upon earth that I desire besides You.

—Psalm 73:25

Jesus made no secret of the fact that following Him would come with a cost. You may recall His saying, "In the world you will have tribulation" (John 16:33). Have you ever felt that by following Jesus you missed out on something?

Maybe you worked really hard for exemplary sales numbers this year, but a colleague cut corners in his work and received the big promotion. Or you chose to give generously to sponsor a missionary, then saw your sister's newly remodeled kitchen, and you felt envious. This happens all the time, in big and small ways, and Asaph, the psalmist who wrote Psalm 73, admitted it is difficult: "For I was envious of the boastful, when I saw the prosperity of the wicked" (v. 3). He observed that they seemed "always at ease" (v. 12) and grew their wealth.

Take heart! Asaph realized his perspective was skewed. He was lamenting things that are certainly impactful in this life, but they are also temporary. He saw that honoring God and His commands brought a satisfaction that nothing else—more money, more success—could ever create! You're not missing any good thing (Psalm 84:11).

Lord, inspire me with confidence in Your plan and provision. Thank You!

FEBRUARY

What Am I Worshiping?

"Where your treasure is, there your heart will be also."

—Matthew 6:21

aybe you've heard it rightly said that every human being worships something. Sometimes our choice is deliberate and even well researched: we decide to follow a certain religious or political leader. Sometimes our choice is more obsessive, and we find ourselves dedicating time, energy, and finances to one thing at the expense of everything else. And sometimes we try to divide our attention by worshiping God and some other thing, person, idea, or goal. God and money is a popular combination that Jesus spoke about.

Jesus has always known that a person "cannot serve both God and money" (Matthew 6:24 NIV). As C. S. Lewis put it, "Prosperity knits a man to the World. He feels that he is 'finding his place in it,' while really it is finding its place in him."

Think about the way prosperity may be knitting you to the world. Then prayerfully consider: What place in your heart and life does prosperity have? If everyone worships something, make sure yours is something eternal.

Thank You, Lord Jesus, for revealing truths I may avoid about myself and reminding me that You will help me change.

People and Porcupines

*Breaking bread from house to house, they ate their food with
gladness and simplicity of heart, praising God.*

—Acts 2:46–47

amilies can be wonderful and joy filled, a blessing from
God for which we praise and thank Him. Yet, as someone
has observed, families can also be like porcupines in a snowfall:
we need each other to stay warm, but we poke each other when
we get close.

And that poking is just evidence of the ways we are separate individuals. We don't always make the same decisions. We
have different tastes. We can become cranky and critical. We
can groan that we're doing all the work. We forget that we are in
our families because our sovereign God ordained it.

Yes, our sovereign God placed us in the families He did for
our good, for His glory, and for purposes we may not always see
or understand. Trusting in God's goodness, let's ask Him to
give us tolerance and love for our family members. Let's do our
part to make family a wonderful and joy-filled thing.

*Teach me, Lord, to live out my gratitude for my life by loving the
people—and the porcupines—in my family.*

The Maker of All Things

"I am the LORD, the Maker of all things, who stretches out the heavens, who spreads out the earth by myself."

—Isaiah 44:24 NIV

Imagine you are meeting with a surgeon about a major heart surgery. He is the top cardiologist in the world. But when you ask questions about his experience, he answers hesitantly and downplays his education and expertise. Although you know he is renowned, you don't feel confident about him. You wonder, *Is he all others claim him to be? Does he believe in himself?*

Imagine a different surgeon. She is the top cardiologist in the world. When you question her, she answers quickly and with authority. She doesn't take an "Aw, shucks" approach to her expertise; she is completely certain about her skills as a surgeon, and she communicates that.

When God states who He is, He does so with authority. He is God, the Maker of all things. He is the One for us to worship; he is the One to believe. What a comfort to know our God is all He says He is—and we can trust Him without hesitation. Thank Him for being a trustworthy and all-powerful God, as the psalmist did: "I will praise the LORD at all times. I will constantly speak his praises. . . . Taste and see that the LORD is good. Oh, the joys of those who take refuge in him!" (Psalm 34:1, 8 NLT).

Father, I am grateful for Your Word. Grow my confidence in You as I remember how awesome You are.

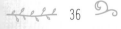

Pause for a Moment

"In the same way, let your light shine before others, that they may see your good deeds and glorify your Father in heaven."
—Matthew 5:16 NIV

When was the last time you complained about something? Maybe it was five seconds ago, and you grumbled about your temperamental coffeemaker. Or yesterday when you vented to a colleague about your boss. It could have been an annoyed comment made about traffic, the fact that your toddler wouldn't eat the dinner you prepared, or your frustration with a parent. After you complained, did you feel happier? Did it bring a smile to your face?

Complaining is so easy to do. In the moment it feels cathartic! But it sure doesn't bring about anything good, does it? Instead, your colleague may agree with your complaints and add his frustration to the mix, leaving you more upset than before. Your exasperation with your toddler might propel her to throw her dinner on the floor.

Do you ever brace yourself when you see a friend, knowing a long list of complaints is headed your way? You don't want to be that type of person. The next time a complaint begins tumbling out of your mouth, pause. Are those words going to bring joy or tension? Will you feel good later about what you say now? The fact is, a grateful heart is uplifting to everyone.

Lord, help me spread my delight in Your goodness, not my complaints.

Hannah's Request

Hannah prayed and said: "My heart rejoices in the LORD . . . I rejoice in Your salvation."

—1 Samuel 2:1

When have you *really* wanted something? We all know what it feels like to long for something desperately, for something, such as a life-giving job, a significant other, a repaired relationship, a sense of purpose, or a friend to connect with.

In the Bible Hannah desired something with every fiber of her being—a child—and this yearning caused her deep pain. The Bible says Hannah finally went to the temple to seek the Lord's help. There she "prayed . . . and wept in anguish" (1 Samuel 1:10).

You may know how the story goes. When Eli the priest saw her pray, he accused her of being drunk. Hannah explained she was full of sorrow, not wine: "[I] have poured out my soul before the LORD. . . . Out of the abundance of my complaint and grief I have spoken" (vv. 15–16). Taken aback, Eli then blessed Hannah and asked the Lord to grant her request. Eventually Hannah got her happy ending: a son, then five more children.

When you deeply long for something and pour out your heart to God, do you finish with gratitude, knowing He hears you? Or do you wait to respond until you receive? Be thankful, for the God of all creation hears your prayers, just as He heard Hannah's.

Father, I rejoice in Your gifts even as I wait for them. Thank You for all You send my way.

The Lord Was Near David

My mouth offers praises with joyful lips.

—Psalm 63:5 NASB

The Bible tells us David was often in danger, especially while King Saul was intent on taking his life. In fact, Psalm 63 is titled "A Psalm of David when he was in the wilderness of Judah." How frightening, to spend years of your life hiding from someone so powerful—someone who searched for you every single day (1 Samuel 23:14). If you were in David's shoes, what would you pray about?

David spent most of Psalm 63 praising God. Note that he focused not on fear or anxiety but on thankfulness for the Lord's nearness. Even as he was in hiding for his life, David prayed, "Because Your lovingkindness is better than life, my lips shall praise You" (v. 3).

Isn't it amazing he didn't show fear or resentment, even though he must have been miserable? Scripture says David felt hunted like a "partridge in the mountains" (1 Samuel 26:20). He must have felt lonely and terrified in the wilderness. Yet David said, "Because You have been my help, therefore in the shadow of Your wings I will rejoice" (v. 7). Despite the danger, David's gratitude and love for the Lord drowned out any fear.

Lord, help me, like David, to feel Your nearness when I fear people and events. Thank You for being closer than I can even understand.

Spring Cleaning

Cleanse me from secret faults.

—Psalm 19:12

Carrie confirmed details with the moving company first thing in the morning. Yes, she thought, she was excited about the new home, but she wasn't naïve. Getting everything from one house to the other would be a lot of work—and of course the move was scheduled during the heat of summer.

Those issues aside, Carrie was also truly glad for the excuse to clean out closets, sift through drawers, and give away things she didn't use! And then there was the fresh start of clean paint, a new address, and a different drive to work and family.

Then Carrie's thoughts changed course. As she reflected on that morning's Bible reading in Psalm 19, the idea came to her that cleaning out the closet of her heart and sifting through the drawers that held her thoughts would be a worthwhile activity also. Not easy, but good. Like the move to the new house.

"Lord," she found herself praying, "please show me my hidden faults. I am so comfortable with some bad habits that I don't even notice them. Please forgive me and lead me in Your way."

Just as in a physical move you keep only beneficial possessions, during a spiritual inventory you can do the same with behaviors and thoughts.

Thank You, merciful and gracious God, for always leading me in the everlasting way of holiness.

Teacher, Victor, Savior

In Christ all shall be made alive.

—1 Corinthians 15:22

We can be very thankful for Jesus' teachings—for what He taught about God's kingdom and how He showed us God's love with His very life. But we can be exponentially more thankful that Jesus was not merely an effective Teacher: He is Victor over sin and death; He is our Savior.

The apostle Paul acknowledged that Jesus' resurrection is key to our faith: "If Christ is not risen, then our preaching is empty and your faith is also empty" (1 Corinthians 15:14). New York City pastor Tim Keller described it this way in his book *The Reason for God*: "If Jesus rose from the dead, then you have to accept all that he said; if he didn't rise from the dead, then why worry about any of what he said? The issue on which everything hangs is not whether or not you like his teaching but whether or not he rose from the dead."

In our postmodern day of moral relativity and discussions about whether truth even exists, aren't you grateful that for you, Jesus' teachings are clear? Because you believe in Jesus as not just Teacher but risen Savior, you have received life abundant and life eternal!

Father, thank You for the saving knowledge of Jesus my Savior. I'll always be praising You for this gift.

Examples of Faith

Faith is the substance of things hoped for, the evidence of things not seen.
—Hebrews 11:1

aith is a hard thing to define. We can be grateful for the examples we have in Hebrews 11 and elsewhere, for the pictures they paint of faithfulness are indeed worth thousands of words.

- Noah built a massive boat to house pairs of all the animals and birds on the earth.
- Commanded to lead God's people out of Egypt, Moses and Aaron confronted the most powerful man in the land, Pharaoh, and demanded their release.
- Facing 450 enemy prophets, Elijah set up a sacrifice and drenched it with water three times before inviting God to set it afire.
- Daniel risked death in the den of hungry lions.

Circumstances varied, and the faith of these human beings probably wavered at least a little along the way. But God's working in the situations they faced was not dependent on their faith—and that is true for us today. It is God's power that saves us.

While faith may be hard to define, we know it when we see it. Can others see it in you?

Thank You for Your example of faithfulness, Lord Jesus. Help me be as faithful.

His Precious Gift

"I have prayed for you, that your faith should not fail."

—Luke 22:32

Who prays for you? Who lifts your name before God and entreats Him to bless, shield, and guide you? A parent, a grandparent, a dear friend? A church, a preacher, or a teacher perhaps? When someone takes the time to pray for you, to lay his or her love and concern for you before the throne of God—how precious is that gift?

And how much more precious when the someone is the very Son of God Himself! Yes, Jesus prays for you.

Before He went to the cross, Jesus prayed for His followers: "Father, I want those you have given me to be with me where I am, and to see my glory, the glory you have given me because you loved me before the creation of the world" (John 17:24 NIV). He didn't want a single soul to be snatched out of His hand. He wants you to be with Him.

But the prayers of Christ didn't stop at the cross. Even in heaven, even this day, He continues to speak to God on your behalf: "Christ Jesus died for us and was raised to life for us, and he is sitting in the place of honor at God's right hand, pleading for [you]" (Romans 8:34 NLT). Jesus lays His love and concern for you before the throne of His holy and heavenly Father. How precious is that gift?

How humbling, how wonderful to know that You, Lord, pray for me!

Please and Thank You

The one who offers thanksgiving as his sacrifice glorifies me; to one who orders his way rightly I will show the salvation of God!

—Psalm 50:23 ESV

When praying, are you better at saying "Please" or "Thank You"? Ponder that question for a few moments. Do you find yourself praying, "God, please _____" or do you start your prayers with praise?

In my experience, it's easier to ask God for something than to give thanks. Maybe it's because the "please" seems more urgent than the "thank You." You might ask Him for a clear cancer scan, relief from anxiety, provision for financial needs, help with a whiny toddler, or strength to get through a demanding day. He wants to hear our requests! But let's praise as we petition. Make it a point to have thanksgiving on your lips as often as you raise requests to God. Not only is gratitude glorifying to God, it also reminds you of His faithfulness in the past and lightens your burdened heart; saying "thank You" recalls what you have already been given.

Be faithful to say "Please," but be especially skilled at saying "Thank You."

Father, thank You for always hearing and answering.

A Limitless God

Your name, O Lord, endures forever, Your fame, O Lord,
throughout all generations.

—Psalm 135:13

The phrase "endures forever" appears more than fifty times in the Bible (NIV), primarily in the Psalms, though it's in both the Old and New Testaments. This phrase "endures forever" is always linked to praise of the Lord and acknowledgment of His goodness. It describes several aspects of God that last eternally: lovingkindness, mercy, grace, righteousness, His name, and His Word, just to name a few.

Do you know anyone who has limitless grace, compassion, and mercy? It's impossible for us as humans! Sometimes being gracious and compassionate and merciful is challenging minute by minute! But for the Lord, it's engrained in who He is and who He'll continue to be, forever. His character will never change. We can be so grateful for that!

In Psalm 136, "his love endures forever" is repeated twenty-six times (NIV)—half of the total number in the Bible. We need to be reminded often of God's steadfast love. It endures forever. It endures forever. It endures forever.

While the phrase appears more than fifty times in the Word, let it resound inside you countless times!

Lord, I want my love for You to endure forever as well!

Yesterday's Thanks

I will praise the LORD according to His righteousness, and will sing praise to the name of the LORD Most High.

—Psalm 7:17

et me ask you this: What if you wake up tomorrow with only the things you thanked God for today? When I first stumbled across that question, it stopped me in my tracks. *Would I wake up with anything?* It's a humbling and provocative idea.

I don't ask this question to make you feel guilty or to coerce you to painstakingly list every single blessing every single day. It's simply a good reminder to keep gratitude at the forefront of our minds—to intentionally thank the Lord for all the gifts He gives us.

While this is an extreme example, writer Barbara Ann Kipfer published a book called *14,000 Things to Be Happy About.* The book lists delights from "rabbit tracks in the snow" to "20 minutes all to yourself" and "strawberry ice-cream shortcake" as reasons for joy. The author started the list when she was younger, and it turned into quite the popular compilation—over one million copies in print.

Again, if you wake up tomorrow with only what you've said "Thank You" for today, what would you have? Let's challenge ourselves to spend a few minutes every day thanking the Lord for His countless blessings.

Lord, my thanks will never be enough, but let me offer them anyway. I praise You for giving so beautifully to me.

I *Get* To!

I will love You, O LORD, my strength.

—Psalm 18:1

You're familiar with the concept of *I have to* versus *I get to*, right? These opposite attitudes create very different outcomes.

- We *have* to clean up our own kitchens; we *get* to clean up a friend's who has welcomed us for dinner.
- We *have* to wash the windows, or we *get* to clean off the winter grime so we can watch spring *spring*!
- We *have* to go to the grocery store—or we *get* to buy an abundance of food from the wide variety available on well-stocked shelves.
- We *have* to give thanks to God—or we *get* to thank Him for who He is and what He does for us.

God created human beings with free will; He didn't construct robots and program us to love and praise Him. After all, forced love and worship would be fraudulent. God wants a relationship with us, and we build our friendship through expressing our love for Him in praise. But God never forces relationship or gratitude. As we come to love God more, we no longer *have to* but more freely and joyfully *get to* offer our thanksgiving.

Thank You, Lord, that I never have to love and praise You! The truth is I get to love You and offer You my thanks!

Who's Praying for You?

"I do not pray for these [disciples] alone, but also for those who will believe in Me through their word."

—John 17:20

It's a risk. It requires honesty. It means choosing vulnerability. It takes courage. And it can be a life-giving blessing that helps us forgive ourselves, fuel our hope, and make God's love for us very real.

"It" is being prayed for by a fellow believer.

We can get tired of praying for the same people and situations when we see no sign that God is at work. Sometimes we struggle to pray for ourselves for the same reason. But when we step forward and ask a brother or sister in Christ to pray for us, we feel less alone, situations look less grim, and God's presence with us becomes more recognizable.

Other Christians, however, are not the only ones who pray for us. As the apostle Paul taught, "The Spirit himself intercedes for us through wordless groans. . . . Christ Jesus who died—more than that, who was raised to life—is at the right hand of God and is also interceding for us" (Romans 8:26, 34 NIV).

Find comfort in the truth that Jesus and the Holy Spirit lift your name to the Father, whether you sense it or not. And never be afraid to ask other believers to pray for you.

Thank You for praying for me—and thank You for Your people who pray for me too.

Breakfast of Gratitude

Where morning dawns, where evening fades, you call forth songs of joy.

—Psalm 65:8 NIV

Omelets. Orange juice. Raisin Bran. Oatmeal. Fruit. Toast. Breakfast is an important meal because it fuels us *for* the day. Even if you don't eat breakfast, you've probably heard others talk about the various benefits from breakfast, including energy, a lower level of bad cholesterol, or healthier food choices for the rest of the day.

Picture yourself in a morning job interview after skipping breakfast. Your stomach is growling, you're beginning to feel sluggish, and you can't concentrate on the interviewer's questions. Now, picture yourself in the same interview, this time after eating a substantial and healthy breakfast. Your performance will be better because you're not distracted by hunger or its side effects.

Gratitude is like breakfast. It impacts your entire day. If you begin the morning with eyes wide open to God's blessings, you'll feel a lot better than if your morning kicks off with a list of complaints.

Try filling your mind and heart with gratitude while filling your body with breakfast.

Lord, thanks for good food that starts me on a path to success.

From Spring to Winter

Be glad, people of Zion, rejoice in the LORD your God, for he has given you the autumn rains because he is faithful. He sends you abundant showers, both autumn and spring rains, as before.

—Joel 2:23 NIV

Unless you're living in a place like Santa Barbara, California, where the weather is mild and hovers around 60 degrees most days, you probably experience seasons to some extent. Everyone has a personal idea of ideal weather. You might revel in Southern summers with sky-high humidity and temperatures. Or autumn may be your favorite season, with its milder temperatures, colorful leaves, and plethora of pumpkins. Some love the life spring brings while others absolutely love bundling up and snowshoeing in the winter.

Since we all appreciate different types of weather, it's good to have four seasons. If you're a snow bunny, and the weather was always 96 degrees, life wouldn't be terribly fun. Likewise, if you are thrilled at the crocuses and daffodils that come with spring, you wouldn't be thrilled with the monotony of winter's bare branches and frozen ground.

Whether you live in Santa Barbara or somewhere with more vivid seasons, praise the God who created sunshine, individual snowflakes, burnt orange leaves, and tender yet powerful plants.

Father, thank You for all the creativity found in the seasons and these ways You display Your love.

God's Track Record

*My heart is confident in you, O God; no wonder I can sing your
praises with all my heart!*

—Psalm 108:1 NLT

The Olympics are always full of intense, hold-your-breath
moments. Will the swimmer pull ahead in the last few strokes?
She needs to stick her vault landing for a shot at the medal
podium. That speed skater needs to have the race of his life—
will he pull through?

If you're watching a rookie in that pressure-filled position,
it's nerve-racking. No one—not even the coach—knows how she'll
perform under the immense Olympic pressure. But if you're
watching a five-time Olympic medalist and you're asking the
same questions, it's not quite as stressful; he has proven himself
time and time again. Your confidence in him is extremely high;
he has always pulled through, even in impossible situations.

God has a proven track record, doesn't He? He never makes
promises in vain; He means what He says. He is the epitome of
faithfulness.

Abraham knew this. Romans 4 says, "He did not waver at
the promise of God through unbelief, but was strengthened in
faith, giving glory to God, and being fully convinced that what
He had promised He was also able to perform" (vv. 20–21). In
life there's no need to hold your breath. *What God has promised He is
also able to perform.* Let that resound in your grateful heart today.

Faithful God, thank You for Your impeccable track record!

Your Shepherd's Voice

"My sheep hear My voice, and I know them, and they follow Me."
—John 10:27

Not every shepherd names the sheep in the flock, but every sheep in the flock comes to know the shepherd's voice. That knowledge means survival as the flock traverses rough terrain, perhaps along cliffs, near unsanitary water, or close to a predator's den. Following the shepherd means life.

And where does the shepherd lead? The shepherd David mentioned green pastures and still waters, places that benefit sheep. David also mentioned "the valley of the shadow of death" (Psalm 23:4). Sometimes getting to lush pastures and clean water means passing over rugged ground and through dark valleys.

Jesus has for you the green pastures and still waters of family, friends, healing, hope, joy, and much more. Along the way, however, you will encounter difficulties, pain, and loss—and Jesus Himself has experienced hardship just as you do. He knows rejection, physical pain, false accusations, isolation, being misunderstood, the loss of friends, and many other forms of rocky ground you and He cover together. Remember, though, that Jesus knows your name: keep listening for His voice, and follow this Shepherd who loves you.

Thank You, Jesus, for always being with me.

Two Simple Words

One of them, when he saw that he was healed, returned, and with a loud voice glorified God, and fell down on his face at His feet, giving Him thanks.

—Luke 17:15–16

What is the most memorable thank-you you have ever received? What made it memorable?

Jesus might answer the first question with the experience recorded in Luke 17:11–19. Once when He entered a village, ten lepers cried out to Him from afar, "Jesus, Master, have mercy on us!" (v. 13). Jesus responded with the instruction to go to the priests, who alone were able to declare a person free of leprosy and free to reenter society.

Luke reported that "as they went, they were cleansed." Only one turned around, went back to Jesus, and "fell down on his face at His feet, giving Him thanks" (vv. 14, 16). This one man knew the blessing that comes from doing what is right and saying "Thank You."

Then Jesus asked, "Were there not ten cleansed? But where are the nine?" (v. 17). His words suggest sadness and disappointment. And we risk disappointing the people we interact with when we fail to express our thanks. Think back to the most memorable expression of gratitude you have received, and deliver that same expression to the Lord and others.

Lord Jesus, train my heart that I may please my heavenly Father by consistently saying, "Thank You."

Glorifying God

I will praise the name of God with a song, and will magnify Him with thanksgiving.

—Psalm 69:30

*W*hy am I here? What is the meaning of my years on this earth? Questions like these are not modern innovations.

Back in the garden of Eden, God gave the first human beings a specific assignment: "Be fruitful and multiply; fill the earth and subdue it; have dominion over the fish of the sea, over the birds of the air, and over every living thing that moves on the earth" (Genesis 1:28). But do responsibilities fulfill the human desire for significance?

The Westminster Shorter Catechism asks, "What is the chief end of man?" The answer: "Man's chief end is to glorify God, and to enjoy him forever."

One way we can both glorify and enjoy God is to, as David phrased it, "magnify Him with thanksgiving." We magnify—exalt, honor, glorify—God when we offer Him our praise and thanks. Acknowledging God as our Creator, Provider, Sustainer, and King gives Him the glory for all we are, all we have, and all we've done. Then we know why we're here and our meaning on earth. We shine the light on His greatness as we give Him our heartfelt thanks.

Thank You, Lord, that my giving You thanks satisfies my heart at the same time it pleases You.

Knowing Whom to Thank

Have faith in the LORD your God and you will be upheld.

—2 Chronicles 20:20 NIV

Today many individuals define their own right and wrong. Society now allows ideas and behaviors that would make our grandmothers faint. Other people's rights are not as important as our own, hate speech seems more prevalent than free speech, and respect for laws and public servants has almost disappeared. Yet people are still interested in spiritual matters. Some are even vocal about having faith without explaining the object of that faith. But faith needs to be placed in a person or a thing, or it is just wishful thinking.

Also characteristic of our postmodern age is a sense of entitlement that doesn't necessitate gratitude. But being thankful is a lovely trait. A general sense of gratitude may make us nice to be around, more positive than negative, sunny as opposed to cloudy. But just as faith is faith only when it is placed in someone or something, our thankfulness makes more sense when we know whom to thank.

Let's pray the people who put faith in luck or good fortune in this era one day exchange their free-floating faith and gratitude for a relationship with Jesus.

I am blessed, gracious God, to know You, to put my faith in You, and to thank You! I love You, Lord!

A Taste of Heavenly Glory

I will give You thanks in the great assembly; I will praise You among many people.

—Psalm 35:18

We can praise God and give thanks by ourselves, with a handful of others, or as part of a large group—and something is remarkable about singing songs of worship and gratitude with many people. Fueled by heartfelt love and by gratitude to our Savior and Lord, voices unite to glorify the King.

Maybe thanking God "in the great assembly" is a rich experience not only because it foreshadows heaven but also because it gives us a taste of heaven on earth. The apostle John, for instance, saw four living creatures saying, "Holy, holy, holy, Lord God Almighty, who was and is and is to come!" John heard the twenty-four elders proclaim, "You are worthy, O Lord, to receive glory and honor and power." Many thousands of angels rejoiced: "Worthy is the Lamb who was slain to receive power and riches and wisdom, and strength and honor and glory and blessing!" And every creature—in heaven, on earth, and under the earth—cried out praise "to Him who sits on the throne, and to the Lamb, forever and ever!" (Revelation 4:8, 11; 5:12–13).

The worship assembly in heaven will be glorious, and God graciously gives us a taste of it from time to time.

Thank You, Lord, for those moments of worship when I sense I'm doing exactly what You created me to do!

Did I Really Say That?

Even a fool is counted wise when he holds his peace; when he shuts his lips, he is considered perceptive.

—Proverbs 17:28

We can marvel and thank God for giving us the ability to speak. But wouldn't it have been nice if He had wired us so that before we spoke, we always carefully thought about the words we were going to say and how those words might affect people?

"Think before you speak" is counsel we all find valuable. We know that being careful with our words can prevent misunderstandings, hurt feelings, lost friendships, and failed job interviews, but still we struggle to think before we speak.

All of us can remember times when we heard words come out of our mouths and immediately thought with horror, *Did I really say that?* Scripture says pointedly, "The words of the reckless pierce like swords, but the tongue of the wise brings healing" (Proverbs 12:18 NIV). While we thank God for the ability to express ourselves, let's also ask Him to make us wise so that our words may bring healing, not wounds.

Lord, thank You for enabling me to choose words that are true, helpful, inspiring, kind, and grateful.

God's Fingerprints

"I set My rainbow in the cloud, and it shall be for the sign of the covenant between Me and the earth."

—Genesis 9:13

The hiker had hesitated at the suspension bridge. But in a few seconds the breathtaking view from the slightly swaying bridge made her happy to have crossed, thankful for the panorama that rewarded the risk.

That day the pine trees were a deep green, tall and majestic. The river itself was a deep blue with the white water bubbling up in sharp contrast. On the other side of the bridge, a waterfall spilled its foamy water into the river, fueling the rapids and adding a lush sound to the beautiful sight. And the spray from that foam offered a reminder of God's Genesis 9 promise: the light shining through the spray made a rainbow.

That unexpected fingerprint of God—that unanticipated "I'm here with you" from the Lord—enriched the beauty of the spot and filled the hiker's heart with gratitude. The Creator had shown up, signing His name with a rainbow.

Yet "I'm here with you" is true always and everywhere. A sharpened ability to sense God's presence with us and to be attuned to evidence of His goodness and grace wherever we are will help us grow in gratitude.

Thank You, Lord God, for letting Your presence with me be known. Please help me see You more clearly.

Doing What Doesn't Come Naturally

Give unto the LORD the glory due to His name.

—Psalm 29:2

The encouragement and commands to give thanks that we find in God's Word suggest that we don't easily or readily do so on our own. Why do we struggle to give thanks? One reason is envy. We don't mind that other people have nice houses, accomplish big things, or have amazing kids—as long as our houses are nicer, we accomplish bigger things, and our kids are more amazing.

In this unseen race—a race happening only and completely in our minds—another person can suddenly take the lead from us. When that happens, our homes don't look quite so nice, our accomplishments do not seem all that remarkable, and even our kids seem more, well, average.

Such disappointment that we don't have *this* when we were satisfied with *that* just yesterday can make us heavyhearted. Envy and thanksgiving can't coexist: envy fuels a restless dissatisfaction, and thanksgiving creates contentment. Let's avoid the error of envy by heeding the Bible's exhortations to praise and thank God for what we have.

Please keep my eyes on You, not on what other people have and do,
and fill my heart with gratitude.

Choosing Gratitude

Praise the LORD! . . . For I know that the LORD is great.

—Psalm 135:1, 5

One reason we human beings struggle to give thanks is pride. Whenever we reach a goal, are awarded a prize, earn a bonus, or exceed expectations in a volunteer position, the human default is to say, "Look at what I did! Look at what I did *all by myself*!" Our pride fuels illusions of self-sufficiency, and our satisfaction in a job well done can increase our self-confidence. Are we finding our value in other people's opinions of us more than in the Lord's?

Gratitude to God can reveal the lie of this sense of self-sufficiency because our giving thanks acknowledges that we had help—that our heavenly Father gave us the opportunity, the abilities, and the success, that He protected us and empowered us. When we thank God for our accomplishments and successes, we are admitting to ourselves that we aren't all-powerful, all-wise navigators of life.

Let's struggle through our resistance to give praise. Let's look at the cross, marvel at God's grace, and choose to live with gratitude.

Jesus, You humbly died for my sins. Thank You for that and all the blessings You give.

Not as Easy as Expected

I thank God—through Jesus Christ our Lord!

—Romans 7:25

Giving thanks should be easy, but a heart matter that impedes our thanks is our expectation of an easier life than we are experiencing. More specifically, we may expect God to protect us from the kind of pain and loss, from the reasons for fear and the levels of anxiety, that we have dealt with or are dealing with. This sense that God has let us down can definitely suppress feelings of gratitude. We may struggle to give thanks for the simple details of the day as well as for the courses of our lives.

One thing that helps us escape this expectation is time with our holy God. In the presence of His purity and splendor, His goodness and grace, we can't help but recognize our sinfulness and God's generosity. Then thanks can bubble up to the surface without our even planning it!

Envy, pride, and unmet expectations: don't let any of them halt your constant flow of praise.

Thank You for enabling me to see Your holy grandeur and my own sinfulness so that gratitude might crowd out expectations.

Called to Praise

Enter into His gates with thanksgiving, and into His courts with praise. Be thankful to Him, and bless His name.

—Psalm 100:4

It's a principle we understand better once we become parents: God, our heavenly Father, issues commands *for our benefit.* Consider Psalm 100, for instance, where we read God's command to "enter into His gates with thanksgiving." Why would God want us to do that? What good does He have for us if we give Him our praise?

Perhaps God issued this command to help us remember that He is God and we are not. Maybe He is prompting us to lift our eyes above life's challenges and beyond the world's priorities to Him—to His power, His guidance, His moral standards, and His truth. The eternal King may want to remind us that this world is not our home or prompt us, in light of His holiness, to modify our behavior. And the list of good reasons to praise God goes on.

After this call to worship, the psalmist listed three such reasons: "For the LORD is good; His mercy is everlasting, and His truth endures to all generations" (v. 5).

Let's savor the benefits God offers through His commands!

Lord, thank You for the privilege of worship that recalibrates my priorities, refreshes my eternal perspective, and reminds me of Your goodness.

MARCH

The Sacrifice of Thanksgiving

I will offer to You the sacrifice of thanksgiving, and will call upon the name of the LORD.

—Psalm 116:17

We may have heard of God's people sacrificing lambs and pigeons, bulls and rams in the Old Testament. But what does the psalmist mean here by a "sacrifice of thanksgiving"?

Nineteenth-century English preacher and commentator Charles Spurgeon offered this perspective: "Having received spiritual blessings at thy hands I will not bring bullock or goat, but I will bring that which is more suitable, namely, the thanksgiving of my heart. My inmost soul shall adore thee in gratitude."

Thanking God, spending time praising Him, telling others of His goodness, journaling so you have a record of His loving care: these actions require time and energy that you could use elsewhere. When you choose to make thanking God a priority—when you choose to invest time and energy in your relationship with God like this—you won't regret it. You will recoup whatever the cost of your saying "thank You" to God as you enjoy a closer relationship with Him.

Aren't you glad you don't need a lamb or bull to appropriately thank the Lord?

Lord, help me never to be too busy or too tired to say "Thank You" for Your grace, generosity, and love.

Impossible? Not for God!

Jesus took the loaves, and when He had given thanks He distributed them to the disciples.

—John 6:11

Maybe you recognize this verse and know it comes from an account of Jesus feeding a multitude. But beyond the miracle, do you see a personal application that may help you today?

Jesus knew the people were hungry and that His disciples had no idea what to do to help. After all, they had only five barley rolls and two small fish provided by a young boy who was willing to share. Undaunted, Jesus thanked God for the rolls and fish. Then Jesus handed food to each of His disciples, who walked into the crowd of five thousand men, plus women and children.

The disciples passed out bread and fish until the people had eaten "as much as they wanted" (John 6:11). The people ate until they were no longer hungry—and then the disciples gathered twelve baskets of leftovers!

The well-fed crowd was the miracle. And here's the personal application: What might happen if you thanked God for the limited resources you have as you face a seemingly impossible situation? Try it!

Lord God, You love to bless Your people! The apparently impossible doesn't keep You from providing for us. Thank You for that.

Braced by Gratitude

I will hope continually, and will praise You yet more and more.

—Psalm 71:14

Robbie's passion for soccer started early, and his disciplined training was remarkable even when he was young. He was always eager to get to practice, and game days were the highlight of each week.

Then one day the opponent's slide tackle took Robbie down. The emergency-room doctor recognized immediately that this injury would require surgery and a lot of rehabilitation.

Although surgery went well, physical therapy was painful, but Robbie was determined to get back on the soccer field. He struggled through the rehab until his leg was almost as good as new. Excited to rejoin his teammates and play again, Robbie was careful not to strain his leg . . . but then the other leg started to hurt. Another injury meant another surgery, a leg brace, and another tough rehab. This time Robbie faced not only an uncomfortable recovery but the heartbreaking realization that his injuries meant he would never again play competitive soccer.

His passion seemingly thwarted, Robbie wonders what kind of good God will bring out of this turn of events. Choosing hope, Robbie thanks Him as he waits.

Lord, You know "Thank You" doesn't always come easily. Help me choose to have hope in You.

Thankful *In* . . .

In everything give thanks; for this is the will of God in Christ Jesus for you.

—1 Thessalonians 5:18

*G*od helps those who help themselves. Charity begins at home. Love the sinner; hate the sin.

Good truths? Yes. Bible verses? Not one of them. But these wise words are often mistaken for biblical truths.

Give thanks for *everything. Give thanks* in *everything.* Good instruction? Only the second statement. The first is too often considered a biblical truth, but the difference between *for* and *in* is huge. God does not call us to thank Him for every event, every relationship, every circumstance. He does not expect praise for heartache, betrayal, job loss, bankruptcy, illness, or death. Yet God does command us to thank Him *in* these tough situations and as we go through the hard times. Why? Because He is our hope and our comfort when we are broken. He can redeem the tragedy of the very situation we cannot thank Him for. By God's grace, unforeseen goodness can follow tragedy.

Let's not mistake good ideas for Scriptures, and let's not confuse ourselves by misreading God's Word!

Lord, help me be thankful in You whatever circumstances I'm experiencing.

A New Way to Praise

*Since we are receiving a kingdom that cannot be shaken, let us be
thankful, and so worship God acceptably with reverence and awe.*
—Hebrews 12:28 NIV

In Gary Chapman's book *The Five Love Languages*, he explores his
concept of five emotional love languages: gift giving, quality
time, words of affirmation, acts of service, and physical touch.
Each person, according to Chapman, has one primary or sec-
ondary way he or she most often gives and receives love. When
you want to show a loved one just how much you care, what do
you do? You might pick up flowers for your mom, schedule a
date with your spouse, compliment your child on his test scores,
do the dishes for your roommate, or give your friend a huge hug.

When you want to express your thankfulness to God, what
action do you gravitate toward? Do you pray, sing, play an instru-
ment, journal, serve others, joyfully follow His commands, or
tell others about God's faithfulness? There are many other
ways to convey your love and thankfulness. This week, consider
thanking God in a new love language.

Father, please show me what new ways I can show You love.

When Words Fail

Praise the Lord, my soul; all my inmost being, praise his holy name.
—Psalm 103:1 NIV

Hallmark Cards, Inc., began in 1910 when a teenaged Joyce C. Hall arrived in Kansas City, Missouri, with two shoe boxes full of postcards. Over a century later, Hallmark has produced billions of cards sold in more than one hundred countries. With so many cards, you'd guess there would be a perfect sentiment for every occasion, emotion, and personality.

But sometimes you can't find words for the amount of love you feel for someone or for the deep grief you are facing. When a family member goes through tragedy, you might think, *I have no idea what to say.* Facing the greeting-card aisles you may think, *None of these cards accurately communicates what's in my heart.*

You might feel the same way about God at times. Maybe you experienced a miraculous answer to prayer, and you're overwhelmed with joy—words don't do it justice! Perhaps you're going through a really tough time and it's hard for you to talk to the Lord; you're confused and tired. At these times, you can use God's Word to give voice to your prayers. Read Psalm 88 aloud if you need to cry out to God. Or pray Psalm 98 aloud if your soul longs to praise Him.

If even Hallmark's words fail you, the Bible has plenty you can borrow. And those words are better than any greeting card.

Father, when words are hard to find, remind me to search Your Word for help.

The Greatness of God and Stars

*He counts the number of the stars; He calls them all by name. Great
is our Lord, and mighty in power; His understanding is infinite.*

—Psalm 147:4–5

Where you live, when you look into the night sky, can you see
many stars? If you live in the city, all the lights can make
stars hard to spot. But in the country, especially if you live in
the middle of nowhere, it seems as though you can see millions!
The stars shine brightly against the jet-black sky. Yet even in
the best of conditions and with really good eyesight, you can see
only about two thousand stars at a time.

You may think, *That's still quite a few stars*, and it is—but do you
know how many stars there are? In the Milky Way alone, there
are as many as 400 billion! *Wow*.

Read Psalm 147:4 again; it states God counts the number of
the stars—and He calls them all by name. Not one has escaped
His sight.

The psalm continues by saying, "Great is our LORD, and
mighty in power; His understanding is infinite." After reading
the facts about stars, you can see just how mighty our Lord is!
The next time you look at the heavens, remember He is powerful—He created every single star. And He keeps track of all of
them. What a glorious God we serve!

*Father who created the heavens and the earth, thank You for creating
me and calling me by name.*

Say "Thank You!"

Every good gift and every perfect gift is from above.

—James 1:17

Children need to be taught to say "Thank you!" Doing so does not come naturally, and developing the habit doesn't happen quickly. In fact, from time to time throughout life, many of us will need some prompting to be grateful for "every good gift" we enjoy.

Silencing that gratitude is, among other social factors, the abundance of what we Americans have. When we possess just about all we want and much more than we need, we get used to that lifestyle, and we come to think we deserve whatever we want whenever we want it and at no real cost to us personally.

If our parents have gone before us to overprotect us from challenging situations, frustrating friends, and difficult science fair projects, we learn to think not only that life *will* be easy, but also that we *should* have easy lives. Why say "thank you" when we have come to expect and take for granted all we have?

Why? As children need to learn and adults often need to be reminded, because every good gift comes from God. All we have—life, salvation, family, friends, clothing, food—is because of His grace.

Lord, forgive me for thinking I deserve what You give me. I want to live in humble gratitude to You!

Three Days and Three Nights

Salvation is of the LORD.

—Jonah 2:9

The story of Jonah and the whale is always a favorite of children because they can't believe he was swallowed by a giant fish—and lived. If you're not familiar with the story, God told Jonah to go to Nineveh and preach repentance to the people. Jonah didn't want to, so he ran. He boarded a ship that faced a life-threatening storm sent by the Lord. Jonah knew he was the reason for the storm, so he told his fellow passengers and the captain, "Pick me up and throw me into the sea; then the sea will become calm for you. For I know that this great tempest is because of me." When they did, "the sea ceased from its raging" (Jonah 1:12, 15).

Once the fish had swallowed Jonah, he cried out to God for deliverance. After three days the fish spit him out onto dry ground. By the end of the story Jonah finally obeyed God, gave His message to Nineveh, and the city was saved from destruction.

Even when we, like Jonah, run from the Lord, we can't escape Him; He is all-knowing and ever present. And even when we disobey, if we cry out to Him He hears. How merciful! Jonah and the whale may be popular with children, but it benefits adults who need God's grace as well.

Father, as You saved Jonah from a frightening fate, please save me in my situation. And please help me to obey.

A Giant Fish

The LORD will guide you always; he will satisfy your needs . . . and will strengthen your frame.

—Isaiah 58:11 NIV

Yesterday you read about God's mercy to Jonah and to us. Let's go back to the raging sea where Jonah was tossed overboard. Imagine: You have no life jacket, the waves are monstrous, and you know you are no match for the sea. You cry out to God as your mouth fills with water. Then you travel down the throat and into the stomach of a fish! Jonah wrote, "The waters closed in over me to take my life; the deep surrounded me; weeds were wrapped about my head" (Jonah 2:4–5 ESV).

Then God saves you. But it isn't a "normal" answer to prayer. The Coast Guard doesn't show up, and you aren't rescued by kind folks who saw you being washed into the fish's mouth. No, the fish actually spits you out onto land. And this time, when God calls you to preach to Nineveh, you go.

God's answers to our prayers are often surprising and unexpected—mysterious, even. He isn't limited to predictable, obvious solutions; He shows us His mind is much bigger than ours. God's answers are not our answers, just as His mercy is not ours. They're better.

Father, when the answer to my prayer takes a different shape from what I expected, help me trust Your ways and Your mercy.

Come Join the Feast!

*For the despondent, every day brings trouble; for the happy heart,
life is a continual feast.*

—Proverbs 15:15 NLT

When times get tough, what happens to your heart? When we're discouraged, many of us focus on the negative and fall into a hole of despair. But if our hearts are joyful and hopeful, the verse says life is a "feast"; in other words, full of delight, joy, and pleasure. A person who embodies these traits is one who lives a grateful life.

Notice the verse says nothing about circumstances you're in right now. It simply says there are two different camps for your heart: happy or despondent. *So many hard things happen to me,* you may think. *It's easy for someone to be happy if her life is easy and she doesn't have a care in the world.* True, it's sometimes very hard to be content, but it's naïve to think anyone has a completely "easy" life. Each life has its own share of good and bad, and Proverbs says our circumstances don't need to dictate how we act or feel.

How is your heart today? Come join the feast!

Lord, I want to live in joy and gratitude. When my heart succumbs to despair, lead me up and out.

Small Pleasures, Big Gratitude

Great is the LORD, and greatly to be praised.

—Psalm 48:1

What comes to mind when you hear the phrase *life's simple pleasures*? Summertime-fresh corn on the cob? Autumn leaves to crunch? A sparkling Christmas tree and crackling fire to sit in front of? The first irises in spring?

Maybe it's the opportunity to sit with a good cup of coffee and a good book, or a walk with a friend in the cool of the evening. Maybe it's the dog's welcome, a loved one's voice, or a child's hug.

Life's simple pleasures: Wouldn't a focus on these touches of joy and those hints of God's grace increase our gratitude?

What else qualifies as life's simple pleasures? Maybe a warm shower. Soft sheets. The freedom to worship. The colors of a sunrise or a sunset. A new recipe that everyone likes. A good workout at the gym. A clean kitchen. A freshly mown lawn. A sweet time of prayer. The unexpected phone call. Eye-to-eye communication without words. A new insight about a familiar Bible passage.

God's goodness to us is evident in little ways and big. We can ask Him to help us notice life's simple little pleasures so they fuel the fire of our gratitude to Him.

Great God and generous Father, may the grace of life's most basic pleasures ignite big gratitude in me!

It's Contagious!

Declare His glory among the nations, His wonders among all peoples.

—Psalm 96:3

"Be nice or be quiet" is a simple guideline for children to remember. Whatever our age, this variation of that statement can be helpful: be thankful—or be quiet.

You have probably noticed that negative attitudes can be contagious. Someone having a bad day snaps at you in line at the grocery store. Your stressed-out daughter is crabby and uncommunicative. Pressures at work make your spouse irritable . . . and your quiet contentment is swept aside. You can snap right back at the person in the checkout line, forget that you're the adult and give your daughter the same attitude she gave you, and pout, get angry, or play the martyr around your spouse. Negativity can spread like disease!

What about the positive attitude of thankfulness? Can it be contagious? Perhaps some people will find themselves smiling along with you when you exclaim, "What a gorgeous sunset!" Maybe others will see your kindness to the clerk at the grocery store and follow your example. If your grateful heart and the ways you manifest it aren't contagious, at least your positivity might curb the negativity.

Try being thankful today—or just be quiet.

Lord, help me stand strong in my gratitude even when those around me are angry or frustrated.

Humble Gratitude

King David went in and and sat before the LORD; and he said: "Who am I, O Lord GOD? And what is my house, that You have brought me this far?"

—2 Samuel 7:18

When David spoke so humbly to God in this passage, the prophet Nathan had just shared with David a report of the glorious future God had for the king's descendants. Nathan said, for instance, that God would have David's son "build a house for My name" (v. 13). As if this promise weren't amazing enough, Nathan concluded, "Your throne shall be established forever" (v. 16). And what was King David's response? To sit modestly before God and express thanks.

What is your response when you receive unbelievably good news? Perhaps the long-awaited baby was born, the job secured, or the home purchased. Perhaps the prodigal child returned to his spiritual home or your loved one's cancer is in remission. What is your response?

Let's learn from David's example. Let's talk humbly with the Lord. Can we bask in the truth that the Author and Sustainer of life knows us and cares for us? "Who am I?" began David. "Who am I that You have blessed me so richly by . . . ?" Finish the sentence.

I want to learn from David and, when You bless me beyond expectation, sit with You in awe and wonder and gratitude.

Empowered and Blessed

He is the tower of salvation to His king, and shows mercy to His anointed, to David and his descendants forevermore.

—2 Samuel 22:51

In 2 Samuel 22 King David praised God as "the tower of salvation to His king." David was a man of war whom God enabled to be an effective commander, and David led the army of Israel to many victories.

David's praise continued for God's power, deliverance, mercy, guidance, protection, and victories. Interspersed are details about enemies who scattered, were subdued, and destroyed. David's proclamation was triumphant and joyful as he gave credit for the battlefield success where credit was due—to God Almighty!

Like David, we would do well to humbly acknowledge that the victories we experience are due to God's goodness, involvement, power, and love. Such thankfulness honors God, blesses Him, and glorifies Him. Thanking God also strengthens our trust in Him and prepares us for life's future battles. Therefore give thanks and acknowledge the tower of your salvation!

Glorious God, may I always give You praise, thanks, and credit for the good You do in my life!

Everyday Courage

"Take courage! It is I. Don't be afraid."

—Mark 6:50 NIV

We've all seen great acts of courage on the news: the hero who rushes into the burning building to save the child, the soldier who braves the heat of battle to save a friend, the young woman who donates a kidney to help a stranger.

But another kind of courage doesn't make the news. Robert Louis Stevenson reportedly said, "Everyday courage has few witnesses. But yours is no less noble because no drum beats for you and no crowds shout your name."

Quiet, everyday courage says no to evil—even when those around us ridicule us for doing so. It chooses the important over the urgent. It sets aside fear and doubts, and it steps out in faith to do what is right and good. It routinely proclaims the power, goodness, and reality of God in a world that would rather forget Him.

God knows we need courage in this world—that's why He sent us Jesus. So when you're out in the middle of the everyday rocky waters of life, Jesus calls to you, "Take courage! It is I." Whether you're performing a remarkable feat of courage or just a small act of it in a mundane setting, He walks out on those waters to be with you and help you.

Thank You, Lord, for giving me Your courage—not only in big moments, but also in all the everyday moments of life.

Our Good God

You are good, and what you do is good.

—Psalm 119:68 NIV

Although our feelings may occasionally (or even often) tell us otherwise, we always have many reasons to be thankful. Sometimes to see those reasons we need to look past our circumstances. In this verse of praise to God, the writer gives us the fundamental reason we can always make that choice: simply, the Lord is good.

What does it mean that God is good? God's goodness is evident in His character—in, for instance, His purity, holiness, kindness, love, mercy, and grace.

God's goodness is also evident in His actions. We see His goodness in sending His Son to die on the cross for our sins. We see God's goodness in His forgiving us, guiding our steps, providing for our needs, protecting us, blessing us with family and friends, and so much more.

Both aspects of God's goodness—who He is and what He does—give us many reasons to praise Him. When the circumstances of life make it tough to feel thankful, ask your wonderful God to help you look past them to His character and His actions.

Lord, remind me of all You do and are. I praise You for Your goodness to me.

Diverse Personalities

Worthy are you, our Lord and God, to receive glory and honor and power, for you created all things, and by your will they existed and were created.

—Revelation 4:11 ESV

Often people categorize personalities as extroverted or introverted, type A or type B, and so on. Yet there's a plethora of different personality traits you may not think of: adaptable, competitive, enigmatic, mellow, friendly, loyal, curious—and that's just the tip of the iceberg! You could list hundreds, if not thousands, more.

What is one of your favorite personality traits in yourself or in others? Let's say it's enthusiasm. An enthusiastic person eagerly approaches life; she is passionate and energetic, animated and full of ardor. She's likely the one cheering on others and focusing on the positive. Enthusiasm is a great trait to have! But what if our world were comprised of only enthusiastic people? It could be a bit overwhelming, couldn't it? On the other side of the spectrum, a low-key personality could be both positive and negative as well.

God created humans with a diverse range of personalities, and they often complement each other. Whatever your personality type, you have potential to bless others.

Father, show me how to use the personality You've designed me with, and let it bring praise and gratitude to You.

Thank God for Dirty Dishes

I have learned in whatever state I am, to be content.

—Philippians 4:11

We may believe that in general we appreciate what we have. But when we suddenly don't have something we rely on, we realize maybe we had been taking that something for granted.

A storm causes the electricity to go out. That means no phone recharger. It means no microwave, and it may mean no stove. It means you miss the big game on TV or the end of that miniseries. When was the last time you thanked God for electricity?

A flat tire makes the morning routine anything but routine! Will you miss your appointment, be late for work, or fail to reach the airport on time? Do you trade cars with your spouse or your adult child—or do you call an Uber and worry about the tire later? When was the last time you thanked God for the tires on your car?

You no longer find empty glasses in unexpected places, an unwashed frying pan on the stove, or wet clothes in the washing machine. Now your high schooler is in college halfway across the country. When was the last time you thanked God for dirty dishes and clothes left for you to dry and fold?

No matter how thankful we think we are, all of us can grow in gratitude.

Lord, please help me be grateful for what I have without having to do without it!

Showers of Compassion

The Lord is good to all, and His tender mercies are over all His works.

—Psalm 145:9

ake a moment to reread today's verse. Notice that these are statements of fact, not questions or queries, not hopes or wishes. These two things are true: "The Lord is good to all" and "His tender mercies are over all His works."

The Message says it this way: "God is good to one and all; everything he does is suffused with grace," while the New Living Translation says, "The Lord is good to everyone. He showers compassion on all his creation."

It's easy to see God's goodness and "tender mercies" on days when everything is going just right. But on those not-so-good and downright-terrible days, when everything seems to go wrong—can you find God's goodness and grace then? Because it is there. Look for it.

God promises that if you search for Him, you will find Him (Jeremiah 29:13) and His showers of compassion in the friend who calls just when you need her, or in the song on the radio you needed to hear. His compassion is in the thousand and one good and tender mercies God gifts you throughout your day. Look for them. And when you find them, thank the God who is good to all.

Open my eyes, dear Lord, and show me the wondrous details of your "tender mercies."

A World Without the *Mona Lisa*

Each of you should use whatever gift you have received to serve others, as faithful stewards of God's grace in its various forms.

—1 Peter 4:10 NIV

God gives each one of us specific talents. You know the dessert at your favorite restaurant? God gave that chef a specific culinary talent. He blessed your son's teacher with the ability to teach, and He gave your financial advisor skill in working with numbers. Everywhere you look—at your office, in your home, in the community—talented people abound.

What if Steve Jobs hadn't exercised his talent to create innovative products? Or imagine a world without such classic books as *Pride and Prejudice*, *The Adventures of Huckleberry Finn*, or *A Christmas Carol*. If Da Vinci hadn't cultivated his painting talent, the *Mona Lisa* wouldn't exist today.

Let's give thanks to our creative Father who generously gives us each different strengths. Our world is more beautiful, interesting, and functional because of those who use their talents to serve the world.

Father, help me put my gifts to work to bless, beautify, and aid the world.

Shining a Light of Gratitude

Those who are wise shall shine like the brightness of the firmament,
and those who turn many to righteousness like the stars forever and
ever.

—Daniel 12:3

Many acts of kindness, expressions of gratitude, and wisdom for
navigating life can make us shine.

Being people who are peaceful at our core, who live with
hope, and who choose to be grateful makes us different from
those who don't yet know the Lord. Pastor and author John
MacArthur agrees:

> A thankful heart is one of the primary identifying characteris-
> tics of a believer. It stands in stark contrast to pride, selfishness,
> and worry. And it helps fortify the believer's trust in the Lord
> and reliance [on] His provision, even in the toughest times. No
> matter how choppy the seas become, a believer's heart is buoyed
> by constant praise and gratefulness to the Lord.

Our gratitude may be a winsome light that attracts the lost
even as it grows our relationship with God and our trust in Him.

Lord, please fill my heart with gratitude so that You are glorified,
people are drawn to You, and my faith grows.

Step by Step

Your word is a lamp to my feet and a light to my path.

—Psalm 119:105

In this much-loved verse we find comfort, peace, and hope in knowing that the Lord will show us the way through life. But that lamp doesn't always shed as much light as we'd like. In certain circumstances we realize that God will lead us a step at a time—and not necessarily giant ones. We still feel some comfort, but the peace can waver a bit.

In *Breathing Room: Letting Go So You Can Fully Live*, Leeana Tankersley shared her thoughts about these smaller revelations:

> Our job is to take the very next step. . . . Our job is to trust that more will be revealed. If we could see the answer from here, we wouldn't need courage. We wouldn't need God. We wouldn't need each other. We wouldn't need faith. . . . Sometimes all we've been given is a match when what we were hoping for and waiting for was high beams. But if we'll commit to what's right in front of us, we can make the long journey with just a little light at a time.

Psalm 119:105 is always true. Thank God that He does show us the next step and that He gives us the courage we need as we wait for more instructions.

Lord, thank You for Your wisdom: if I saw the entire path of my life, I wouldn't need You or faith.

From the East to the West

"I have swept away your offenses like a cloud, your sins like the morning mist. Return to me, for I have redeemed you."

—Isaiah 44:22 NIV

At some point someone has hurt or wronged you, and you needed to forgive. It may have felt impossible to pardon that particular betrayal. It might have taken minutes, weeks, or even decades for you to truly forgive and let go of resentment. The same may have been true for someone who needed to absolve you. Being on either side of forgiveness—the one seeking or the one giving—is difficult. It requires humility, love, and grace.

Maybe you're thinking of someone right now you haven't forgiven. What he did was crushing, and you're still smarting from the wound. Friend, consider the Lord's forgiveness for you and for me. When we ask Him to forgive us, He goes above and beyond what we as humans usually do. He forgives us that instant!

In *The Message* translation, Psalm 103:10, 12 says, "He doesn't treat us as our sins deserve, nor pay us back in full for our wrongs. . . . And as far as sunrise is from sunset, he has separated us from our sins."

Forgiveness is often painful no matter which side you're on. The next time you're tempted to hold a grudge, remember how the Lord forgives. What a loving and gracious God!

Thank You, Lord, for showing me how to forgive, even as You have forgiven me.

Light in the Darkness

It is the God who commanded light to shine out of darkness, who has shone in our hearts to give the light of the knowledge of the glory of God in the face of Jesus Christ.

—2 Corinthians 4:6

We find new reasons to thank God as the play of light impacts how we see the world around us. Wispy, low-lying fog adds a hint of mystery to the mountains in the distance. A setting sun paints the sky with vivid colors. A dark night provides a velvety background for brilliantly sparkling stars. The stars and the sunsets, the meadows and the mountains, as well as the heavens truly declare God's glory (Psalm 19:1). We marvel at the beauty of the physical light God gives us, light that He commanded to "shine out of darkness." We can be thankful that God, the Creator of light, makes His presence known in the handiwork of His entire creation.

The same God who called physical light out of physical darkness "has shone in our hearts" a spiritual light that enables us to understand the gospel of Jesus and recognize God's glory in the face of Jesus. We marvel at God's plans for us, His oversight of all history, our charge to share the gospel around the globe, His grace and His mercy.

We can be thankful both for our physical light and for the spiritual light God shines into lives and hearts.

Thank You for the beautiful light in Your creation and especially for the spiritual light of truth, forgiveness, hope, guidance, and love.

The Risen Christ

The LORD lives! Praise be to my Rock! Exalted be my God, the Rock, my Savior!

—2 Samuel 22:47 NIV

Sugary marshmallow treats in the shape of chicks or bunnies, in pastel hues, and covered with glistening sugar: What pops into your mind? Peeps! For more than sixty years, Peeps have been filling the mouths of sugar lovers. When you think of Peeps, other things may come to mind: jelly beans, new spring dresses, colorful plastic eggs, or a very large white bunny. They're all associated with a very important holiday: Easter.

When you hear the word *Easter*, what comes to mind? For many the resurrection of Jesus Christ is not just strongly associated with Easter; it's the only reason for Easter. But it's also easy to associate Easter with customs like eating ham, putting together Easter baskets, and decorating eggs with the holiday as well. Those things aren't necessarily bad, but it's important to remember *why* Christians celebrate Easter. It's a celebration of a risen Savior, the One death could not defeat. It's a reminder of what has been done for us on the cross, giving access to eternal life. It's absolutely central to the Christian faith.

Even while you're eating Peeps or picking out a ham, keep the real reason for Easter at the forefront of your heart, and praise God from whom all blessings flow! *Christ is risen!*

Lord Jesus, thank You for dying—and rising—for me!

Being Present in the Present

"Don't worry about tomorrow, for tomorrow will bring its own worries."

—Matthew 6:34 NLT

The past, the present, the future—each can prompt our gratitude. We thank God for yesterday as we look back and see His hand of provision, protection, and guidance. We find our hope strengthened as we recognize God's great faithfulness through the inevitable storms of life.

We thank God for tomorrow—for the fresh start of a new day, for a future that invites bold dreams and steps of faith, and for the eternal future He promises those who name Jesus their Savior.

We realize only today is available to us. We show our gratitude for the present by savoring the moment rather than regretting the past or worrying about the future. For example, consider the first-time grandmother visiting her son's home. Recently retired, she's discovering a new occupation. Her toddler granddaughter puts in Grandma's eyes a twinkle not seen in the workplace. Clearly relishing the moment, she smiles contentedly as she relaxes in the joy of this giggling granddaughter.

Though we're grateful for past and future, let's take a lesson from Grandma: learn to be present in—and thank God for—each precious moment of life.

Thank You for reminding me that I have only today. Teach me to live fully in the moment.

"Abba, Father"

You received the Spirit of adoption by whom we cry out, "Abba, Father." . . . We are children of God.

—Romans 8:15–16

Were you blessed by a wonderful mom and/or dad? Have you thanked God for that gift? Maybe you've been a bit irritated by their still acting like parents even after you've grown up. Be gracious. Your mom and dad can't help it because once a parent, always a parent!

A mom of young adults will find herself swaying in time with the new mom who is swaying while she holds her baby. However old his own kids are, a dad always turns and looks when he hears "Dad!" Thankfully, the "once a parent, always a parent" principle applies to your Creator God: He will always be your Father. Whatever your earthly parents were like, know these truths about your heavenly Dad: He is good and wise, compassionate and gracious, faithful and yes, unchanging. He is the sovereign King and the Author of history. Your heavenly Father who orchestrates the seasons also gives you your every breath, and He comforts and heals your heart.

Be sure to thank and honor your parents for all they've done, and thank God for His perfect, His constant, and His never-ending parenting as well.

What a blessing to be able to approach my Lord and King as my Father! Thank You—and I love You.

You Have Everything You Need to Be Grateful

I will sing the LORD's praise, for he has been good to me.

—Psalm 13:6 NIV

He's fed. He's being held nonstop. I know his tummy isn't bothering him. His diaper is clean. He should be happy—why is he crying? He has everything he needs.

If you've ever been a new parent or around one, you know some newborns are easily consoled while others . . . are not. Some babies are perfectly content after a good nap, some food, and a clean diaper. It doesn't take much for them to settle into peaceful bliss. Other babies are harder to please!

Are you more like the contented baby or the grumpy baby who never seems to have what he wants? Look at your life. You have been given food, clothing, shelter. More important, you have a God who has sustained you every day of your life. Why are you still unhappy?

Someone in a developing country with two shirts in his possession could be happier than a billionaire with two private jets and every material item he wants. It's not a matter of what they have; it's the state of their hearts.

Check the state of your heart today. Like a contented newborn, you have everything you need—and you are loved by the God who created the universe.

Father, help me find contentment in what I have rather than dissatisfaction in what I don't.

The King . . . on a Cross

Behold, your King is coming to you; He is just and having salvation,
lowly and riding on a donkey, a colt, the foal of a donkey.

—Zechariah 9:9

As Jesus entered Jerusalem just days before His crucifixion, people lined the road. They waved palm fronds and cried out, "Hosanna! 'Blessed is He who comes in the name of the LORD!' The King of Israel!" (John 12:13). That crowd anticipated the coronation of the long-awaited King Jesus and the overthrow of Rome. The people joyfully shouted, "Hosanna!" which meant "Save us!"

Jesus, however, rode into Jerusalem that Passover week not to ascend a throne but to die on a cross. He was the perfect Lamb of God, whose blood would take away the sin of the world. Jesus' kingdom was a spiritual one. Jesus would overthrow sin and death, not Roman rule. So that day, riding on a donkey, Jesus moved toward His death.

Not even His disciples fully understood what would happen to Jesus. Many years later the disciple Peter wrote that we are redeemed not "with corruptible things, like silver or gold . . . but with the precious blood of Christ, as of a lamb without blemish and without spot" (1 Peter 1:18–19).

While the crowd in Jerusalem was ecstatic with hope, we are humbled by gratitude.

Thank You, King Jesus.

Faith Like a Child's

"Anyone who will not receive the kingdom of God like a little child will never enter it."

—Luke 18:17 NIV

We can thank Jesus for not making it a guessing game or keeping it a secret—His teaching about the kingdom was clear. We may wonder, though, *how* to "receive the kingdom of God like a little child." What does childlike faith look like?

If you have spent time around young children, you have seen how they trust. If an adult yells, "Jump into the pool! I'll catch you!" the child jumps. When a parent says, "I'll make sure you have your costume for the play on time," the child relaxes into that certainty. Tell kids "Jesus loves you," and they accept it as fact. They don't question God's reliability or care—they count on it! That is childlike faith.

We can do more than just thank God for telling us how to receive His kingdom. Let's follow the children's example by resting in our Father's love, praying about all that concerns us, and knowing He can do anything.

Father, I want to love You with childlike faith, rest in rather than question Your love, and pray with confidence. Please guide me into the kingdom.

APRIL

Prepped for Heaven

"If I go and prepare a place for you, I will come again and receive you to Myself; that where I am, there you may be also."

—John 14:3

Have you ever noticed that the preparation time a project requires takes longer than the enjoyment of the end result?

- Making dinner takes longer than eating it. Let's thank God that we have food to fix and people to feed.
- Wrapping gifts takes longer than opening them. Let's thank the Lord that we are able to give gifts and we have people we want to give them to.
- Prepping to paint a room takes longer than putting the paint on the walls. Let's thank God not only for a home we can live in and paint, but also for the fact that the paint lasts much longer than the prep takes.

It takes a lot of time to prepare for a big project. Case in point: it takes our lifetime for God to ready us for heaven. God knows the best way to make us more like Jesus. He uses hard times to purify our faith and teach us to trust—and He will often take seven or eight decades to do so. But thankfully His prep work pays off for eternity!

Thank You, Lord, that life's challenges and triumphs ready me for heavenly living.

Serving with Love

"Now that I, your Lord and Teacher, have washed your feet, you also should wash one another's feet."

—John 13:14 NIV

Maybe at work you've been asked to do something outside your job description. You might be thinking, *That's not really my job. I'm grateful I don't have to do it all the time.* Perhaps during Saturday chores you hear the kids debating—loudly—about where one person's vacuuming duties stop and another's begin: "That's not my job!"

Upon entering the Upper Room with Jesus, the disciples saw the basin and towel ready for a servant to use to wash their feet. But no servant appeared—initially. Jesus' followers must have thought, *Well, I'm not going to do it. That's not my job.*

But knowing "that the Father had put all things under his power, and that he had come from God and was returning to God," Jesus made it His job. Confident of both God's plan and His role, Jesus stood up "from the meal . . . and wrapped a towel around his waist" (John 13:3–4 NIV)—and He washed all those tired, dirty feet.

Washing His disciples' feet was not Jesus' job. Washing our sinful selves was not His chore either, but He did it willingly. When you're asked to do something outside your normal duties, think of Jesus, and do it with love.

Thank You, Lord Jesus, for Your model of servanthood and the privilege of serving You. Help me do so with joy and gratitude.

Our Creator Is Alive

I know that my redeemer lives, and that in the end he will stand on the earth. . . . I myself will see him with my own eyes—I, and not another. How my heart yearns within me!

—Job 19:25, 27 NIV

If you live in an area where seasons change noticeably from winter to spring, you've seen winter ebb and newness blossoming. The garden, still tangled in a web of dead leaves, begins showing signs of life. Tiny green shoots push their way above the previously frozen ground. Birds begin serenading.

In spring, God's creation once again proves that death doesn't have the final say. It feels almost possible to hear all of nature whispering, "It's time!"

In the book *Gardening in Eden*, author Arthur T. Vanderbilt II gave voice to the promise that the season change holds, the physical reminder that our Creator is alive and near:

The hosannas of the lilacs, can you hear them shout and sing? The greening of the grass. The leafing of the trees. How could anyone not see what's happening, how could anyone miss it? There is nothing subtle or cryptic about it. Who wouldn't be a believer, watching breathlessly in reverential awe, as unfathomable wonders, one after another, reveal themselves to us?

Father, thank You for the wonders You unfurl all around us in spring. Glory to You!

A Beautiful Promise

"The Son of Man came to seek and save those who are lost."

—Luke 19:10 NLT

In the New Testament, with the coming of Jesus, we are given such a beautiful promise: Jesus came to seek and save lost human beings. And once He arrived, whom did He seek? The legalistic, already-have-it-all-figured-out, pharisaical crowd? No, He sought people like Zacchaeus—a dishonest little tax man up in a tree. A scandalous Samaritan woman fetching water from a well. A demon-possessed man hanging out in a grave-yard. Jesus came for adulteresses and drunkards, for lepers and the lame. In short, Jesus came to save those who realize they need Him: the sick, the sinful, the broken.

When asked why He deigned to dine with sinners, Jesus answered, "It is not the healthy who need a doctor, but the sick" (Mark 2:17 NIV). He knew the sick sought a healer, and He wanted to provide that healing.

Luke 19:10 promises that Jesus came to save those who know they need saving! In what ways do you need Him today? Will you let Him find and save you?

Thank You for always seeking—and saving—me.

Only God!

The multitude of those who believed were of one heart and one soul.
—Acts 4:32

The people in this crowd "were of one heart and one soul." Granted, they had in common that they "believed," but even when we have something in common, we aren't always of one heart and one soul! And too often we focus on what we don't have in common.

Variety, however, is clearly a trait God values. Think about the different kinds of weather you experience. Rain, snow, clouds, and sun each offer a unique beauty. Think, too, about the wide variety of flowers God created—and the different colors each of them features. God's botanical rainbow suggests He loves variety as much as He loves beauty.

And back to people: reflect on the range of appearances, personalities, backgrounds, ideas, passions, opinions, and idiosyncrasies. Think about your family, your neighborhood, your workplace, your gym, or your church. Every one of those settings is a microcosm of the world's wide variety of human beings.

We can thank God for the diverse people we know and, as today's verse reports, the ways He makes eclectic groups of opinionated and passionate people form multitudes "of one heart and one soul." Only God can do that!

Thank You, God, for the variety You wove into Your creation—and thank You for bringing unity among very different human beings!

The Value of Variety

All of you together are Christ's body, and each of you is a part of it.
—1 Corinthians 12:27 NLT

When have you been grateful, relieved, encouraged, or motivated by another person's perspective? Sometimes a fresh take on an idea can be an answer to prayer, a life-changing insight, or a simple relief from worry.

If all of us looked at challenges the same way, the range of responses would be quite limited. It's therefore good when a team is comprised of a variety of people: introverts, extroverts; musicians, athletes; married, single; those especially gifted with wisdom, others deeply committed to prayer.

As Paul wrote, "How strange a body would be if it had only one part!" (I Corinthians 12:19 NLT). If the human body were only an eye, how would we hear? If a body were only an ear, how would we smell? Clearly we can appreciate this kind of variety and even embrace the ways we are different from our brothers and sisters in the Lord.

We can also thank God for "I never thought of it like that!" moments that make for healthy discussion, thorough analysis, and solid decisions. God's people—the different parts of His body—exist as variety with a purpose.

Thank You, Lord, that in Your body, all of us together count and bring value to the whole.

"Not as I Will . . ."

He went a little farther and fell on His face, and prayed, saying, "O My Father, if it is possible, let this cup pass from Me; nevertheless, not as I will, but as You will."

—Matthew 26:39

Biblical folks responded to commands differently:

- God said, "Noah, build an ark because it's going to rain. A lot." It was a massive project that appeared purely impossible, but Noah did what God commanded.
- God told Moses to go before Pharaoh and demand he let the Hebrew people go. Moses did God's will reluctantly.
- To bridge the gap between Himself and sinful people, our holy God wanted Jesus to die on the cross. Beyond the agonizing physical pain would be the spiritual pain of being separated, because of our sin, from His holy Father. Fully aware of the cost, Jesus asked His Father to, if possible, let Him avoid the cross. But knowing that His shed blood was necessary for our forgiveness, Jesus did not what He wanted, but what God wanted.

When God commands us to do something, we are wise to follow Jesus' example: consider the cost, yet always choose God's will over our own.

Lord Jesus, please strengthen me. Enable me to choose God's will for my life whatever the cost.

Do What You Can

"She has done what she could."

—Mark 14:8

When speaking of a woman with a now-empty alabaster flask, Jesus said, "She did what she could do."

"She" was a woman who slipped into a dinner party to anoint Jesus' head with a costly perfume—because that was what she could do. She couldn't stop the crucifixion that was coming, even if she'd known of it. But she could honor and anoint Him, deliver a gift of gratitude for her Savior. Those who witnessed her worship criticized, "Why was this fragrant oil wasted?" (Mark 14:4). But even today her story is remembered.

Throughout the Bible, we see God's people simply using what they had, wherever they happened to be, to do what they could. Rahab hid the spies. Nehemiah prayed. Abigail rode out to meet David. Mary and Joseph believed. The old woman gave her pennies to the temple treasury. Each did what he or she could—and God made those efforts effective.

This day God asks you to do what you can do. He doesn't ask for perfection, only effort. He will graciously take what you have and make it enough.

Open my eyes, Lord, to see what I can do for You, with what I have, where I am.

God's Love Letter

*Pleasant words are like a honeycomb, sweetness to the soul and
health to the bones.*

—Proverbs 16:24

Think about the most wonderful piece of mail or email you
have ever received. What made it special—the person who
sent it, the message, the timing? We can thank God for the
many ways we are able to connect with people we love.

One way God connects with us is through the Bible. Some
call it "God's love letter to His people." But do we open it with the
kind of excitement we felt when we opened that most wonderful
piece of mail? Do we treasure it the way we do that email?

Consider now who sent it, the message, and the timing of
this Letter. The Bible gives us a clear picture of the Sender—His
character and His desired relationship with His people—and
enables us to experience the joy of communing with Him. Our
hearts warm at messages about God's faithfulness and grace.
Our love for Jesus is rekindled as we marvel at His sacrificial,
selfless love. The Spirit uses the words on those pages to breathe
life into our faith, proving this Letter to be truly timeless in its
relevance and power.

Now what would you identify as the most wonderful piece of
mail you've ever received?

*Your Word shows me a picture of You, connects our hearts, and
reminds me of Your faithfulness. Thank You for the Bible.*

Relentless Love

He said to His mother, "Woman, behold your son!" Then He said to the disciple, "Behold your mother!"

—John 19:27

A common cold can make us preoccupied with ourselves. Wearing a cast can be itchy and inconvenient and leave us focused on our discomfort. A migraine forces us to lie quietly in a dark room, uninterested in doing anything for anyone.

Yet as Jesus hung on the cross, pain searing His muscles, He thought about what His mother would need after the death of her firstborn son. With an economy of words, Jesus arranged for this faithful follower to care for her.

Also as Jesus hung on that cross, He asked His Father to forgive the soldiers who had nailed Him to the crossbeam, "for they do not know what they do" (Luke 23:34). Then, when a criminal being crucified next to Jesus recognized Him as God and asked to be remembered after death, Jesus took time to reassure him, "Today you will be with Me in Paradise" (v. 43).

No head cold, let alone a crucifixion, could make Jesus self-centered. Despite pain and His imminent death, Jesus refused to be preoccupied with Himself. Instead He provided for His mother, forgave the soldiers, and reassured a criminal of his salvation. What amazing love!

Thank You, Jesus, for Your relentless love for others—and for me.

Worthy

"Do not worry. . . . Look at the birds of the air; they do not sow or reap or store away in barns, and yet your heavenly Father feeds them. Are you not much more valuable than they?"

—Matthew 6:25–26 NIV

It's an important yet challenging thing to feel worthy, worthwhile. This world is so often careless with us. A dismissive comment, a disapproving glance, or a snide remark—each can conspire to steal our sense of value.

You might even find yourself questioning God, wondering as David did, "What is man that You are mindful of him?" (Psalm 8:4). *Who am I, Lord, that You trouble Yourself with me?*

Allow the Son of God to answer that question for you: "Look at the birds of the air." They don't hustle off to work to gain a boss's approval. They don't agonize over clothing styles or how to fit in with the "right" crowd. Yet God considers these small winged ones worthy of His care. And you, Jesus says, "are you not much more valuable than they?"

As you go through your day, take time to look at the birds. See how God cares for their every need. Then rejoice in knowing that the God who deems such little ones deserving of His loving care—that same God declares that you are infinitely more deserving than they!

Thank You for the love You pour into my life . . . and for declaring me worthy of Your tender care.

Consider the Brain

How precious also are Your thoughts to me, O God! How great is the sum of them!

—Psalm 139:17

When was the last time you thanked God for your brain? These facts may prompt you to praise Him:

- Information in your brain can travel up to 268 miles per hour—faster than a Formula I race car with its limit of 240 miles per hour.
- Experts estimate that the average brain generates around 50,000 thoughts per day!
- About 400 miles of blood vessels are in your brain.
- Your brain has a virtually unlimited capacity to store data.

Yet even with this astounding mental ability, we cannot *fully* fathom our heavenly Father. The brain He designed, however, does enable us to know God, to read, study, and memorize His Word, to articulate the gospel and share it with others, and to pray to Him and hear His response.

What stunning creations our brains are! What an even more marvelous Creator we are privileged to know!

Your thoughts are indeed precious, and the sum of them, great.
Thank You for enabling me to know them at least in part.

Reflecting Jesus

You, O God, have tested us; You have refined us as silver is refined.
—Psalm 66:10

Are tests of faith ever fun? Perhaps the only way we can honestly thank God for challenges we're experiencing is by thanking Him for the good He will bring from them. Some biblical writers referred to this testing as *refining*, and the metaphor is rich.

A silversmith holds a piece of silver in the hottest part of the fire. Those flames are the most effective at removing the metal's impurities. The silversmith is not a distant observer using a remote control; he or she is present throughout the process, actually holding the silver in the flames.

The silversmith is careful not to heat a piece of silver too long: even a second can render the piece unusable. How does the silversmith know when the silver is free of impurities and fully refined? The answer to that question is the most wonderful aspect of the biblical analogy of a silversmith refining silver and God refining His followers. A silversmith knows that the silver is fully refined when he can see his reflection in it.

Tests of faith are rarely enjoyable, but we can thank God, our Silversmith, for being present with us in the hottest of flames and for keeping us there only until we reflect the image of our Savior.

Thank You, Lord, for using tests of faith to make me stronger and better.

Reaching Out

The angel answered and said to the women, "Do not be afraid, for I know that you seek Jesus who was crucified. He is not here; for He is risen, as He said. . . . Go quickly and tell His disciples that He is risen from the dead."

—Matthew 28:5–7

Their world had crumbled around them as the skies had darkened, the Roman soldiers mocked, and the crucified Jesus died on the hill of Calvary. After the Sabbath, Mary Magdalene and another Mary hurried to the tomb. The earthquake was unnerving, but not as much as the angel sitting on the stone he had rolled away from the opening to the tomb. Then the angel spoke the most glorious news ever: "He is risen from the dead"—and He spoke it to women. That was astounding because in Jesus' day, women were not even allowed to testify in court. And here two women were entrusted with life-changing news.

Throughout His life, Jesus reached out to the marginalized—to demoniacs, adulterers, tax collectors, Samaritans, the diseased, the proud, the poor, and yes, to women. Today we can be thankful for that dark day Jesus died because His rising means He still reaches out to those hurting physically or emotionally, to those who love God and to those who don't know Him, to the lonely and to those lost in their sin. And He loves them all.

Thank You, resurrected Lord, for loving me and for showing me how to approach others with empowered-by-the-gospel love.

When Words Won't Do

"Let your light shine before others, that they may see your good deeds and glorify your Father in heaven."

—Matthew 5:16 NIV

The faith of Esther and her uncle Mordecai are undeniable—as are the workings of God's hand in the saving of His people. In today's world, you will often find yourself in places and situations where you cannot openly proclaim the words of God. Perhaps it's at work or school—where you're told to keep your faith to yourself. Perhaps it's in the political arena, where faith can be seen as a liability instead of an asset. Or perhaps it's simply in the everyday with someone who isn't quite ready yet to talk about God. But remember, words aren't your only method of communication.

Let your actions speak for you. Kindness in the face of hatred, compassion in the face of cruelty, courage in the face of fear: these things can proclaim the name of God just as loudly as your lips. And they can further His plans for His kingdom just as effectively—perhaps even more so.

Consider the ways Esther and Mordecai expressed their faith, if not the actual name of God. When words won't do, what will you do? How will you show the world the Savior who loves you—and them?

Lord, I pray that the light of Your love and glory would shine through me when I speak . . . and especially when I don't.

Choosing to Worship

The LORD gave, and the LORD has taken away; blessed be the name of the LORD.

—Job 1:21

*J*n His Word God graciously provides role models of faith. One such individual is Job: "That man was blameless and upright, and one who feared God and shunned evil" (Job 1:1).

Yet not many verses later, we read that Job's oxen, donkeys, and camels were stolen, his sheep destroyed, and the servants tending all those animals killed. In addition his children died when the house in which they were dining collapsed in a strong wind.

Then we learn why those tragedies happened: God allowed Satan to test Job to see if his loyalty to God would last when the material blessings vanished. Did it?

The grief-stricken Job "tore his robe, and shaved his head." Heartbroken by the loss of his children and the reality that his life had changed forever, he "fell to the ground and worshiped." His words are striking: "The LORD gave, and the LORD has taken away; blessed be the name of the LORD" (vv. 20–21).

When God's ways are hard to figure out, can we yield to His will, choosing to believe in His goodness even when circumstances scream otherwise? Can we thank Him for Job's model of worshiping as we weep?

Thank You for the example of Job, who even in his heartbreak found reason to praise You, Lord.

A Wardrobe Worthy of the King

He has clothed me with the garments of salvation, He has covered me with the robe of righteousness.

—Isaiah 61:10

It's morning and time to get dressed. Are you a denim-and-T-shirt person? Or is it a business suit and heels for you? Clothes make the man (or woman)—at least that's how the saying goes. Of course, as followers of Christ, we know it's not the outward appearance that's important. But still, there is some truth to the saying, especially in a deeper spiritual sense.

Left on your own, you are "clothed" in your sins. Every wrong choice, every moment of rebellion hangs on you like tattered clothing. And just as you wouldn't stroll up to greet an earthly monarch in flip-flops and cutoff shorts, you cannot stand before the King of all creation in your sin-stained rags.

That's when Jesus steps in and gifts you with a whole new wardrobe, one worthy of a King. He covers you with His own "robe of righteousness." And those rags of yours? He takes those for His own.

This morning as you're getting dressed, consider what you're wearing physically—and spiritually. Now that's something to be grateful for.

Cover me, Lord, with the robe of Your righteousness so that I may stand spotless before You, the King.

Nothing!

I am convinced that nothing can ever separate us from God's love.
—Romans 8:38 NLT

$\mathcal{I}$n these words the apostle Paul proclaimed the life-giving, gratitude-fueling truth that nothing could block him—or us—from God's love. Consider this declaration in light of Paul's experiences. Five times Paul "received forty stripes minus one": forty lashes kill people. He was beaten, stoned, and shipwrecked as he served his Lord. Paul endured "a thorn in the flesh . . . a messenger of Satan to buffet me, lest I be exalted above measure" (2 Corinthians 11:24; 12:7). Three times Paul pleaded with God to remove the thorn. God said no.

Couldn't such challenging times sow seeds of resentment rather than faith? Yet Paul trusted God's goodness. The apostle was undoubtedly grateful God had seen him through hunger, thirst, and injury. Again and again God spared his life. Again and again Paul experienced God's strength when he was weak (2 Corinthians 12:9). Through it all, God grew Paul's faith.

Are you feeling shipwrecked or otherwise defeated in some way? Are you suffering from a thorn in the flesh? Will you daily choose gratitude for the rock-solid truth that *nothing* can separate you from God's love?

However tough life gets, Lord, help me relish the fact that I am always enveloped in Your love.

Eyewitness Accounts

Death has been swallowed up in victory.

—1 Corinthians 15:54 NIV

Aren't you glad God provided so much biblical reporting to prove that Jesus rose victorious over death?

Consider, for instance, the witnesses the apostle Paul listed: "He was seen by [Peter], then by the twelve. After that He was seen by over five hundred brethren at once. . . . After that He was seen by James, then by all the apostles. Then last of all He was seen by me also" (1 Corinthians 15:5–8). Luke reported that Jesus "presented Himself alive after His suffering by many infallible proofs, being seen by [the apostles] during forty days" (Acts 1:3).

And let's face it: if the disciples had stolen Jesus' body, as Roman soldiers were paid to say (Matthew 28:13), and the resurrection is a myth, would His followers have preached so boldly? Would Jesus' people have risked their lives and even died for the sake of a lie?

All this evidence of Jesus' life, death, and resurrection underlines the certainty of our position as Christians: Christ has risen indeed!

Thank You, God, for raising Jesus from the dead—and giving me proof I can rely on.

Our Unchanging Lord

Jesus Christ is the same yesterday, today, and forever.

—Hebrews 13:8

What does it mean to you in the day-in, day-out routines of life that Scripture says Christ is unchanging?

Imagine if Jesus were gracious, kind, gentle, strong, and loving only some of the time. What if He were truthful or forgiving only on occasion? Praying to Him would be much trickier, and trusting Him might be close to impossible. We would probably be less likely to talk to other people about Him, and we might wonder if heaven truly awaits. In addition we would probably struggle to be grateful to a fickle Lord.

But when we meet Jesus in the Bible, we learn about His character—and we also learn that His character will never change. So rather than worry, we can pray to the Jesus we meet in the Bible who is loving and faithful to us. And rather than carry around a burden of guilt, we can go to Jesus and know that He will forgive us just as He did yesterday (and just as He will when we stumble tomorrow). And rather than fret about how far short we fall from being the people He wants us to be, we can rest in the unwavering love of our unchanging Savior.

In a world that spins with busyness and noise, I am grateful for You, my unchanging Jesus, my Fortress and my Rock.

No Fine Print

*Love . . . bears all things, believes all things, hopes all things,
endures all things.*

—1 Corinthians 13:4, 7

Did you notice the fine print in these words from
1 Corinthians? Trick question: there *is* no fine print. There
is no "love bears all things—except a, b, and c" disclaimer. We
don't read "love endures all things—except x, y, and z." Instead
we find the unwavering guarantee that God's love for His children bears and endures *all* things.

No matter, for instance, how often we do what we don't want
to do and don't do what we want to do, no matter how many
times we lose our tempers or falter in our faith, our gracious
and loving God bears all things. He puts up with us, and, He
will always welcome us home when we have strayed. This kind
of love is different from the kind reflected in greeting cards,
seen in chick flicks, and found on "reality" television. This
1 Corinthians 13 kind of love is divine in its origin. After all, as
the apostle John put it, "God is love" (1 John 4:8).

With the love of God, no fine-print exceptions exist. Let's
celebrate with gratitude and joy!

Lord, thank You for Your awe-inspiring love.

Finding Beauty in the Weeds

Lead me in Your truth and teach me.

—Psalm 25:5

One day along a road in the Grand Tetons, Wyoming, nature provided an unexpected lesson. In mid-May the mountains had snowy peaks, some lakes were still frozen, higher elevations were not yet open to visitors, and snowbanks lined the cleared roads. Yet the clear, bluer-than-blue skies and warmish sunshine clearly indicated that spring was arriving.

A rustic split-rail fence marked the border of a lovely meadow that stretched to the foothills in the distance. The lush green grass seemed to cry out, "Picnic time!" In this small patch of God's glorious creation, even the weeds looked beautiful!

Everyone's life has its share of weeds—loss, disappointment, brokenness, failure, and closed doors. But by God's grace those weeds come to have an unexpected beauty of their own. There may be a long winter wait before we can identify the beauty in our weeds, but when the time comes, we can finally see from a God-given perspective.

Wherever you are today, can you recognize a life-giving lesson in your recent difficult experiences? Can you find in your life's "weeds" some unanticipated beauty?

Lord God, thank You for the ways You bring beauty from the "weeds" of life.

Your Anchor

We have this hope as an anchor for the soul, firm and secure. It enters the inner sanctuary behind the curtain, where our forerunner, Jesus, has entered on our behalf.

—Hebrews 6:19–20 NIV

An anchor holds a boat in place. It keeps the vessel from being dragged away by winds or waves or storms. An anchor is a good thing to have—not only in a boat, but also in your life.

Who or what is your anchor? What keeps you from being dragged away by the winds, the waves, the everyday ups and downs of life? Is it a job? Family? Friends? Though these are all wonderful and even needed things, they are not meant to be your anchor. They are temporal and of this world, and they can change or slip away like the shifting of shadows or the turning of the wind.

Only Jesus never changes. Only He is worthy of being your life's anchor. Yes, the winds and the waves of this world will still come, will still rock and rage. But you can trust Jesus not only to keep you safely moored to His side, but also anchored in the very presence of God. He will not let you be moved (Psalm 55:22).

Let Jesus serve as your holy Anchor throughout all the storms life brings.

When the winds and waves threaten to pull me away, secure me, Lord, to Your side.

A Place for You

"There is more than enough room in my Father's home. If this were not so, would I have told you that I am going to prepare a place for you?"

—John 14:2 NLT

More than enough room." How often do we really hear those beautifully welcoming words? Isn't it far more often that we hear the words of the innkeeper—"No room!"—as he turned Mary and Joseph away? No room for you—at the party, at the boardroom table, in that circle of friends.

But with God (and have you ever considered just how lovely those three words are: *but with God*?), "there is more than enough room." Room for you at the table, room for you in heaven, room for you in the very heart of God. As Jesus said, "If this were not so, would I have told you that I am going to prepare a place for you?"

Not only is there wonderfully welcoming room for you, there is a place prepared *just for you*. You aren't merely welcomed, you are thought of, considered, and prepared for! Jesus has gone to a lot of trouble to make sure there is plenty of room and that your place is ready. Let's thank the Lord today who provides so bountifully for us, both here and in heaven.

How wonderful to know that there is a place in heaven prepared just for me—by You! Thank You, Lord, for making room for me!

Time-Tested Faith

Who is God, except the LORD? And who is a rock, except our God?
—Psalm 18:31

Do you marvel at the fact that people hundreds and even thousands of years ago recognized Jesus as God's Son? How do you feel about your beliefs being time-tested? Do you thank God for being part of this glorious family of believers?

Thoughts like these filled Ellen's mind when, during her visit to Greece, she was enjoying the deep azure waters, bright blue sky, and craggy black-lava cliffs of the island of Santorini. On one of those cliffs sat an old church, whitewashed and weathered. Its bell may not have rung for decades, but the cross at the top of the bell tower clearly proclaimed the resurrected Jesus.

Who knows how many ocean storms and gale-force winds the cross has endured? Who knows how many souls have found encouragement looking up at that cross standing boldly against the backdrop of God's heavens?

Centuries after this church's construction, its cross still offers encouragement to those who see it, to God's people who are, metaphorically speaking, experiencing the storms, gale-force winds, and battles of life.

Be encouraged by and thankful for your time-tested faith; there truly is no rock except your God.

For centuries people have put their faith in You, Jesus. You are the Rock I need during life's battles. Thank You.

Shalom!

The Lord will bless His people with peace.

—Psalm 29:11

What a glorious promise! What a cause for thanksgiving! God knows we need the tranquility only He can give and that we will never find genuine, lasting peace in our own power.

The Hebrew word for the peace God gives is *shâlôwm*, or *shalom*, a term that *Strong's Exhaustive Concordance* defines as "completeness, soundness, welfare, peace." This term refers to an individual's internal contentment and to harmony between two entities (people, groups, nations, and God). Consider these aspects of the *shalom* that comes only as a gift from God:

- When Jesus died on the cross for our sins, God made possible relationship between Himself in His holiness and us in our unholiness.
- God alone makes us complete—another aspect of *shalom*— when He makes us new creations (2 Corinthians 5:17).
- God's love and forgiveness help us know peace within.
- God enables relationships of *shalom* between family members, friends, church members, coworkers, and neighbors.

Receive with gratitude the blessing of *shalom*, the peace that God wants you to have and that He alone provides.

Thank You, Lord, for the peace I have with You because of You.

Too Busy to Know Peace

Surely I have calmed and quieted my soul, like a weaned child with his mother; like a weaned child is my soul within me.

—Psalm 131:2

We have much to be thankful for, and therefore much to keep us busy. But are we too busy? Are we running through life? Are we gasping for breath?

If experiencing peace and finding opportunities to take slow, deep breaths feel more like distant memories than present-day realities, think about how you may have gotten to this point. The doable pace probably intensified degree by degree. You took the pace up a notch when you added another extracurricular to the kids' schedule. The cars and the house still needed to be cleaned. You wanted not only to pay the bills but also to work for advancement. A few overtime hours here and there became the seemingly required Saturdays in the office.

But on a drive one day, you may find yourself looking at rolling green hills sprinkled with oak trees and accented by a blue sky. A couple of horses stand in a field outlined by a split-rail fence. You see no other human beings; you hear absolutely no noise. Simply put, you taste peace and you gain perspective.

Be thankful for all you have to keep you busy, and for the sense not to get or stay too busy! Thank God for insight and His help in slowing the pace.

Thank You, Lord God, for the ways You use Your amazing creation to speak to my soul.

Bank on It

It is impossible for God to lie.

—Hebrews 6:18

ibs, falsehoods, and fabrications. Little white lies and whoppers. We use all sorts of words to describe it and dance around deception, but the fact is that we all hear and face lies. And worst of all are lies said to you about God.

Once you've suffered the effects of life, you can be left feeling more than a bit wary, unsure of what is truth and who can be relied on to tell it. Let the words of Hebrews 6:18 reassure you: "It is impossible for God to lie."

What does that mean for you? It means you can believe that God will do what He says He will do, every single time (Numbers 23:19).

So when God says that He loves you and sent Jesus to save you (John 3:16); He will wash away your sins (1 John 1:7); He has a place in heaven for you (John 14:3); He will answer when you call (Psalm 91:15); He will never leave you (Deuteronomy 31:6); and you are His own beloved child (1 John 3:1–2), you can bank on it. If God says it, it is true.

Forget fibs and falsehoods. Here is one Person who will never, ever lie to you! Let's be grateful for a God who does not deceive.

You, Lord, are the God of truth—and I'm so very thankful I can always count on You.

His Reasons

This is how God showed his love among us: He sent his one and only
Son into the world that we might live through him.

—1 John 4:9 NIV

Jesus had His reasons for leaving heaven, for coming to earth, for dying on a cross. He certainly didn't do it for money or the things of this world—the things that motivate so many today. While here He didn't even have a home to call His own, for "foxes have holes and birds of the air have nests, but the Son of Man has nowhere to lay His head" (Luke 9:58). As for the lure of riches, Satan offered Him everything, but Jesus said only One was worthy of His worship (Matthew 4:8–10).

Jesus didn't come for power either. When the crowds tried to seize Him and make Him their earthly king, "he slipped away into the hills by himself" (John 6:15 NLT).

Jesus came because He loved His Father, and His Father asked Him to show God's love for us "that we might live through him." What astounding reasons brought the Son of God from heaven to earth!

You came for Your Father, for love, and You came for me. Thank
You, Jesus.

Your Gift

Do not neglect the gift that is in you.

—1 Timothy 4:14

God has given you a gift, something you can do in a way that is uniquely your own. And while the furtherance of the kingdom of God does not rest solely on your shoulders, if you neglect using your gift, His kingdom will be missing that special little touch that is you.

Your gift may be one of words: you write, you teach, you sing. You may have a talent for encouragement: you lift up and strengthen. Perhaps yours is a gift of the hands: you build, you create, you cook or sew, you touch. You may have the gift of presence: you come alongside, you sit with, and you listen.

Your skill may be big and bold and for all the world to see. Or it may be calm and quiet and shared in the hidden places of the heart.

Whatever your talent, the responsibility is the same: use it for the glory of God. Your gift is the thing that enables you to shine for Him and for His kingdom. It is your way to be "the light of the world" (Matthew 5:14).

Gratefully give your unique gift back to the world—and back to God.

Thank You, Lord, for this ability You've given me. Show me how to use it to bring glory to Your name.

MAY

A Little Salt

*"Salt is good, but if it loses its saltiness, how can you make it salty
again? Have salt among yourselves, and be at peace with each other."*
—Mark 9:50 NIV

Salt: it sits on most every table and flavors many of our foods.
Not only is it a necessary part of our diets, it is also handy
for so many other purposes. Bakers use it to make sweet foods
taste even sweeter. A sprinkle in your coffee grounds takes the
bitterness away. And as a scrub, salt can be used to cleanse. In
the past, salt was often used to preserve foods.

When Jesus said, "Have salt among yourselves," He was
reminding His disciples to always have *Him* among themselves.
It is the salt of Jesus and His teachings that preserves our "peace
with each other." What good does it do to say we are Christians
if we have lost the flavor of Christ? A life without the salt of
Christ certainly doesn't promote peace!

And the salt of Christ does more: It cleanses us of our sins
and freshens our souls before God. It takes the bitterness of
this world's hurts and stings away. It makes even the sweetest of
moments that much sweeter.

This type of "salt" is far from everyday! Sprinkle a bit of
this throughout your day, and give thanks to the One who gives
your life such wonderful flavor.

*How wonderful my life is because of the salt of Your love and grace;
help me to share it with all I meet this day.*

The Strength of Three Strands

If two lie down together, they will keep warm; but how can one be warm alone? Though one may be overpowered by another, two can withstand him. And a threefold cord is not quickly broken.

—Ecclesiastes 4:11–12

Friendships are one of life's blessings. Here, wise Solomon was talking about the value of having a friend alongside us as we journey through life—and who can argue with his reasoning? Two friends will definitely be warmer together than either will be alone. Two can also stand strong against an enemy who would easily defeat just one. And of course a cord of three strands is stronger than a cord of only two.

In terms of friendships—and hopefully you've experienced this—the heart connection between two people is strengthened when the Lord is that third strand.

When have you met someone, experienced an instant connection, found conversation easy, and felt as if you'd known that person for a long time? When have you seen a couple work through the issue of unfaithfulness to their vows, untruths told about finances, or an unexpected tragedy? Again, it's often because of the third strand: God enables forgiveness, provides hope, and brings comfort that two people alone may not have. Thank God for the blessing of relationships rooted in and sustained by His power and love.

Thank You, Jesus, for modeling how to be a friend and for blessing my friendships.

Overcomer—That's You!

*Who is it that overcomes the world? Only the one who believes that
Jesus is the Son of God.*

—1 John 5:5 NIV

Merriam-Webster's dictionary defines *overcome* as "to get the better of." Certainly that's a good definition. But the real meaning and impact of the word depends upon whether you are the one *being overcome* or the one *doing the overcoming*.

For the child of God, it is always the latter: *you* are the overcomer. You belong to the One who overcame! From the very first moments of creation, the light of Jesus cast away the darkness (John 1:4–5), and today He gives you this word of hope: "In this world you will have trouble. But take heart! I have overcome the world" (John 16:33 NIV).

Merriam-Webster's dictionary aside, for the child of God the word *overcomer* isn't about getting the better of someone else; it's about getting the best of God. It's a promise that says you needn't worry about being conquered by anything in this world because you belong to the ultimate Overcomer. Believe in Him, follow and obey Him. And He will shine His light into your life, He will bless you with peace . . . and He will help you prevail over every foe.

*How wonderful to know that You have already overcome this world,
and when I follow You, You make me an overcomer too. Thank You,
Lord!*

The Fragrance of Forgiveness

Forgive as the Lord forgave you.

—Colossians 3:13 NIV

The sense of smell is a powerful thing. Not only does it inform us of our surroundings, but certain scents can bring memories and emotions rushing back to us. But it's not just the scent of places or things that tickles our noses. Even our emotions and actions can have a fragrance all their own. (Perhaps you've heard someone talk about the *smell of fear.*)

An old saying goes, "Forgiveness is the fragrance that the violet sheds on the heel that has crushed it." These words call to mind those of God when He had discovered Adam and Eve's sin and the punishment He pronounced upon the serpent: "I will put enmity between you and the woman, and between your offspring and hers; he will crush your head, and you will strike his heel" (Genesis 3:15 NIV).

A curse, yes, but look closer. For within the words of that long-ago curse we also find the whispers of a promise and the first gentle stirrings of the beautiful fragrance of the forgiveness Christ would bring.

As you move through this day, give as you have been given: let the fragrance of Christ's forgiveness linger with you wherever you go.

Fill my senses, Lord, with the fragrance of Your forgiveness—and help me, in turn, to share that precious scent with the world around me.

Spiritual Adulting

The waters which came down from upstream stood still, and rose in a heap very far away. . . . And all Israel crossed over on dry ground.
—Joshua 3:16–17

*I*t's an occasion for heartfelt thanksgiving when we see God figuratively "part the waters."

Claire realized it was a long shot, but she had a freshly minted college diploma in hand and enough of an adventurous spirit that she bought a plane ticket to Los Angeles. It was time for her to start *adulting*.

After contacting a church for possible roommates, Claire had Facebooked with a young woman who truly seemed a kindred spirit—and Claire had signed a lease. God parted the water.

Claire had been a Lakers fan all her life. Her degree in communications just might land her a place with the organization, and her résumé reflected her four-year involvement with the college basketball team. A position had just opened, and Claire was the perfect fit. Could she start Monday?

Claire is also adulting spiritually. She has been building a community in her weekly Bible study. She has friends to text with prayer requests, friends to go to the beach with.

As Claire has learned to "adult," God has cleared her path every time. In your continuing journey to "adult," when have you seen the Lord "part the waters"?

Lord, thank You for blessing our steps of faith and our spiritual adulting at all ages and stages of life.

Faithful in the Little Things

"Because you were faithful in a very little, have authority over ten cities."

—Luke 19:17

$\mathcal{I}$n the story Jesus was telling in Luke 19, the master had entrusted his servants with a mina, about three months' earnings. And the master rewarded each servant who proved a faithful steward by gaining a profit on his investment.

Our stewardship involves using wisely not only our finances, but also our time and the talents God has blessed us with. And He calls us to be responsible, godly, and attentive stewards of our spouses and our children.

Our financial stewardship, though, means more than giving tithes and offerings. Financial stewardship means using well the money God has enabled you to earn. So when the box of contact lenses is about ninety dollars at the doctor's office, it's nice to find the pack online for eighty-five dollars, but it's very exciting to find the pack for sixty-eight dollars at the local warehouse store. Sold!

What has God entrusted to you to use well? Using God's money well brings joy. Find fulfillment in being faithful in the little things, thanking God for guiding and blessing your efforts.

Thank You, Lord, for the finances, time, and skills You entrust to me. Please help me be a careful steward.

Never Forgotten

"I will not forget you. See, I have inscribed you on the palms of My hands."

—Isaiah 49:15–16

God is perfect in every way: He forgets absolutely nothing. So why does He tell us in Isaiah 49 that He will not forget us? For our sake.

Back in pre-smartphone days—if you were even alive in those dark ages!—how many times did you write a phone number on your hand so you wouldn't forget it? Or maybe you wrote on your hand the four things you needed at the grocery store so you wouldn't get home with only three.

God has something on His hands that will last longer than a phone number written with a ballpoint pen or even with permanent ink. We read in Isaiah that God has "inscribed" your name on His hands. And He has put your name there *not* so He will never forget you, but to help *you* know that He will never forget you. This image of your name on the palms of God's hands underscores that you are always part of Him.

God forgets nothing—especially you, His child.

Thank You, Lord, for the love that took You to the cross, for the love that will never forget me.

Thanks to the Man Above

"Well done, good and faithful servant. . . . Enter into the joy of your lord."

—Matthew 25:21

In June 2017 the National Basketball Association named Russell Westbrook of the Oklahoma City Thunder Most Valuable Player. In his acceptance speech, Westbrook said, "First and foremost, thank you to the man above. Without his blessing, without his honor, I wouldn't be standing here today. . . . I'm very, very blessed to be in the position I am today."

Westbrook then thanked the Thunder organization, his teammates, his parents, his brother, and his wife, but those thanks came only after he boldly thanked God. Westbrook acknowledged from this unique platform his awareness that he held the MVP trophy only because of the Lord's blessings. What an honor to have one's hard work recognized, and God is blessed when we thank Him in those moments when we are acknowledged.

Imagine the joy, though, of being recognized by God Himself, our Maker and King, for the ways we lived out our love for Him during our years on earth. Maybe we won't be declared the Most Valuable Player, but like Russell Westbrook, we'll say, "I'm very, very blessed to be in the position I am today."

Thank You for helping me live so that one day I will hear You say, "Well done, good and faithful servant."

Stories That Teach

Jesus went up into the temple and taught. And the Jews marveled,
saying, "How does this Man know letters, having never studied?"

—John 7:14–15

Even people who don't accept Jesus as their Savior and Lord will acknowledge He was a wise and remarkable teacher. Jesus often told parables—stories based on common situations of the time—to teach a principle or truth. Even today Jesus' parables speak to us in terms we understand and with images we remember.

Among the lessons of His parables, Jesus taught that God's Word goes out to everyone, but only some people respond, and that God's kingdom is more valuable than the treasure the world offers (Matthew 13:18–23, 44–46). Some of Jesus' parables taught about the great love of God, who pursues sinners the way the shepherd seeks lost sheep and welcomes sinners the way a father joyfully receives his returning son (Luke 15:4–7, 11–32). Jesus' parable of the good Samaritan teaches us how to love, and His story of the persistent widow calls us to persevere in prayer (Luke 10:25–37; 18:1–8).

The great Teacher Jesus used parables to teach us truths of God. We can be thankful for these stories that show us God's ways.

Thank You, Jesus, for teaching us by means that help us learn and
remember.

God's Hidden Work

"The kingdom of heaven is like leaven, which a woman took and hid in three measures of meal till it was all leavened."

—Matthew 13:33

Today's headlines and the impossible-to-ignore reach and impact of evil are hardly seeds of gratitude and joy, until you consider these realities in light of Jesus' Matthew 13 parable. Leaven actually offers an encouraging truth in this dark world that does not invite the growth of God's kingdom.

The American Heritage Dictionary defines *leaven* as "an agent, such as yeast, that causes batter or dough to rise, especially by fermentation" and more metaphorically as "an element, influence, or agent that works subtly to lighten, enliven, or modify a whole." In Jesus' parable, this "element, influence, or agent" that modifies the three measures of meal is the gospel that modifies the world as more people recognize its truth and accept Jesus as their Lord.

Consider the ways leaven is like the gospel: the work of leaven is hidden, gradual, and somewhat mysterious. A little bit of leaven, working silently and relentlessly, impacts an inordinately large amount of meal.

Despite the headlines, be encouraged and thankful: God's unstoppable gospel truth *is* at work.

Thank You, Lord, for working in this lost world even when we're unaware of it.

Guided by God's Word

The entrance of Your words gives light; it gives understanding to the simple.

—Psalm 119:130

These days technological resources help us figure out how best to get from point A to point B. When we're lost and panicky, a little help from GPS, Google Maps, mapz, or an Uber driver can get us back on track. But when point A is where we are now and point B is a life of intimacy with the Lord and faithful service to Him, we need only one resource: God's Word.

Throughout the Psalms, writers describe God's Word as a source of wisdom, joy, and direction. In Psalm 119:130 the psalmist is grateful for the way Scripture lights his path and guides his steps. The Bible helps us recognize obstacles, avoid falling down, and stay on the path God has for us.

Knowing God's Word can keep us from sinning (Psalm 119:11) and, as Jesus Himself modeled, help us resist temptation. Challenged to turn stones into bread, Jesus told the devil, "It is written, 'Man shall not live by bread alone, but by every word that proceeds from the mouth of God'" (Matthew 4:4).

When we're lost between point A and point B, let's put God's written Word to the test—and be grateful for it!

Thank You, Lord, for the ways Your Word shapes my life.

The Gift of Quiet Companionship

[Job's three friends] sat down with him on the ground seven days and seven nights, and no one spoke a word to him, for they saw that his grief was very great.

—Job 2:13

We can't thank God enough for people who know how to be friends in both the best and worst of times. We don't always rush to the side of someone who is hurting. We know we can do absolutely nothing to change the circumstances, and we have no idea what to say. But we find in the book of Job some ideas about how—and how *not*—to come alongside a grieving friend.

First, the "how not." If you know the book of Job, you know how long-winded and unhelpful Job's friends were as they accused Job and defended God. These fellows—and this is the "how"—would have been better friends had they continued their Job 2:13 approach. Honoring Job's grief without trying to find a reason for it would have provided real comfort; their challenges to Job's record of righteous living only stirred bitterness.

We can thank God for skilled friends and for teaching us how to be real companions to others. We can find it challenging to sit quietly with our hurting friends, but our presence with them truly is more healing than our words.

Thank You, Lord, for friends who listen when I'm in pain. Their encouraging presence makes Your love more real.

Telling Your Story

Oh, give thanks to the LORD! Call upon His name; make known His deeds among the peoples!

—Psalm 105:1

Me? An evangelist? Yes, you! You have a story to tell—with gratitude—about meeting Jesus.

Evangelism doesn't happen only on the big stage with a famous evangelist such as Greg Laurie or the late Billy Graham. Since God calls people to Himself one by one, everyone who knows Him can be an evangelist. Witnessing for the Lord on a smaller scale matters in big ways. Sharing Jesus with your neighbor, a coworker, a friend at the gym, the distant cousin, or the checkout person at the grocery store may be the very reason you are in that person's life.

The best way to obey Jesus' command to "make disciples of all the nations" (Matthew 28:19) is to simply tell your story: "make known His deeds among the peoples." Your giving thanks for all God has done in your life—including helping you recognize your need for a Savior—is an excellent way to share the gospel with people who have not yet named Jesus their Savior and Lord.

Yes, you, an evangelist! You have a story to tell. Tell it with gratitude.

Lord, show me opportunities to tell others about Your work in my life.

He Is Able

God is able to bless you abundantly, so that in all things at all times,
having all that you need, you will abound in every good work.
—2 Corinthians 9:8 NIV

With God you will never face a situation in which you are forced to admit defeat and say, "I can't." With God it is always, "I can." It may take bravery, it may take strength, it will definitely take faith—and the victory may look a little (or a lot) different from what you expect. But with God, all things are possible (Luke 1:37).

Just ask that young shepherd David as he stared down at the fallen giant. Just ask Noah as he stepped out of the ark into a fresh, new world. Ask Esther as she stood outside the king's throne room after their fateful conversation.

The list could go on of the people who trusted God in the face of impossible situations and learned that He is indeed able. Lepers, outcasts, ordinary—and not-so-ordinary—people like us.

In this life, you'll face some tremendous challenges. But don't worry. God is able to handle every one of them. In fact, He "is able to bless you abundantly" so you will have "all that you need." Impossibility doesn't even exist for you. Thank the Lord!

No matter what comes my way this day, I know that You are able to
see me through—and for that I praise You, Lord.

Friends Who Carry Us

They made an opening in the roof above Jesus by digging through it and then lowered the mat the man was lying on. When Jesus saw their faith, he said to the paralyzed man, "Son, your sins are forgiven."

—Mark 2:4–5 NIV

When have you, like the paralytic man, found yourself thanking God for people whose faith strengthens your own? Consider the paralytic's remarkable experience.

The roofs in the Middle East were thatched: mud held together the rushes, and this final product rested on wooden crossbeams. Clearly, when they arrived at the home where Jesus was teaching, the paralytic's four friends had work to do.

Getting themselves and their friend on top of the house would have been no easy feat. Then came the challenge of breaking through the hardened mud. Undaunted, the paralytic and his friends were up for the task, and their efforts were rewarded: Jesus forgave their friend's sins and healed his legs.

The friends had demonstrated their faith by working hard to place the paralyzed one before Jesus. The paralytic himself had faith enough to consent to his friends' crazy plan. Jesus saw the faith of the five and granted healing.

Thank God for people who strengthen our belief.

Lord, I am grateful for friends who carry me to Jesus' feet—and for the privilege of carrying my friends.

God's Power for Your Goliaths

David said to the Philistine, "You come to me with a sword, with a spear, and with a javelin. But I come to you in the name of the LORD of hosts, the God of the armies of Israel, whom you have defied."
—1 Samuel 17:45

Young David held only a sling and five stones, the weapon he had used effectively to protect the sheep in his charge from lions and bears. In contrast, the Philistine Goliath had not only an impressive résumé of battlefield victories but also "a bronze helmet on his head, and he was armed with a coat of mail, and the weight of the coat was five thousand shekels of bronze. . . . His iron spearhead weighed six hundred shekels" (1 Samuel 17:5, 7).

The combatants did not look at all evenly matched, but David had a secret weapon that he didn't keep secret. David was fighting for God's honor and in God's power, so he was fearless.

Whether you're battling fear, anxiety, guilt, or shame, the challenges of marriage or parenting, or persecution for your faith, you can have the confidence David had. When you remember that you are fighting in God's power and that He will help you defeat your foes, you can stand strong before the enemy.

When you have only what appears to be a slingshot and stones to fight with, hang on: the Lord will deliver you just as He delivered David. Praise Him!

Thank You for Your invincible power for good in this world!

Teaching Our Children Well

These words which I command you today shall be in your heart. You shall teach them diligently to your children.

—Deuteronomy 6:6–7

When we are thankful for the children God has entrusted to our care, we obey His command to teach them about Him.

"Why do I have to do chores?" or "Why don't we have school on Memorial Day?" offer teachable moments. TV news can do the same: "What causes a hurricane?" or "What is the legislature?" Certain truths are too important for us to merely wait for an opportunity to arise. We need to initiate conversations about the foundations of our faith. God's words provide not only purpose, direction, and guidelines for this life but the path to eternal life as well.

Helping teach these vital truths are family devotions and holiday celebrations that focus on Jesus. In addition, family and bedtime prayers, family service projects, and dinner discussions of what happened (good and bad) in each person's day can help children learn about loving God and loving others. They also learn by watching you walk with the Lord through ordinary days, special seasons, good times and bad.

We express our gratitude for our children to the Lord by acting on His commands to train them well.

Lord God, help me teach the children You've entrusted to my care to love You and love others.

Seen, Known, and Loved

You know when I sit and when I rise; you perceive my thoughts from afar. You discern my going out and my lying down.

—Psalm 139:2–3 NIV

Sometimes we feel small and insignificant, such as at a busy airport where people are rushing to catch a flight, excitement and anticipation filling the air. We can easily feel invisible on an airplane, looking at huge clouds beneath us and miniature houses and cars farther below. Unnoticed and unrecognized, we may feel sad and lonely in this big world populated by billions of people. Yet God crafted each of us uniquely, and He knows every one of us by name.

God actually knows much more about you than your name. Jesus taught that "the very hairs of your head are all numbered" (Matthew 10:30). God knows your words before you speak them, and God knew you before you were born (Psalm 139:4, 16).

God also knows why you're at the busy airport. And He knows your heart—the joy, the sorrow, or the bittersweet combination. God knows when you sit down, when you stand up, when you go out, and when you lie down.

You may feel small and insignificant in this big world, but you are known and loved by a much bigger God. Choose gratitude for this marvelous truth, and some sadness and loneliness may fade away.

Father, I am grateful that You see me, know me, and love me.

Precious to the Lord

You formed my inward parts; You covered me in my mother's womb.
I will praise You, for I am fearfully and wonderfully made.

—Psalm 139:13–14

How many reasons to give thanks do you see in those three lines? Read the verses out loud. Do these truths make you feel a little uncomfortable?

If so, the reason may be that we too rarely hear that we are wonderful, special, delightfully unique, or created by God for His good purposes. What a blessing, though, if you have an affirming spouse or dear friend who speaks to you about your value and God's great love for you. Even then the messages of the world can drown out the most affirming voices—and even God Himself.

The people on magazine covers and in print ads unwittingly set standards that we mere mortals can't achieve without Photoshop. Television programs and movies offer a false picture of reality. In these ways and others, the world tells us we don't measure up. This ubiquitous message makes it all too easy for us to accept as truth the idea that we are somehow "less than." If someone significant in life communicated that to us early on, the world reinforces it.

Reread Psalm 139:13–14. Can you accept it as truth? If you can, you'll find many reasons to thank the Lord.

Thank You for helping me believe that I am more than precious to You.

The Grace of Forgiveness

Lord, You know all things; You know that I love You.

—John 21:17

𝓘t's easy to be annoyed: whether it's our child's "Why?" many times in a single conversation or our teen's "Can I have the car?" multiple times a week. But in the John 21 scenario, the repetition was necessary.

Peter was understandably upset when the risen Jesus asked him the same question. Yet it is surely no coincidence that Jesus repeated, "Do you love Me?" three times to the person who had denied knowing Him three times (John 21:17; 18:17, 25–27).

Another element of this scene hearkens back to an earlier moment in Peter's life. The first words Jesus spoke to Peter as the fisherman was casting a net into the sea were "Follow Me" (Matthew 4:19). Significantly, after the back-and-forth of the questions He had for Peter, the resurrected Jesus said to Peter once again, "Follow Me" (John 21:19).

Jesus acknowledged Peter's three denials by giving him three opportunities to affirm that yes, he loved Jesus. Then Jesus' "Follow Me" reassured Peter of his forgiveness.

We understand Peter's annoyance, but our takeaway is gratitude to God for this lesson about His readiness to forgive our sins.

Thank You, Jesus, for Your gracious forgiveness of my sins—and for this reassuring picture of reconciliation.

Multitasking . . . Your Faith?

Very early in the morning, while it was still dark, Jesus got up, left the house and went off to a solitary place, where he prayed.
—Mark 1:35 NIV

An epidemic is sweeping across our society. It's injuring our relationships, contributing to overeating, and damaging our creativity!

What is it? Multitasking. With all the rush-and-hurry pressures we're under, it seems wasteful, almost decadent to focus on one thing at a time. So we fold laundry while we cook dinner—and chat on the phone. We check our phone for emails and texts while waiting for the stoplight to turn green. We create meetings while half listening to meetings.

We feel as if we're getting more done, but are we really? Or are we missing out on the beauty of the moment?

There's one place where multitasking has no place: your faith. Sure, you might say a prayer in the shower or listen to a podcast devotion in your car, but don't neglect your focused, one-on-one time with God. Slip away to a quiet place and simply sit with your Father.

Don't let this epidemic keep you from giving God your full attention . . . and be grateful for a God who's always ready to focus on you.

Quiet my churning thoughts, still my restless spirit, and help me to focus on You.

By Design

"Everyone who is called by My name, whom I have created for My glory; I have formed him, yes, I have made him."

—Isaiah 43:7

Who among us regularly thanks God for the gifts of sight and hearing? The abilities we human beings have to see, to hear, and to learn, remember, and imagine are quite remarkable.

The cornea, iris, pupil, retina, optic nerve, and visual cortex help us see. The outer ear, ear canal, eardrum, hammer, anvil, stirrup, and cochlea help us hear and maintain our balance. Then, of course, there's the human brain that processes sight and sound.

The odds of these incredible structures "just happening" are beyond determining. Still, people hesitate to believe in an intelligent designer.

But imagine such people walking along the beach and finding on the shore something unlike anything they had seen before. They pick up the very strange pocket watch and open the cover. Upon seeing its inner workings, wouldn't they logically conclude that a designer was behind its existence?

We find in our bodies, especially the organs allowing us to see and hear, countless reasons to praise God for His breathtaking handiwork.

Creator and Sustainer of life, I marvel at the human body. Thank You for helping me see Your hand in its design.

The Best Choice

Choose for yourselves this day whom you will serve.

—Joshua 24:15

*I*sraelite leader Joshua knew that he couldn't force the people of Israel to make a heartfelt, genuine commitment to God. Yet only that dedication to the Lord enables His people to be faithful despite life's wildernesses. That foundational choice to live as God's people also guides how we spend our time and money; whom we have as friends; what we read, listen to, watch.

In her book *Choosing Gratitude: Your Journey to Joy*, Christian radio host, speaker, and author Nancy Leigh DeMoss wrote about a choice we face multiple times each day:

> I have learned that in every circumstance that comes my way, I can respond in one of two ways: I can whine or I can worship! And I can't worship without giving thanks. It just isn't possible. When we choose the pathway of worship and giving thanks, especially in the midst of difficult circumstances, there is a fragrance, a radiance, that issues forth out of our lives to bless the Lord and others.

Joshua knew that choosing to serve God was choosing a life of worship. And it is a very good choice.

Lord God, please help me make the best choice—to serve You—in big ways and small, with my life and in my days.

Why?

"I, even I, am He who blots out your transgressions for My own sake; and I will not remember your sins."

—Isaiah 43:25

Why? Just a simple word, but it's the one that's really at the heart of so many questions about God, isn't it? It is the one word that sometimes makes it so hard to believe. Not just the why of things that happen, but all those other whys too:

- Why did God rescue His rebellious people time and time again?
- Why did God plan for His Son to leave His side?
- Why did God place all the darkness of sin on the One who never sinned?
- And . . . *why does God love, forgive, and redeem someone like me?*

Why? is a simple question with a simple answer. Because of His great love for you, God created a way to blot out your transgressions, to wash away your sins, to make you whiter than snow. He did it for His own sake, so that He wouldn't have to live forever without you.

Thank You, Lord, for a love so great that it answers my "Why?" with "Because I love you."

Beating the Odds

Philip found Nathanael and said to him, "We have found Him of whom Moses in the law, and also the prophets, wrote—Jesus of Nazareth, the son of Joseph."

—John 1:45

The Old Testament prophets wrote about Jesus, and they did so in different places and at different times, some of them five hundred years before Jesus walked the earth and some of them a thousand years before.

Consider six of the sixty-one Old Testament prophecies about Jesus. The Messiah would be born in Bethlehem (Micah 5:2). A person—whom we know as John the Baptist—would "prepare the way" by calling people to repent of their sins (Malachi 3:1). There, a friend would betray Jesus (Psalm 41:9), and the friend would receive thirty pieces of silver for doing so (Zechariah 11:12). The accused but innocent Christ would be silent during His trial (Isaiah 53:7), and that trial would lead to His being crucified (Psalm 22:16).

The odds that a single person would fulfill these six prophecies are astronomical. Yet Jesus fulfilled all six listed as well as the remaining fifty-five.

Today thank God that He is faithful to do what He says He will do—in your life and in history—whatever the odds.

Thank You, Lord, for Your written and reliable Word, for prophecies made as well as promises fulfilled.

The Perfect God for You

"To whom will you compare me? Or who is my equal?" says the Holy One.

—Isaiah 40:25 NIV

Do you thank God for variety that makes life interesting? You thrive on any unknown that suggests adventure and discovery. Or do you thank God for your comfortable routine? Routine keeps you calm. Life is nice and predictable. You could stay in your cozy pattern forever!

If you are someone who doesn't like newness or change, then the God of the Old Testament and the New, the God who sent Jesus to die for your sins, is the One for you! After all, He is "the Father of lights, with whom there is no variation or shadow of turning" (James 1:17).

If you are someone who is energized by newness and change, then the God of the Old Testament and the New, the God who sent Jesus to die for your sins, is also the One for you! Why? Because "His compassions fail not. They are new every morning; great is Your faithfulness" (Lamentations 3:22–23). Every day the manifestations of God's mercy and compassion are different and unique.

Thank God that He never changes and for the infinite variety of ways He shows His love.

I praise You for being the everlasting, never-changing God who will always love me as well as the extravagantly creative God who blesses me with such variety.

Love *and* Action

Dear children, let us not love with words or speech but with actions and in truth.

—1 John 3:18 NIV

The life of Jesus was and still is a life of love, from before His life's earthly beginning to forever after its earthly end. But His years on earth were also much more than that. His was a life of both love and action.

- He walked on water and offered His living water to a woman by a well.
- He prayed to His Father and taught His followers to do the same.
- He touched the lepers and gave sight to the blind.
- He raised Lazarus from the dead and an adulteress from the dirt.
- He forgave the disciples who deserted Him.

Jesus lived a life of perfect faith to show us the way to do it too. It was not a passive life; rather, it was a busy one filled with acts of love.

Will you let His love be active in your life this day? And will you then praise Him by letting His love be active through you?

Help me, Lord Jesus, to live the kind of life You did.

Faith Steps Out

If we are thrown into the blazing furnace, the God we serve is able to deliver us from it, and he will deliver us.

—Daniel 3:17 NIV

Charles Blondin was the first person to cross Niagara Falls on a tightrope. On his first of seventeen crossings, the three-inch hemp cord stretched eleven hundred feet across the river. Crowds on both sides roared at his success. It was 1859.

Blondin crossed in a variety of ways: on stilts, pushing a wheelbarrow, blindfolded. Whatever his feat, the crowd cheered loudly and enthusiastically. At one point he offered to carry one of his spectators, the Prince of Wales, on the rope over the Falls. The prince demurred, but Blondin did carry his manager over.

Had you been present, and had Blondin asked, "Do you think I could carry a person across in this wheelbarrow?" what would you have answered?

As we all know, talk is cheap. It's easier, for instance, to say we have faith than to ride across Niagara Falls in Blondin's wheelbarrow. But without actions, ours is not genuine faith. Like the three young men in Daniel 3 who assured a powerful king that their God was even more powerful, we can opt to believe in the Lord's promises. Let's thank God that, day by day, He gives us opportunities to learn to trust Him more.

Thank You, Lord, that I can fearlessly step out in faith and sit in Your wheelbarrow.

"I Will Give You Rest"

"Come to me, all you who are weary and burdened, and I will give you rest."

—Matthew 11:28 NIV

Weary, *exhausted*, *drowsy*, or *drained*: we have so many words to describe that one feeling of just being tired. The truth is that we live in a wearying world. There's so much pressure to do, to be, to accomplish that rest—even necessary, needed sleep—feels like a guilty pleasure. So we push through. We rise early and go to bed late. But if we aren't careful, we can find ourselves going through the motions, living our days in an exhausted haze of checking off boxes on a to-do list that will never be completely finished.

More than once Jesus invited His disciples to step away from the rush. He urged them to "come with me by yourselves to a quiet place and get some rest" (Mark 6:31 NIV). Why? Because Jesus knows it's easier for us to neglect our rest and our time with Him than to neglect our to-do list.

Whatever words we use to describe tiredness, Jesus' invitation serves as a gentle reminder we must take care of ourselves. And when we do step away with Him, He gifts us with a beautiful promise: He will give us rest.

How wonderful to be loved by such a Savior as You, Lord—to know that You understand my need to rest.

Two Kinds of Hearing

"He who has ears to hear, let him hear!"

—Matthew 13:9

What have you heard already today? What sounds have you thanked God for? Our ability to hear is a gift for which we can be grateful.

When spiritually deaf people hear the gospel for the first time—when they understand that Jesus died for their sins—their lives can be radically different, and their eternal lives absolutely will be!

Jesus knew, though, that not everyone who hears the words of the gospel *hears*—grasps—what it means. After He told a story about the sower's seed falling by the wayside, on stony ground, among thorns, and on good soil, Jesus acknowledged this about some people: "Seeing they do not see, and hearing they do not hear, nor do they understand" (Matthew 13:13). It is definitely by God's grace when, by the power of His Spirit, He opens our ears and our hearts to His truth.

Whatever you hear today, be grateful for the birdsong, the "I appreciate you," and the laughter you hear. Be grateful too for hearing the "I love you" that God has spoken to you through His Son.

Thank You, God, for enabling me to hear not only sounds in this physical world but also the truth about Jesus!

The Ultimate Sacrifice

"Greater love has no one than this, than to lay down one's life for his friends."

—John 15:13

*I*n the United States, the last Monday in May is Memorial Day. On that day people from Maine and Florida to Alaska and Hawaii remember the men and women who gave the ultimate sacrifice so their fellow Americans could know freedom.

And how many have? According to PBS.org, from the Revolutionary War to the ongoing War on Terror—and that time span includes the War of 1812, the Civil War, the Spanish-American War, World Wars I and II, Vietnam, and the Persian Gulf War—more than 1.1 million Americans have died.

Let's pause and consider how big a number a million is. Well, one million seconds is 11.574 days. If you were driving at 100 miles per hour with no stops for gas or bathroom breaks, it would take you 1.14 years to drive one million miles. And to reach one million hours at work—eight-hour days, Monday through Friday, with no time off for vacations, holidays, or illness—480.8 years. (Make Math a Game website)

Our freedom has cost more than one million individuals their lives or functionality. This Memorial Day, let's be grateful for these courageous American heroes.

Lord, thank You for the freedom we enjoy because of Americans willing to make the ultimate sacrifice.

JUNE

"Be of Good Cheer"

"Be of good cheer, daughter; your faith has made you well."
—Matthew 9:22

Imagine the blessing of living in Jesus' day and actually encountering Him. Certainly the people who knew Jesus' physical touch experienced indescribable peace, comfort, and hope. What gratitude they must have felt!

Consider the woman who found the courage to touch Jesus's clothing and was healed. A woman's bleeding, whether by menstruation or disease, made her unclean and therefore unable to interact with others. The woman in Matthew 9 had been bleeding, isolated, and physically weakened for *twelve years*. Now she risked the shame of having to describe her illness and a rebuke for being out among spiritually "clean" people.

Yet this woman had hope in Jesus: "If only I may touch His garment, I shall be made well." Her touch did not go unnoticed. Jesus knew someone had accessed His healing power, and when He saw her, His "Be of good cheer, daughter" calmed her heart, and she "was made well from that hour" (vv. 21–22).

Today, live with gratitude for your Savior Jesus, who comes near and heals you so that, like the woman in Matthew 9, you can also "be of good cheer."

Jesus, thank You for healing and comforting. Please touch me today.

Never Greater Than God's Grace

He . . . Himself bore our sins in His own body on the tree, that we,
having died to sins, might live for righteousness.

—1 Peter 2:23–24

Adam and Eve had one rule to follow in Eden: "Of the tree of the knowledge of good and evil you shall not eat" (Genesis 2:17). Nudged by the deceiver, "when the woman saw that the tree was good for food, that it was pleasant to the eyes, and a tree desirable to make one wise, she took of its fruit and ate" (Genesis 3:6). Haven't we all done something similar?

Through the millennia, however, our sin was never greater than God's grace. He already had a plan for restoring our relationship with Him.

The night before Jesus was sacrificed on the cross, He shared a meal with His disciples. Matthew reported, "As they were eating, Jesus took bread, blessed and broke it, and gave it to the disciples and said, 'Take, eat; this is My body'" (26:26).

Did you notice the parallel? Eve took and ate and introduced death into the world. Jesus invites us to "eat" of His sacrifice, restoring life to the world.

Eve broke the one deadly rule, and Jesus overcame the consequences for all humankind.

I praise You and thank You for Your sovereign grace.

An Open Door

"I know your deeds. See, I have placed before you an open door that no one can shut. I know that you have little strength, yet you have kept my word and have not denied my name."

—Revelation 3:8 NIV

Your heart and your life are like a door. But whether to open or close it, whether to let others in or keep them out—that is up to you. Most people will knock on a door, but if no one answers they will go away. They might try another time, or they might not. But Jesus stands at the door of your life, your heart, and just keeps knocking (Revelation 3:20). Sometimes He knocks softly, sometimes He pounds, but He doesn't ever go away. He waits until either you welcome Him inside or it's too late.

Some people are afraid to let Jesus inside because of the mess that He'll find there: mistakes, shambles of sins, untidied thoughts and desires, a chaos of questions and confusion. But just look at what He says, "I know your deeds." Another translation says, "I know everything you have done" (CEV). Jesus has already seen what's on the other side of the door—and guess what? He loves you so much that He still wants in!

Each time you open or close a door this day, be thankful for the One who is always eager to come inside—and let your door swing open wide!

So often I am weak, but I will always strive to follow You, Lord. Thank You for coming into my life.

Faith and Respect

Only speak a word, and my servant will be healed.

—Matthew 8:8

A Roman centurion spoke these words of Matthew 8:8. This military man—who of course understood the hierarchy of leadership and authority—had respectfully asked Jesus to heal his servant, who was "lying at home paralyzed, dreadfully tormented." Jesus didn't hesitate: "I will come and heal him" (Matthew 8:6–7).

That's when the humble soldier pushed back a bit, confessed his sense of unworthiness, and suggested that Jesus simply speak the healing words rather than go to his home. This commander of a hundred soldiers knew about authority: "I say to this one, 'Go,' and he goes; and to another, 'Come,' and he comes; and to my servant, 'Do this,' and he does it." Jesus "marveled" when He heard the centurion: "Assuredly, I say to you, I have not found such great faith, not even in Israel!" (vv. 9–10).

Jesus has ultimate authority over everything and everyone. The centurion recognized and respected Jesus' position, giving us an example to follow. Thankful for His absolute righteousness, may we recognize and respect Jesus' authority as well.

Today, how might you, like the centurion, display your respect for Jesus' righteous authority and your faith in His ability to act on your behalf?

Help me to respect Your authority in all I think, do, and pray.

Precious People

I thank my God every time I remember you.

—Philippians 1:3 NIV

There's that one person who is just a little extra special. You know the one. He or she never fails to bring a smile to your face and a little leap of joy to your heart.

Perhaps it's a treasured grandparent who always provides a loving and safe place to land. Perhaps it's a friend who's seen you through the ups, the downs, and the everydays, and who's never too busy to listen. Perhaps it's a child who fills your heart with so much love you wonder if it might burst, or a spouse who can brighten your whole day with just a smile.

God gifts us with those whose gentle hands and wise advice shape and mold us. He blesses us with people of strength who reach out, who help and hold us. These special ones, created in the image of God Himself and reflecting His love in our lives, lift our spirits and smooth our frayed edges. They help us be who God created us to be.

Yes, thank God for that special one who lights up your life, but don't stop there. *Be* one of those precious people. Be someone who is always remembered with thanks.

You fill my life with people who make this world better and help me to be a better person in it. Teach me to be that kind of person too.

The Right Word

A word fitly spoken is like apples of gold in settings of silver.
—Proverbs 25:11

Are you one of those people who always seems to know just what to say? The right word at the right time in the right way is a beautiful and powerful thing. And Jesus was the Master of always knowing the perfect thing to say.

- To a father grieving the news of his daughter's death He said, "Do not be afraid; only believe" (Mark 5:36).
- To a downhearted disciple He inspired confidence by urging, "Feed My sheep" (John 21:17).
- To the Pharisees trying to trap Him with questions about taxes He replied, "Give back to Caesar what is Caesar's, and to God what is God's" (Matthew 22:21 NIV).

Whether it was to comfort, encourage, challenge, or deftly dodge a Pharisee's snare, Jesus' words were always flavored with wisdom. How did He manage to do that every single time? I suspect it had something to do with this habit: "Jesus often withdrew to lonely places and prayed" (Luke 5:16 NIV).

Will you do the same? If you do, you'll probably find that same heavenly wisdom flavoring your own words. You'll be one of those people who always says the right thing!

Lord, I am so grateful for the wisdom of Jesus' words as they guide my life.

A Feast for the Soul

Oh, taste and see that the LORD is good; blessed is the man who trusts in Him!

—Psalm 34:8

It was the first feast of summer. The red-and-white-checked tablecloth covered the picnic table, and wildflowers smiled from the vase in the middle.

Slices of watermelon, cantaloupe, and honeydew made a rainbow of sweet refreshment. Tomatoes, lettuce, and red onions waited for a home on a burger—and the burgers would be off the grill any minute. Right now the aroma was whetting appetites as the potato salad, corn on the cob, and chips called people's names. Soon they would taste and eat; soon the flavors would satisfy!

When we taste the truth of our Lord, the flavor of His goodness satisfies our souls. Just as a child might hesitate to taste a foreign-looking casserole, some people might hesitate to risk seeing if the Lord will indeed be faithful, generous, forgiving, and loving. Those of us who have learned that, yes, God is always good, can encourage the reluctant by sharing our experiences of God's kindness.

Summer picnics aside, once we taste God's goodness, an amazing feast for the soul is ours. When we read His Word, sing His praises, worship, and hear His voice as we pray, we are indeed relishing God's greatness!

Thank You, Lord. Your goodness satisfies my soul like nothing else!

Speak Life-Giving Words

An encouraging word cheers a person up.

—Proverbs 12:25 NLT

Isn't it amazing that with the same tongue we can bless God and wound others? That we can speak words that save and heal or discourage and hinder? The challenge of taming our tongues may be second only to the difficulty of corralling our thoughts. In the same way that unhelpful thoughts pop into minds, unhelpful words pop out of mouths.

Most of us, for instance, can recall a painful statement made to us when we were young that impacted our thoughts about our value, wounded us emotionally, or crushed our dreams. On the other hand, can you recall a statement that affirmed your value, energized you for the future, or increased your passion to pursue your dreams?

We can choose to praise our God and bless other people. Indeed, we who are made in God's image reflect Him when we speak words that hearten and build up others. Let's strive to be people who help, not hurt, others by what we say!

Thank God for the blessing of life-giving words and the opportunity to say them to others.

I am grateful, almighty God, that You can supernaturally help me speak good into the world.

Paid in Full!

God wiped out the charges that were against us for disobeying the
Law of Moses. He took them away and nailed them to the cross.

—Colossians 2:14 CEV

Isn't it wonderful to see the words "Paid in Full" stamped across a bill? Perhaps it's a car note, a mortgage, or a nagging medical or credit card bill that you have finally managed to pay off.

Debt can be a terrible thing. Huge debt can weigh on you like a boulder, so that you can't eat, can't breathe, can't sleep. But even a little debt can be a source of constant irritation. That is why those three little words—"Paid in Full"—can bring such relief and joy. It may take a little extra work; often it takes a lot of sacrifice. But paying off debt is a wonderful thing!

There's only one debt you can never pay off. No amount of work or sacrifice will ever make it right. That's the debt of your sins against God. But when you decide to follow Jesus, He hands you (figuratively speaking!) a bill with the words "Paid in Full" stamped in bright red across the top. The blood of Jesus "wiped out the charges that were against us." Your work, your sacrifices aren't required—and they wouldn't work anyway.

God knew you could never pay the debt you owe Him, so He sent Jesus to take care of it for you. Your debt is "Paid in Full"!

I cannot fully imagine my debt to You, Lord, but I know I could
never repay it. And so I thank You for a love so great that You paid
it for me.

The Music of Gratitude

Be filled with the Holy Spirit, singing psalms and hymns and
spiritual songs.

—Ephesians 5:18–19 NLT

All of us can thank God for the gift of music, but not all of us are especially musical! Karen, for instance, was not a musician, a worship leader, or a Sunday school teacher who knew the hand motions to children's favorite songs. Neither did Karen go around humming or whistling.

But Karen did make melody inwardly to the Lord, and people recognized it. Karen had an amazing way of making everyone feel like her best friend. When she said hello, people sensed her joy at seeing them and her thankfulness for their place in her life. Encountering Karen was like hearing a favorite song that plays all day long. The contagious music in Karen's heart made people smile long after they saw her.

Key to that tune in Karen's heart or ours is a spirit of gratitude. Thanking God for a few things leads us to thank Him for more—and the Spirit lightens our hearts as our lists grow.

Whether you're musically inclined or tone-deaf, let gratitude form lyrics in your heart, and share the joy.

Thank You for helping me be thankful and then using that gratitude
to put a contagious song in my heart.

Find Strength in Community

Let us consider one another in order to stir up love and good works,
not forsaking the assembling of ourselves together.

—Hebrews 10:24–25

We can easily know the right course of action, but acting on it—especially acting alone—can be difficult. God not only understands that, He planned for it!

God's plan involves His people, our fellow Christ-followers, the community of believers, finding strength in one another. When we waver about taking a right direction, we have brothers and sisters stirring us up to do those "good works" and often doing those works with us.

Taking any unpopular stand is less daunting when other believers speak as well. Bravely making waves when it's appropriate best happens when other believers support you and your values.

We lose vital support for our walk with Jesus when we forego gathering with other believers. Oh, we may not always appreciate being "stirred up" and encouraged to do what we know is right, but sometimes that nudge is exactly what we need.

Let's thank God for the freedom to further His kingdom with fellow believers as well as the encouragement we give each other to do good works for God's glory.

Thank You for Your people who motivate me to act rightly when I'm tired, distracted, or far from my comfort zone.

A Key to Christlikeness

I urge you, dear brothers and sisters, to pay attention to what I have written in this brief exhortation.

—Hebrews 13:22 NLT

By God's design, we who follow Jesus are part of an assembly of believers who, also by His design, encourage one another to do His will. And knowing us well, God also seems to acknowledge here that some of us may—at least from time to time—need more than just being nudged to do good works. Some of us need to be *exhorted*, which according to *Merriam-Webster* means to "incite by argument or advice: urge strongly."

This call from Hebrews 13, however, impacts us in two ways: we are called to graciously receive exhortations, and perhaps by implication we are urged to graciously exhort others at the same time. Both are invitations to rely on God, asking Him for wisdom about if/when/with what words to exhort a fellow believer, and for the ability to receive His exhortations as they're spoken through His people.

Our God wants us to grow, so He designed a safe context in which to do so. Let's be prayerfully and faithfully involved with other believers.

Thank You, Lord, for life in community that grows my faith and makes me more like Jesus.

Responding with Prayer

"You will hear of wars and rumors of wars, but see to it that you are not alarmed."

—Matthew 24:6 NIV

Today, with twenty-first-century technology and social media, we hear about "wars and rumors of wars" and much more. Of course we don't thank Him for these events, but we can thank Him for the fact that we know about them.

Why? Because we can receive bad news as a call to pray. Responding with prayer does not preclude acting: We pray for the refugees *and* we write a check to a reputable missions organization. We pray for the African children orphaned by AIDS *and* financially support efforts to house and feed them. We pray that cruelty to animals will stop *and* we volunteer at a pet shelter.

We pray not just once but regularly. We pray for God's light to prevail against the world's darkness. We pray for His will to be done as we witness international and domestic accidents, natural disasters, and misunderstandings. We pray for the victims as well as their loved ones and friends. We may even pray for the perpetrators who are so clearly misguided.

We don't thank God for "wars and rumors of wars," but we can thank Him that knowledge of these events is an opportunity to pray.

Thank You that I can hear and respond to today's news stream as a chance to talk to You.

Humble, Thankful Prayer

Be anxious for nothing, but in everything by prayer and supplication,
with thanksgiving, let your requests be made known to God.

—Philippians 4:6

When you read "Be anxious for nothing," what people and circumstances come to mind? If worry is threatening your peace of mind, the apostle Paul offered a few steps toward experiencing freedom from anxiety.

Paul's first instruction is *pray*! Go before your heavenly Father, the almighty King of kings, and the Author of all history and your history. Let Him know what is heavy on your heart. Yes, He already knows, but He wants your relationship with Him to grow, and that requires communication. So pray.

Supplicate. This old-fashioned word means more than just asking. The act of supplication, according to the Merriam-Webster. com website, is more passionate: among its synonyms are *beseech*, *implore*, *beg*, and *entreat*. Feel free to beg Him to act as you approach Him in humility.

Paul then offered a how: *pray thankfully*. What can you be thankful for when you're worried? That you can choose prayer rather than fear, that you can pray to a high and holy God, and that God loves to respond in His perfect timing and way.

Don't be anxious. Be prayerful, thankfully so.

Thank You, Lord, for the practical wisdom of Your Word, Your
invitation to pray, and Your perfect answers to those prayers.

Trading in Your Worries

The peace of God, which surpasses all understanding, will guard your hearts and minds through Christ Jesus.

—Philippians 4:7

Responding to the call to pray and offer our supplications with thanksgiving is one way we grow our relationship with God. Expressing our hearts to Him means spending time with Him and giving ourselves the opportunity to listen for His voice. Our prayers also lift our eyes to our very big God, and looking at Him can make our concerns seem smaller. He can handle anything and everything that worries us.

Another benefit of praying when we're anxious is described in Philippians 4:7: we will experience "the peace of God, which surpasses all understanding." This peace is also beyond description, a supernatural gift from the heavenly Father, who is the God of all comfort.

When we release to God whatever we are anxious about, He fills with His peace the space those worries were taking in our hearts and minds. By taking deep breaths in His presence, reminding ourselves of His truth, and remembering His great faithfulness to us, we open ourselves to this precious gift of His peace.

As we obey the call to pray, let's be grateful for this promise of peace.

Gracious God, thank You for hearing my prayers and replacing my worries with Your wonderful peace.

What Are You Thinking About?

Whatever things are lovely, whatever things are of good report, if there is any virtue and if there is anything praiseworthy—meditate on these things.

—Philippians 4:8

Too often our thoughts take on a life of their own, wandering freely and sometimes landing in dark places. Our Creator God calls us to be intentional and selective about our thoughts and to use them to enrich our relationship with Him.

Look back over your thought life in the last day or two. What did you think about that was "admirable," "excellent," or "praiseworthy" (Philippians 4:8 NIV)? All of us can improve our habitual thoughts and better manage our wandering minds. If that sounds daunting or even impossible, remember that when God calls us to do something, He enables us to do it. You could start by making a list of some alternate thoughts to those you usually have. You could also memorize Scripture, such as Philippians 4:4–8, Psalm 100, or Philippians 2:5–11.

When our thoughts wander and cause worry, let's thank God that meditating on good things feeds our souls and enriches our relationship with God.

Thank You for an alternative to troublesome thinking: meditating on Your Word.

A Family Tree of Faith

I call to remembrance the genuine faith that is in you, which dwelt
first in your grandmother Lois and your mother Eunice.

—2 Timothy 1:5

𝓘f you look at your family tree and see its branches heavy with the fruit of faithful Jesus-followers, thank your gracious God and know you are blessed.

Young Timothy was doubly blessed to have his grandmother and mother teach him about living for the Lord. Consider the heritage of faith you, like Timothy, have by blood. Maybe your parents have been teachers and role models your entire life. Maybe a grandmother prayed for you for decades. Perhaps an uncle was a pastor or an aunt a missionary.

If your family tree lacks such examples, consider the heritage of faith you have through God's people. Someone invited you to church one day, and you never missed a Sunday after that. The friends who showed you the way to salvation and kingdom living were your Lois and Eunice.

Then there is the treasure literature offers. Believers such as Paul the apostle, Matthew Henry, and C. S. Lewis (among many others) have left you a legacy of theology. Their words guide you to right living.

Whether the heritage of your faith extends back in the family for generations or God has used friends, clergy, or books to teach you, thank Him for the way He led you to know Jesus.

Thank You, Lord, for my unique heritage of faith.

Living with Gratitude

Be thankful.

—Colossians 3:15

As we consider living with gratitude, we realize that having a thankful heart is to some degree a choice we make. In fact, choosing gratitude is choosing to obey God's command: "Be thankful."

Today, think about what you can do to encourage your own sense of gratitude. Put differently, what can you change in your environment to lighten your heart and add some joy to your life? (Joy just may be a close cousin or even a sister of thankfulness!)

Maybe flowers in the center of the dining room table make you smile. Find a few pictures of loved ones you can put in your office, on your desk, in the kitchen—anywhere you spend a lot of time and will see them. Music may ignite joy in your heart. Maybe some days you're listening to your favorite classical composer, but on another day praise and worship songs or folk music will lift you up. Sometimes a plaque with a single word—*Hope* or *Peace*—can bring a touch of joy as it reminds you of your Lord. Try lighting a candle. Pet the family cat on your lap or the dog at your feet.

Help yourself choose gratitude by filling your surroundings with things that bring you joy.

Lord God, thank You for a world of things You use to spark joy and gratitude in my heart.

An Antidote for Envy

Godliness with contentment is great gain.

—1 Timothy 6:6 NIV

Here's a simple truth to help us be more thankful: covetousness and gratitude are mutually exclusive. How can we urgently desire what another person has if we are truly grateful for what we already have? Just as our eyes look right or left, our hearts must choose the direction of either envy or thankfulness.

Our minds can guide our hearts. If you wish for your neighbors' home, realize that you don't know how difficult the upkeep is, how high the mortgage is, how much debt they are carrying, or how happy the family living there is. Someone else's spouse may "show" well, but he or she is still very human and may actually be quite difficult to live with. As for the neighbors' shiny sports car or SUV, the jobs that paid for those luxuries may not be as glorious as they appear, and what car payments, maintenance costs, and sacrifices are they making in order to draw people's admiration when they go to the market for milk?

In God's strength let's fight the covetousness that comes so naturally and instead thank Him for where we live, the spouses He gave us, the jobs He provided, and the transportation we have.

Lord, please transform my covetous heart into a thankful one!

Established Faith

As you therefore have received Christ Jesus the Lord, so walk in
Him, rooted and built up in Him and established in the faith.

—Colossians 2:6–7

It makes sense that being "established in the faith" means "abounding in it with thanksgiving." When we consider where we were before Christ, where we are today, and what awaits us in the future, gratitude follows!

Where we were: We lived by our own rules. We were unaware of being separated from God. At times we might have wondered about the purpose of our decades on earth.

Where we are: Naming Jesus as Savior—"receiving Christ Jesus the Lord"—means God called you to know Him and you responded. He forgave your sins and invited you into relationship with Him. He also gave you a purpose in life: to love others with His love.

What awaits us: eternity with the Lord, as Paul wrote, "Our citizenship is in heaven" (Philippians 3:20 NIV). We will live in heaven with the Lord Himself. What more could we ask?

Becoming "established in the faith" has meant deliverance, purpose, and anticipation. These are great reasons for gratitude.

Father, help me to abound with thanksgiving because You chose me
to receive Jesus as my Lord and "walk in Him."

Mindful of Me?

The Lᴏʀᴅ has been mindful of us; He will bless us.

—Psalm 115:12

It's hard to fully comprehend the fact that our infinite and almighty God is "mindful of us." But we certainly can be thankful for this truth as well as for the evidence of His care that we see every day.

God is the Giver of all the good gifts we enjoy—family, friends, food, and clothing. We also are blessed by the more universal gift of salvation and a future in heaven, as well as by the gifts of music, laughter, beauty, pets, rain, mountain air, ocean power, and significance in His eyes. Anything that makes us smile or laugh is something God has given us.

In fact, all we appreciate in and about life is a gift from God and therefore a reason to thank Him.

Thanking God as we walk through a day for the blessings God bestows could mean a very different experience of life. Recognizing God's hand in all we encounter and His presence with us in every set of circumstances can help us choose gratitude throughout our waking hours.

Our infinite and almighty God is indeed "mindful of us." Let's ask Him to help us become more mindful of Him and His bountiful blessings—and quick to express our gratitude.

Lord, I want to live with respect and gratitude for the fact that You, holy and sovereign One, keep me in Your thoughts.

Live for Jesus

*Whatever you do in word or deed, do all in the name of the Lord
Jesus, giving thanks to God the Father through Him.*

—Colossians 3:17

What does your day hold? Maybe just routine stuff, or appointments that are causing stress; perhaps a long-planned special event, a sure-to-be-difficult conversation, a ministry opportunity, or a dreaded household project.

We can change our attitude toward all a day holds when we decide to do everything in honor of the Lord. The weekly shopping, the yard work, the dirty diapers, the endless laundry, the dinner prep, the meal cleanup, the Sunday school lesson, the car maintenance, the Bible study, the visit to a lonely neighbor, the volunteering in a child's classroom, the evaluation with your boss: whatever you're doing, be aware of the Lord's presence. Adopting His attitude of servanthood, thank Him for being present with you and for the opportunity to serve in whatever task is at hand.

So what does your day hold? Many occasions to honor the Lord Jesus and thank Him for adding significance to all you do by calling you to do it in His name.

Thank You for considering all I do as service to You.

What God Sees

"The LORD does not see as man sees; for man looks at the outward appearance, but the LORD looks at the heart."

—1 Samuel 16:7

Some truths of Scripture—like today's words from God Himself—can both ignite gratitude and make us a little uncomfortable. God had rejected Saul as Israel's king and assigned the prophet Samuel to anoint the next monarch. God sent Samuel to Jesse's house. Even though the oldest son looked the part, he was not God's choice, and neither were any of the next six. The Lord explained Himself in 1 Samuel 16:7.

Clearly God found the heart He was looking for in David the shepherd. What does He see when He looks at you and me? Knowing the Lord's eye is upon us, we may feel regret for all the mistakes we've made, the times we've rebelled against the Lord, the instances we failed a loved one. But we may also rejoice when God sees our hearts because He is full of mercy and grace. In those moments we can feel relieved and grateful that our loving God knows our intentions even though we don't always follow through.

Let the truth of 1 Samuel 16:7 motivate you to more consistent service and deeper gratitude.

Thank You, Lord, for knowing my heart and extending grace.

A Good Habit

"Blessed are the pure in heart."

—Matthew 5:8

Have you noticed that saying "Thank you," regularly and genuinely, is a lifelong responsibility with perhaps a lifelong learning curve?

When we're young and just mastering a few words, we learn to say it phonetically. Having barely conquered *Mama* and *Dada*, we offer our own unique expression of gratitude that only Mama and Dada can understand. As we grow up, we learn the universal rule: always say "Please" and "Thank you." There may be no situation where those words are inappropriate!

Our learning continues as we adults work on saying *thank you* from our hearts. We know when to say it, but does the recipient know we truly mean it? Does the person we're thanking recognize the genuine appreciation we feel?

Giving thanks is a learned skill that we may always be refining. An advanced step might be learning, for instance, how to tailor our thanks to each person we encounter.

Mastering any skill takes practice, and thanking God habitually and from the heart is always a great way to practice thanking others.

Lord God, You give me much to be thankful for. Remind me to thank others consistently and generously.

God Meets You in the Moments

We know that all things work together for good to those who love God, to those who are the called according to His purpose.

—Romans 8:28

All of us have an accuser, one who stands before God pointing out all our sins and mistakes (Revelation 12:10). But here's a truth to hold on to: your accuser loses—though he isn't ready to admit his defeat. Even now, because you belong to Christ, that accuser has no power over you because, as Romans 8:1 declares, "There is no condemnation for those who belong to Christ Jesus" (NLT).

Yes, there will be times when you step away from God's plan. But when you do, because you belong to Him, God doesn't listen to your accuser. Instead, He steps down to meet you on that broken pathway you've stumbled onto. He brushes away the dirt and dust of your sins, your doubts, and your disobedience. And with love and grace, He stretches out His hand and gently guides you back to His perfect path. All the while He heals and teaches and renews so that you grow stronger than ever before.

While the accuser strives to use our stumblings against us, God promises to use them for us.

Thank You for meeting me in the missteps of my life and for guiding me back to the flawless plan You have for me.

Perceived by the Heart

I will praise You, O Lord my God, with all my heart, and I will glorify Your name forevermore.

—Psalm 86:12

Maybe you know someone you just click with: you think alike, you read the same books, you visit the same restaurants, you have similar hobbies, and you finish each other's sentences. That connection is great as far as it goes, but a relationship is richer when a heart connection accompanies a mind connection. We can be thankful that both connections happen in our relationship with God.

In fact we enter a relationship with God via our hearts. Seventeenth-century French inventor, physicist, mathematician, theologian, and philosopher Blaise Pascal reportedly put it this way: "That is what faith is: God perceived by the heart, not by the reason."

As Pascal's résumé indicates, he was definitely a man of the mind, but his relationship with the Lord involved both head and heart. And his point is well taken: if the intellect alone could nail down everything there is to know about God, we would not need faith.

We can be thankful for the close friends with whom we match minds, but the Spirit tends to get our attention via our hearts, and the love story begins.

I am thankful that my relationship with You encompasses my head and my heart, my sense of humor and my logic.

Along for the Journey

You hem me in behind and before, and you lay your hand upon me.
—Psalm 139:5 NIV

This life is a journey. And like any journey, it has its moments of adventure, wonder, and delight—along with its unexpected layovers, delays, and detours. Some days are smooth sailing through friendly waters, while others are filled with turbulence. Though our journey is an ever-changing one, one truth remains ever the same: we do not journey alone.

We are never out of the sight of God. As Psalm 139 says, He hems us in "behind and before." *The Message* says it this way: "I look behind me and you're there, then up ahead and you're there, too—your reassuring presence, coming and going" (v. 5).

In that wonderfully mysterious and omnipresent way of God, there is no place in your life where He is not. When you look to the future, He is there and has already prepared for you everything you'll need to carry on. When you look to the past, He is there as well, covering your life with His mercy and His love. And today? God is right by your side, His "hand of blessing" gently resting upon your head (v. 5 NLT).

Savor this day, and give thanks for it. Not only for the journey of it, but also for the God who never lets you travel alone.

Your presence around me, Lord, is the ultimate reassurance. I covet
Your love, and care, and direction for this journey back home to You.

Our Trustworthy God

It is better to trust in the LORD than to put confidence in man. It is better to trust in the LORD than to put confidence in princes.

—Psalm 118:8–9

Don't you wonder what led to the psalmist's conclusion? What experiences had taught him that "it is better to trust in the LORD" than in people and governments?

One way God has proven His trustworthiness is by making and keeping promises. God promised to deliver His people from slavery in Egypt; He did. God promised to send a Savior and King; He did.

What a contrast to promises we make today. Consider, for instance, how many marriage vows are made "till death do us part"—then broken. Or how many people promise to improve their behavior—and don't. Or how many teenagers promise to be home by curfew—and aren't.

And then there are political promises. These can be so flagrantly broken that we wonder if the promise-maker ever intended to keep them.

Life teaches us, as it apparently taught the psalmist, that trusting God is better than trusting people and governments. Our God has always kept His promises, and He always will.

Thank You for being completely trustworthy, Lord God. You are a Rock for us in this unsteady world of broken promises.

Learning to Be Content

I have learned in whatever state I am, to be content.

—Philippians 4:11

Among the sufferings the apostle Paul experienced were hunger, beatings, and shipwrecks, yet he had learned to be content. The gale-force winds we experience aren't filled with saltwater the way his were; instead we find ourselves buffeted by advertisers' sales pitches and culture's standards. But like Paul, we can learn to be content.

An advertiser's job is to sell, so implied in many ads is the message that this product will mean attractiveness, acceptance, peace, and a general satisfaction with life. At the same time we feel the cultural pressure to fit in, to measure up, to keep up. How can we learn to be content?

Paul said it can be done, and British writer and philosopher G. K. Chesterton offered a how-to: "There are two ways to get enough. One is to continue to accumulate more and more. The other is to desire less."

Contentment comes with desiring less of what the world offers and more of what God offers, which is Himself, His constant presence, and His unchanging love. Paul could look past his sufferings to these gifts from his God. What else could he—or we—possibly need to be content?

Thank You, Lord, for life-changing truths. Please help me desire You more—and to desire more of You!

Praise for God's Handiwork

*Praise Him, you heavens of heavens, and you waters above the
heavens! Let them praise the name of the Lord, for He commanded
and they were created.*

—Psalm 148:4–5

*L*et's join the psalmist in praising God for His amazing works
of creation and for what they reveal about His existence and
His character.

Ex nihilo is the simple Latin phrase used to describe the initial
mind-boggling act of God: He created all that exists "from or
out of nothing." Artists create sculptures using wood, marble,
or granite; chefs create new recipes using edible items; construction workers create buildings using iron, steel, concrete,
and glass: these are all substances that God made out of nothing. Yet still people often fail to credit the existence of anything
to the existence of God.

Many scientific minds insist that nothing can come from a
void; something (or someone) has to cause things like planets,
people, and events to exist. Certainly many who don't espouse
a loving God believe everything comes from somewhere (again,
or someone)—a designer must be behind it all.

The fact is, if we believe in God, the only reasonable response
to the intricacy and complexity of His handiwork is our praise
and thanksgiving.

*You brought everything out of nothing! Thank You for the beauty of
it all.*

JULY

The Potter's Task

We are the clay, and You our potter; and all we are the work of Your hand.

—Isaiah 64:8

Isn't it good that we aren't in charge of making ourselves more like Jesus? That would be an impossible assignment. But how do you feel about being like clay in the hands of God the Potter? We all know the creative process is not easy. Chances are we are not the most malleable, and the necessary softening of our character will be uncomfortable. We may find it difficult to trust the Potter as He does the shaping work He has to do.

Consider, for instance, what is causing you pain right now. Maybe your life seems stalled, or perhaps you are experiencing loneliness or anxiety. Could these tough circumstances be one way God is purifying and softening you? Does He seem to be slapping the clay down hard on the wheel to make it smooth, consistent, and free of air bubbles that can lead to broken pottery? The Potter wants to remove the impurities of our character and teach us to trust: He wants to make us more like Jesus.

The great news is that the pain from the process will not only fade but ultimately prove entirely worthwhile as you recognize the healing and wholeness you experience. The Potter will have made you more the person He created you to be.

The time You spend prepping me as the clay isn't fun, but thank You, Lord, for the more-like-Jesus creation that results.

Awestruck by God's Grandeur

The heavens declare the glory of God; and the firmament shows His handiwork.

—Psalm 19:1

While all of God's amazing creation points to Him, nothing quite proclaims His majesty the way the heavens do. We marvel in response to heaven's declaration of God's glory when, on clear nights, the ink-black sky sets off the timeless and divinely arranged constellations. We find ourselves worshiping the Creator as the setting sun paints the sky with rich lavender and bright oranges. And we are awed when crackling lightning pierces the pitch-black skies and the thunder rumbles forth in a bass voice so loud and low that we feel it.

Clouds, whether puffy white or darkly ominous, also speak of God. Viewed from the ground, the clouds offer either beauty or warning. Viewed from an airplane, the clouds' unique topography and wide range of colors remind us earthbound worshipers of God's vastness and our smallness. On the ground or in a plane, we may find ourselves awestruck and silenced by God's grandeur, His artistry, and His craftsmanship.

The heavens do declare God's glory and His existence! Let us respond with gratitude at this often-breathtaking display of God's power and beauty.

Thank You for feeding my soul with the loveliness of the world You created, beauty that reveals Your power and glory!

Taking God for Granted?

*I do not conceal your love and your faithfulness from the great
assembly.*

—Psalm 40:10 NIV

Would the homegrown tomatoes and the perfectly melty
s'mores of the summer be as amazing if they were readily
accessible 365 days of the year? What about strawberries, pump-
kin pie, Christmas carols, Easter hymns, and fireworks? Would
they be less special if they weren't limited to certain times of
the year?

Scarcity does seem to enhance appreciation in a supply-and-
demand world. Perhaps that is one reason we are not overflowing
with appreciation and thanksgiving to God. After all, He is always
with us, and He is always good, generous, gracious, kind, merciful, and forgiving. What can we do to be more mindful of His
goodness and more faithful in our gratitude?

Reading this book may help! Find a partner who also wants
to develop a habit of gratitude, brainstorm ideas, and pray for
each other. Set a timer: every hour, stop and thank God for
something. Or every time you pick up your smartphone, let that
action prompt a quick "Thank You" to God for who He is, what
He's done, or how He's blessed you.

Though we appreciate summer tomatoes and Christmas songs
in their seasons, let's appreciate the Lord year-round.

*Forgive me for taking You for granted. Please transform me: make
my heart thankful and steadfast.*

A Jump-Start for Your Praise

Sing to the LORD with grateful praise; make music to our God on the harp.

—Psalm 147:7 NIV

Are you having trouble jump-starting your "grateful praise" today even though it's a national holiday on which we celebrate our freedom?

Maybe you didn't sleep well. Or perhaps you're overwhelmed by getting ready for the BBQ at your house tonight. Or you're concerned about your friend's son or your own health.

Now think about those things from a different angle. You didn't sleep well, but you usually do—and you had a bed with clean sheets, in a house, in a nation of liberty, justice, and freedom. As for the BBQ, you have friends and family to invite over, you have income from a job, and you are able to purchase a variety of items from well-stocked shelves. You can pray for your friend's son and thank God for this bump in the road that will grow the young man's trust—and you can pray about your own health. Remind yourself that Jesus is King and sovereign over all of the universe and throughout all time.

I hope you're able to easily jump-start your praise now!

Gracious and generous God, You provide for my needs and many of my wants—and I thank You with all my heart. I receive these blessings with gratitude.

Jesus' Healing Power

*A leper came and worshiped Him, saying, "Lord, if You are willing,
You can make me clean." Then Jesus put out His hand and touched
him, saying, "I am willing; be cleansed." Immediately his leprosy was
cleansed.*

—Matthew 8:2–3

When have you thanked God for the sense of touch? Sometimes a touch means more than any words could; that was undoubtedly true for this leper. Lepers lived with other sufferers, away from society and synagogue life.

When Jesus first encountered the leper, though, He was concerned less about the man's physical health or spiritual uncleanness than about his heart, which had been crushed by the isolation this disease required. Who knows when this leper had last felt the comfort of human touch? Jesus knew, and He first "put out His hand and touched him."

A deeper healing of the leper's heart happened along with the external healing of his skin. Jesus' touch meant acceptance, community, and compassion. The clean skin enabled the former leper to live out his healed life with gratitude.

Pay attention today for touch you receive and give that means life.

*Thank You, Jesus, for healing hidden internal hurts as well as
external ones—and that You do so with Your touch.*

God Makes a Way

*"I am about to do something new. See, I have already begun! Do
you not see it? I will make a pathway through the wilderness. I will
create rivers in the dry wasteland."*

—Isaiah 43:19 NLT

One of the Bible's most wonderful reassurances is this: when
God's people need rescuing from an impossible situation,
He somehow makes a way.

- When thirsty Israelites looked in vain for water, God
  poured it forth from a desert rock.
- When Joshua needed a little more time to win the battle,
  God told the sun to stand still.
- When a few thousand people needed to be fed, He
  provided all that was needed from a young boy's lunch.
- And when His people needed a way to get to heaven,
  God sent His Son.

When God's people need help, He does things that have
never been done before. For "with God all things are possible"
(Mark 10:27). When you face a seeming impossibility, remember the Lord will give strength and wisdom each day. And step
by trusting step, God will make a way for you.

I praise You, Lord, knowing that nothing is hard for You.

Facebook Prayers

You are my Lord; apart from you I have no good thing.

—Psalm 16:2 NIV

𝓘t has its benefits, but it has its downside. It ignites a certain kind of communication at the same time it squelches others. It connects people who wouldn't normally be connected, but it disconnects people who could or even should be connected.

It is social media.

How recently were you having a nice enough day, feeling encouraged and thankful, until you sat down to check your social media of choice?

You know that people don't post hosing out the trash can, cleaning up after dinner, or arguing with a spouse or teenage daughter. You know that you are seeing only high points and fun moments. Yet suddenly you're depressed because your son wasn't accepted at Harvard, you didn't vacation in Tahiti, and you weren't invited to the party that—according to Facebook— everyone you know attended.

We need to protect our hearts. First, if you're sad or lonely, don't catch up on Instagram or Facebook for a bit. Second, ask God to help you share other people's joy and to open your eyes to all that is good in your life. Enjoy social media's benefits, but don't let it create dissatisfaction with your God-blessed life.

Lord, please help me moderate my social media use wisely. Thank You for all that is lovely and abundant in my life!

Conquering the Blues

A merry heart does good, like medicine.

—Proverbs 17:22

We've all done it: awakened on the wrong side of the bed, full of the blues and fresh out of gratitude.

All is not lost! A couple of solutions can turn your attitude and day around. First, get silly. Find something that makes you laugh *out loud*. You may have a favorite book, movie, or website of cartoons that guarantees giggles. Maybe a friend or relative always has a healthy, humorous perspective on life; make a call and get some relief!

Second, do something for another person. It's easy to wallow in misery and spiral downward, but we can be proactive about regaining our equilibrium. Surprise a friend by taking her coffee; make dinner for the young mother or older caregiver who could use a break. Offer to walk someone's dog or watch someone's child (the exercise will perk you up). Say "Thank you" to someone who's often overlooked.

The day that started badly doesn't have to finish that way. It's all up to you.

Choosing to laugh and to help others enables us to choose gratitude.

Thank You, Lord, that I can conquer the blues by finding laughter or being a helping hand.

Times of Refreshment

Times of refreshment will come from the presence of the Lord.

—Acts 3:20 NLT

*I*s there anything more refreshing than an icy glass of lemonade on a sweltering summer's day? Unless perhaps it's a day at the beach, where the rhythmic rocking of the waves lulls and soothes the stresses away. Or perhaps for you it's curling up with a good book, a fuzzy blanket, and a warm cup of tea to sip by a winter's fire.

What do you do when you need to be refreshed? Whenever or wherever you seek your respite, be sure you are also seeking the presence of the Lord. For true refreshment—the satisfyingly soul-deep kind—is found only with Him.

He alone can shoulder all your worries. He alone can handle all your cares. In the presence of the Savior, you'll find not only the strength to keep going, but also the peace and comfort to restore your soul.

Make time today, if only for a moment, to seek out your Savior. He's more refreshing than lemonade and more soothing than the sea! You'll come away renewed by your time with the Savior—your time of refreshment.

I praise You as I come into Your presence; please renew, restore, and refresh my soul.

The Creativity of God

God created the Heavens and Earth—all you see, all you don't see.
—Genesis 1:1 *The Message*

Just step outside, if only for a moment, and take a look around. All you see—and all you cannot see—was created by the hand, the mind, the words of God.

From the sparkling rays of sunshine that warm your face to the tiniest wildflower bravely bursting up through the sidewalk's crack, every bit of creation sprang from the imagination of God. *You* sprang from the imagination of God!

Because you are created in His image, you have inherited something of His imagination, His creativity. As His creation, you have been gifted with the ability to do wondrous and amazing things. As His child, you have been blessed with the privilege of doing them for His glory.

If you paint, write, teach, build, counsel, encourage, cook or sew or serve, do it all to His glory. And in all things, love—both your Lord and your neighbors—to His glory.

The divine creativity you witness every day also burns within you. What can you do today to fan that spark into a flame, in loving gratitude and for His glory?

Make my life a living praise to You, O Lord!

Buried or Planted?

He shall be like a tree planted by the rivers of water, that brings forth its fruit in its season.

—Psalm 1:3

Said writer Christine Caine, "Sometimes when you're in a dark place you think you've been buried when you've actually been planted. You will bring forth life!!" That perspective invites not only thanks but also hope and peace.

What a blessed perspective on the dark places all of us encounter in life! We feel buried, like seeds, but we can choose to trust that God is at work. The germination of what He is growing in us is hidden, and that, along with His timing, can be frustrating and discouraging. Yet the best option is to persevere.

A student feels buried by assignments. A mom feels buried by laundry. A businessperson feels overwhelmed by deadlines. The summer intern feels overwhelmed by projects. "What's next?" looms large for the college grad and the person laid off after decades with the company. And whatever the circumstances, a broken heart seems all-consuming to the person in grief.

Where do we find something to be thankful for in dark places like these? In the hope we feel when we choose to see ourselves as being planted, not buried.

Lord God, thank You for the reminder that much of the work You do is hidden. Help my unbelief.

Your Audience of One

We are not trying to please people but God.

—1 Thessalonians 2:4 NIV

You wouldn't worry so much about what others think of you if you realized how seldom they do," Olin Miller reportedly said. Isn't it possible other people are too busy thinking of themselves—or wondering what you're thinking about them?

Are you grateful to hear those words of freedom? Receive them as an invitation to live your life for your audience of One. Whom do you need to please? Whose opinion matters? Whose rules will you follow, whose values will you adopt, and whose causes will you champion? You will find not only more breathing room but also more joy in life if you stop trying to please everyone around you. Instead, make it your goal to please God.

That assignment sounds simple enough, but it's not easy. It's hard to please someone you can't see and whose voice you're not always sure you recognize. That's why we thank God for His Word, His Spirit, and His people, each testifying of His great love. Don't worry about what others are thinking; live for God's approval alone.

Please teach me to live for You, my audience of One. Thank You!

Choosing to Forget

"I will forgive their wickedness and will remember their sins no more."

—Hebrews 8:12 NIV

Where did I put my keys? I just know I left my phone on the table, but now I can't find it anywhere! Ever say something like that? Or perhaps you've searched high and low for the sunglasses that were already perched atop your head.

So often remembering is a struggle. But in an ironic twist, while we find ourselves struggling to manage the everyday details of life, we have no trouble recalling every aspect of that wrong done to us by a friend at a party more than ten years ago.

Why is it so much easier to remember the moments that hurt and sting rather than the moments that heal and soothe?

Thankfully, God is not like us. He actually chooses to forget the very hurts and slights and stings we tend to remember. When we become His children, He opts to forget our sins.

Let's be more like our Father. While we hate to lose our keys, let's enjoy losing bad memories of perceived slights. Because that's what God does for us.

Bless me with the ability to remember as You remember and to forget as You forget. Thank You, Father.

Called to Be Holy

He has saved us and called us to a holy life—not because of anything
we have done but because of his own purpose and grace.

—2 Timothy 1:9 NIV

Throughout the Bible we see God calling His people to places,
to experiences, to jobs designed just for them.

- Abraham was called to a journey.
- Moses was called to lead.
- David was called to take up his sling.
- Gideon was called to take up a torch.
- Esther was called to stand before a king.
- Peter was called to preach.

Each person's call was unique, but they all shared one particular command: to live holy lives of obedience to God. We think
of the heroes of the Bible with a bit of awe and conclude, *I could
never do what they did.* Chances are you won't be asked to lead a
people out of slavery or take down a giant! But you share that
call to holy living.

How will you answer that call today?

*Fill me not only with the courage and strength to live a holy life, but
with the joy of living it for You!*

Great Treasure

We now have this light shining in our hearts, but we ourselves are
like fragile clay jars containing this great treasure.

—2 Corinthians 4:7 NLT

As children of God, we have been given an amazing treasure. The Lord has entrusted it to us, though we are but ordinary people, fragile clay jars so easily broken.

What is this treasure? It is the gospel, the good news of Jesus, the pathway to salvation. There is no greater treasure! And God has *given it to us*. He has placed it within us so that "we now have this light shining in our hearts."

That light transforms and strengthens us. Though the darkness of the world attempts daily to shatter us, though it presses and pushes and persecutes, it will *never* overcome the light that shines in our hearts. It will never overcome Jesus, our Lord (2 Corinthians 4:8–10).

We may be but fragile clay jars, but our Savior? He is a rock, and by His power, we are made strong. We may be but ordinary people, but by His glory we are transformed into the image of Him.

Lord, thank You for the treasure You have placed within my heart.
Help me to so shine that everyone in my little sphere sees Your light.

The Canvas of Your Life

Everything else is worthless when compared with infinite value of knowing Christ Jesus my Lord.

—Philippians 3:8 NLT

The great apostle was first a great persecutor of the early church. Paul studied under the respected teacher Gamaliel and let that law define his life: "according to the strictest sect of our religion I lived a Pharisee" (Acts 26:5). Self-described as "zealous toward God" (22:3), this Jew's Jew had a passion for Yahweh that led him to track down, arrest, imprison, and vote for the deaths of Jews who had strayed from the Law and begun following the teachings of Jesus.

Unbeknownst to Paul, his life, from God's perspective, was a mess—a complete rebellion against the truth of Jesus Christ and an utter rejection of the Messiah the Jews had long awaited. Consider God's artistry: He transformed Paul's fiery passion and brilliant mind into tools for His kingdom. A bold, articulate spokesperson for God's truth, the redeemed Paul taught, started churches, and wrote more than a dozen New Testament books.

First a persecutor, then an apostle: only God could have done it! We thank God for Paul's life, Paul's writings, and how God uses them to paint His story of redemption in our lives.

Thank You, Lord! I am grateful for Your redemptive work on the canvas of my life.

In His Hands

Lift up your eyes on high, and see who has created these things, . . .
He calls them all by name.

—Isaiah 40:26

We serve an immeasurable God, who knows our words before we speak them and whose presence with us we can never escape (Psalm 139:4, 7–10). What a blessing to know the One who is all-powerful, sovereign, and eternal. We praise Him for His salvation plan of grace, and we marvel at His creation. Consider these facts about God's cosmos.

- The sun contains over 99 percent of the solar system's mass.
- Eight planets orbit the sun, and 140 moons orbit the eight planets.
- Earth's solar system is in the Milky Way galaxy, and the Milky Way galaxy is in a cluster of more than fifty galaxies.
- Andromeda is the closest galaxy to earth, and it is 2.3 million light-years away.

Look at the stars tonight and thank the amazing God who made them for loving you even as He keeps the planets in their orbits.

Thank You, Lord, for taking care of me even as You hold the galaxies in Your hands!

Becoming More Like Jesus

You know what commandments we gave you through the Lord Jesus.
For this is the will of God, your sanctification.

—1 Thessalonians 4:2–3

*G*ratitude is always about perspective, isn't it? Are you discouraged today about your current circumstances, the trajectory of your life, or the impurity of your heart? Choosing thankfulness may be easier if you first adopt the big-picture perspective suggested by Joyce Meyer. She said, "I'm not where I need to be, but thank God I'm not where I used to be. I'm okay, and I'm on my way!"

Like Joyce, we haven't yet become the more-like-Christ people we need and want to be. But we can be sure that He will both bless and enable our progress toward that goal: our sanctification is, after all, the will of God.

The greatest cause for thanks we find in Joyce's words, however, is the truth that even though we won't be completely like Christ this side of heaven, we are not the people we once were! Praise God indeed!

Whatever you're feeling about your growth in Christlikeness so far, check your perspective. Remind yourself of both the progress you've made and the fact that you're moving forward.

Lord God, I want to be more like Jesus. Thank You for making that transformation happen.

Praise, Not Pride

It is good to sing praises to our God; for it is pleasant, and praise is beautiful.

—Psalm 147:1

Why is it so hard to be consistently grateful and overflowing with praise? Of course it makes sense from a human perspective that when the bank account is low, the layoff notice is delivered, or the relationship is rockier than ever, we don't find ourselves with thankful hearts. Puzzling, though, is the fact that when the surprise inheritance check arrives, you get the long-awaited promotion at work, and the relationship is joyful and fun—even then we can find ourselves lacking gratitude!

Why is that? Because our human default is pride. That being the case, some of us think, *We're good people. Of course great things are happening!* or *We deserve all the good we get. We worked hard for it!* Such pride can mean we think we're owed the blessings God gives.

Consistent gratitude comes from putting away pride and accepting all, humbly, as God's gift.

Lord, help me to replace my pride with praise.

The Blessing of Praying Friends

The effective, fervent prayer of a righteous man avails much.
—James 5:16

The email came early one morning—and quite unexpectedly. It was just a note that reminded Laura of the sender's prayers for a personal predicament and asked for a progress report. But that short message started her day with a heartwarming reason to thank God for the body of believers.

What a blessing to have someone faithful in prayer on our behalf! This particular reminder cut through a recurring cloud of loneliness, and the message itself reenergized hope that God hears and would answer. The thought of this friend's concern offered encouragement throughout Laura's day.

With or without technology, you can bless someone today. Spend some time praying for a person you know is struggling and then let that person know. Or contact a friend you haven't talked to in a while and ask how you can pray for him or her. That person will be delighted that you reached out! Remind someone you care, and you will know the joy and gratitude that come from being used by God.

Thank You, Lord, for Your people who are committed to prayer and especially for those who pray for me.

Pleased, But . . .

Let us run with endurance the race that is set before us, looking unto Jesus, the author and finisher of our faith.

—Hebrews 12:1–2

The high school coach offered solid training throughout the track season, and the runners' times were impressive. The coach was pleased, but not satisfied.

Coach was genuinely delighted with the athletes' hard work and their significant improvement. But even as he let them savor the results of their hard work, he encouraged them to do better. He wasn't pushing them toward some impossible goal, but to excellence and an improved personal best. This pleased-but-not-satisfied approach worked well on the track.

Like the coach, God is undoubtedly pleased when we control our speech, make time to be with Him, and turn off the trashy movie. But perhaps like the coach, He wants even more for us. He wants us to know the joy of His presence, the ability to hear His voice, and the peace that calms our hearts. We'll enjoy these benefits as we keep striving toward a deeper relationship, a personal best, in our relationship with the Lord.

God, like a great coach, will always encourage you toward a more rewarding and abundant life. See it as a vote of confidence in a treasured member of the "team."

Thank You, Lord, for wanting a richer relationship with me than I have dreamed of myself. Show me how to go deeper with You.

Hope and Healing

He heals the brokenhearted and binds up their wounds.

—Psalm 147:3

You understand the value of living thankfully, but sometimes your heart is broken and hurting. When that's the case, know that when you go before the Lord in your pain, your actions themselves speak gratitude that He is there for you. Your drawing close in prayer is an act of thankfulness that you don't have to perform for Him, that you don't need fancy words to approach Him, and that you don't have to fake a gratitude you don't feel.

God doesn't want you to waste energy putting on a brave face—you can't fool Him anyway! God knows your heart without your saying anything, although sharing with Him everything about your pain and sadness—what you're thinking, how you're feeling, what you're worried about—can help you heal.

When you are in pain, don't try to ignore it. Only openness and honesty will help. Approach your heavenly Father and thank Him for listening, for holding you close, and for healing your broken heart.

Father, I'm grateful that You know my pain and will listen and comfort the ache.

God's Unexpected Ways

The LORD rescues his people.

—1 Samuel 17:47 NLT

We read in God's Word that He does things in ways we would never expect or even imagine. Three examples:

1. God whittled down Gideon's army from thirty-two thousand to ten thousand to three hundred—and that last cut was based on how they drank from a stream, not on their swordsmanship or battle experience. And God enabled the slimmed-down army to defeat Midian.
2. The Philistine giant, who wore a full set of bronze armor, died at the hands of an Israeli shepherd boy who was skilled with a slingshot.
3. Jesus fed five thousand people—and that number doesn't include wives and children—with a young boy's lunch of only five rolls and two small fish.

Of course these victories prompted heartfelt gratitude and unbridled praise. The soldiers, the frightened Israelites, and the hungry crowd probably didn't expect these outcomes. When we face massive obstacles, let's put our faith in the even-more-massive God. May we live more like David, confident that God is on our side (1 Samuel 17:46).

Please help me live as David did, facing life's challenges head-on!

God's Good Word

The law of the LORD is perfect, refreshing the soul. The statutes of the LORD are trustworthy, making wise the simple. The precepts of the LORD are right, giving joy to the heart.

—Psalm 19:7–8 NIV

In Psalm 19 David celebrated God's law. The truths in these six lines alone contain much to make a heart thankful!

Look at how David described God's Word: "perfect," "trustworthy," and "right." Let's look at each of these qualities more closely.

God's law is perfect. This perfection refreshes the soul with its revelation of sin, call to repentance, and guidelines for holiness. The Bible's teaching about God's forgiveness, our salvation, and our redemption free us from eternal darkness.

God's law is trustworthy. What a blessing to have total confidence that Scripture's truth will make us wise. The counsel of the world is loud, ubiquitous, and often destructive. We need the Lord's reliable instructions for living well.

God's law is right. As the world denies God, dismisses the very existence of truth, and makes morality relative, we can joyfully receive God's instructions knowing they are absolutely correct for us to follow.

Let's join David in praising God for His law!

Lord, thank You for Your Word that refreshes my soul, makes me wise, and gives me joy.

God's Guiding Truth

The commands of the LORD are radiant, giving light to the eyes. The fear of the LORD is pure, enduring forever. The decrees of the LORD are firm, and all of them are righteous.

—Psalm 19:8–9 NIV

Here we read that God's instructions for life are "radiant" and "firm," and that our fear of the Lord—which prompted us to acknowledge Jesus as our Savior and King—results in a relationship with our holy God that will endure forever. As travelers through a dark world, we can thank God for His "radiant" commands specifically but also for His revealed truth in general. Together they shine light on the path He wants us to walk. The twenty-first-century din of culture and redefinition of existential basics may cloud our view, but God's truth cuts through that fog.

We can also be grateful that God's laws are "firm": they won't change as generations, administrations, and fashions come and go. Thankfully, these laws are completely righteous and, as Psalm 19:1 states, absolutely perfect. When we obey, we can be confident we are headed in the direction God wants us to walk.

As David took time to praise God for His instruction, let us do so also: humbly, gratefully, obediently.

Lord God, thank You that Your unchanging, righteous laws light my path.

Only God

*The foolishness of God is wiser than human wisdom, and the
weakness of God is stronger than human strength.*

—1 Corinthians 1:25 NIV

God has blessed us with the ability to do some wondrous and amazing things. But as the beloved poet Elizabeth Barrett Browning once said, "God's gifts put man's best dreams to shame." For while an artist can paint a stunning sunrise upon a canvas, it will never compare to the sunrise God so effortlessly paints upon the sky each morning. Not even the most talented musician can compose a symphony so lovely as a baby's laughter. And a scientist—no matter how brilliant—cannot create a world and then breathe life into it. Only God can:

- speak into nothingness and have it become everything.
- truly love without condition or end.
- step down from heaven to live the life of a man.
- wash away the stain of our sins and make us wholly clean.
- open the gateways of heaven and welcome us in.

We as human beings can dream of, aspire to, and accomplish so much. But even our biggest, boldest, and best dreams are minuscule next to the tiniest gifts of God. This day, open your eyes to the things only God can do. Then praise Him for such glorious gifts.

Thank You, Lord, for everything You do on my behalf!

Sword and Scalpel

The word of God is living and powerful, . . . and is a discerner of the thoughts and intents of the heart.

—Hebrews 4:12

The diagnosis rocked her world: cancer. She thanked God that the enemy had been detected early, a factor in her favor. Then she was grateful when the Lord provided a place in the schedule of the highly recommended surgeon, because the growth had to be removed.

Similarly we have been diagnosed as having a cancer called sin. We can thank God that, by His grace, we have detected the disease and that He is the very best surgeon. The scalpel He uses is His Word, which is "sharper than any two-edged sword" (Hebrews 4:12).

Matthew Henry described Scripture's power this way: "By his Spirit, it convinces powerfully, converts powerfully, and comforts powerfully. . . . The word will show the sinner all that is in his heart."

A diagnosis is only a starting point. When we face the Surgeon, we can do so confident that He will deftly and compassionately remove sin from our lives.

Thank You for Your Word that shows me my sin and how to avoid it.

This Is the Way

Whether you turn to the right or to the left, your ears will hear a voice behind you, saying, "This is the way; walk in it."

—Isaiah 30:21 NIV

This world can be so confusing. Things we know to be right are declared to be wrong. Value and morals waver with the day, and absolutes are lost in ever-shifting shades of gray. Even two plus two might not always equal four!

The only thing that seems to be universally accepted as wrong is declaring anything to be wrong. So how can we know what to do? Who and how are we supposed to be?

The answer lies with God. Look to Him. He is not only the Giver of "every good and perfect gift" but also "the Father of the heavenly lights, who does not change" (James 1:17 NIV). God's word, His character, His promises, and His wisdom remain—wonderfully, faithfully, and refreshingly—ever the same.

And when we look to Him, He blesses us with a promise: "Your ears will hear a voice behind you, saying, 'This is the way; walk in it.'"

Seek the Lord's truth and lay aside your confusion. Thank God for His goodness and His guidance.

Open my ears, Lord, so that I may hear You when You say, "This is the way; walk in it."

The Working of God's Word

All Scripture is given by inspiration of God, and is profitable for doctrine, for reproof, for correction, for instruction in righteousness, that the man of God may be complete, thoroughly equipped for every good work.

—2 Timothy 3:16–17

The Bible is certainly a rich tome! For millennia we have known that we need "every word that proceeds from the mouth of God" (Matthew 4:4). And Paul told us the written Word of God provides us with doctrine, reproof, correction, and instruction in righteousness. When you think about it, that's an enormous amount of information!

In the English language, those four categories sound very similar. But the original Greek makes them more distinct: *doctrine* is teaching and instruction; *reproof* is conviction; *correction* is "restoration to an upright or right state; improvement of life or character"; and *instruction in righteousness* is teaching that leads to being "acceptable to God," *righteousness* being "integrity, virtue, purity of life, rightness, correctness of thinking, feeling and acting" (blueletterbible.org).

Praise God for His abundant Word. When we absorb and obey its tenets, we will find ourselves well equipped, pure in belief, and able to accomplish everything He has for us to do.

Thank You for Your written Word that teaches, convicts, corrects, and shows me how to honor You with my life.

Obey God, and See What Happens

The battle is not yours, but God's.

—2 Chronicles 20:15

There are some battles we simply cannot take on, at least not on our own. But thankfully, we are never left on our own. So what should we do when faced with a battle we cannot fight? Obey God, and see what happens.

For Daniel, faced with the dilemma of either disobeying his God or his king who wanted to be God, Daniel maintained his allegiance to God. The result? A toss into the nearest den of hungry lions. It was Daniel versus several of nature's most powerful predators—all ravenously hungry, of course. This was a battle Daniel could not even begin to fight. But he didn't have to.

God didn't ask Daniel to take on the lions, just to do what was right. And because Daniel did, God sent an angel to "shut the lions' mouths" (Daniel 6:22). When morning came and the king called out to Daniel, the prophet was safe and sound.

You'll likely face some lions today, whether it's in the boardroom, the playroom, or the sickroom, and there will be a battle you cannot even begin to fight. But here's the good news! God doesn't ask you to fight. Your job is to trust Him and simply obey. God will be with you because the battle belongs to Him.

Today, in each situation I face, I will strive to do whatever You tell me to—and trust You to take care of the result.

You're Not Big Enough

Many are the plans in a person's heart, but it is the LORD's purpose that prevails.

—Proverbs 19:21 NIV

You're all grown up now. You're sophisticated enough to drive, to vote, to have your own job, your own home, and your own family. And you're also big enough to make a pretty sizeable jumble of relationships, of your career, and of the plans you have for your life. But—and this is so important—you are not big enough to destroy *God's* plans for your life.

You may have it all figured out—or at least think you do—when suddenly all the pieces you've so carefully set into place crumble. And you've turned everything upside down—or at least think you have. But again, here's a little comfort and grace and reassurance: you're not big enough to derail God's plans for your life.

You're just not that strong or sovereign. But God is big enough, strong enough, and sovereign enough to take that disaster of yours and convert it into a golden opportunity. Just surrender it all to Him.

You're all grown up, but you're not all-powerful. If you've upset your circumstances so thoroughly you're sure God can never redeem them, don't worry . . . you're just not big enough for that.

I am so grateful, Lord, that You are big enough to transform any crisis I create.

AUGUST

Peace with God

I am not ashamed of the gospel of Christ, for it is the power of God
to salvation for everyone who believes.

—Romans 1:16

We can be very thankful for the ways God uses His Word—written, preached, and sung about—to save and nourish our souls. We can hear the gratitude in Martin Luther's statement written after he encountered the Lord while reading the book of Romans:

> I longed to know what I could do to be accepted by God. Now I knew. I could do nothing. What had to be done, Christ had already done. Christ died and rose again to pay for my sin. In paying for my sin, Christ opened the arms of God. God's arms were now . . . welcoming me, and all I had to do was believe. . . . Now I had peace with God.

Luther concluded, "I felt as if I were entirely born again and had entered paradise itself through the gates that had been flung open."

Here God used His Word to save and nourish the man who became the great reformer of the sixteenth century. This understanding of faith is indeed "the power of God to salvation for everyone who believes"!

Thank You for the powerful truth of Your Word, Lord, and for doing for me what I could not do.

Before and After

Put on the Lord Jesus Christ.

—Romans 13:14

We can thank God for the "before" and "after" pictures He gives us of some of His most significant servants. In Augustine's *Confessions*, this respected man of God offered an overview of his life BC—before Christ. He admitted that during childhood he stole, lied, cheated, and shirked responsibilities. As he grew up, Augustine confessed, he was guilty of lust and sexual immorality: he had an affair and fathered a child. As an adult, he continued in his sins of the flesh and added the pursuit of success and glory. Yet in all these things Augustine never found fulfillment or peace.

Then one day he heard a voice from a neighboring house say, "Take up and read." Understanding this to be God's command to read Scripture, Augustine opened the Bible and read the first words he saw. The passage was Romans 13:14, where Paul revealed how the truth of Jesus changes believers and consequently their choices and behaviors.

The "after" picture of Augustine showed a thoroughly changed man who thanked God for saving his soul. Likewise we thank God for the powerful example of His transformational work in this forefather of our faith—as well as for the "after" pictures He's provided of ourselves!

Show me, Father, how to lay aside the flesh and put on Christ.

Remember Whose You Are

"You shall be holy to Me, for I the LORD am holy, and have separated you from the peoples, that you should be Mine."

—Leviticus 20:26

Chuck remembers with a smile hearing the same words every time he left the house to visit his girlfriend (now wife). His mom always said with a smile, *"Vaya con Dios!"* Spanish for "Go with God," this phrase reminded Chuck that whatever he and his date did, they would be doing with God present. The fact of God's presence made Chuck mindful of how he treated Pam, what movies they saw, and how they heeded curfew.

"Vaya con Dios!" is an excellent mind-set for young people heading out for an evening, but it serves well people of every age. What a difference that truth can make in our outlook as our day unfolds! And what a key to living with a thankful heart. Read aloud Leviticus 20:26 and replace *you* with your name. Receive with gratitude the truth of these words. Remembering that we are the Lord's (1 John 3:1–2) and that He is with us always (Matthew 28:20) can be a game-changer for lost, lonely, hurting individuals, as you yourself may have discovered.

How does knowing you belong to God and He is with you always affect you as you work, play, spend time with family, worship? Is *"Vaya con Dios"* something you need to say to a loved one? Is it something you need to say to yourself?

Teach me, gracious God, to live mindfully and thankfully in the truth that I am Yours and You are with me always.

A Foolish Faith?

The message of the cross is foolishness to those who are perishing, but to us who are being saved it is the power of God.

—1 Corinthians 1:18

We can be thankful that God warned us about—and thereby prepared us for—how the world would view not only the gospel but also the way we, His people, live. The world sees our values as utterly foolish:

- *You're not going to live together before you get married? How will you know this is a good match? Besides, you could save money!*
- *You're saving sex for marriage? How old-fashioned and unrealistic!*
- *The baby may have Down syndrome—and you're going through with the pregnancy?*
- *What do you mean, you're praying about the election? Really?*
- *You prayed and God healed her? Riiight!*
- *What do you mean you're in a rough patch but you're staying in the marriage because you took a vow?*

Aren't you glad God warned us we would be considered odd and ill-advised both for our faith in Jesus and for how we live out that faith? We aren't blindsided by the world's criticism, and we know we will find strength in His Word, His Spirit, and His people.

Thank You for opening my eyes to Your truth and for enabling me to stand strong when the world calls me "foolish."

Lean on Him

Pile your troubles on GOD's shoulders—he'll carry your load, he'll help you out.

—Psalm 55:22 *The Message*

*E*verybody needs a shoulder to lean on once in a while. You know that, because even though the days can seem long, there are often too few hours in them. Because you're running as fast as you can, but it's often uphill. And because sometimes life just isn't easy and the people in it just aren't kind.

You carry on. You smile for the ones who need a smile. You hug the ones who need your loving touch. You give encouragement to those who need a little boost to keep going. And you offer a shoulder to lean on for those who look to you for help, for guidance, for strength.

But the truth is you could use a smile yourself, and a hug would be nice too. A little encouragement to keep you going, a little help and guidance and strength. Whose shoulder will you lean upon?

God would love for you to lean upon Him. And when you do, just look at what He promises: "I am with you. . . . I will strengthen you and help you. I will hold you up with my victorious right hand" (Isaiah 41:10 NLT).

When you need a shoulder, God always offers His.

When so many lean on me, thank You, God, for being the One I can lean upon.

God's Saving Grace

By grace you have been saved through faith, and that not of yourselves; it is the gift of God, not of works, lest anyone should boast.

—Ephesians 2:8–9

Praise God for His grace! It not only saved us, it did much more! God didn't stop at the point of our salvation. In fact, once we named Jesus as Savior and Lord He welcomed us into His family.

Having adopted us, God reveals a father's grace. He provides for and protects us; He guides, comforts, corrects, and challenges us. And it is all God's favor poured into our lives despite the unwavering truth that we rebellious people don't deserve it.

Consider now the scope of God's grace: any good time, special friendship, or beloved family member you can think of is evidence of God's grace in your life. Similarly, any award your children earn, any promotion you get, or any goal you achieve is evidence of God's grace.

We thank God for saving us by His grace—and for the countless ways He has poured goodwill into our lives since then.

Thank You for Your immeasurable and unending grace.

God's Amazing Mercy

Hear me when I call, O God of my righteousness! You have relieved me in my distress; have mercy on me, and hear my prayer.

—Psalm 4:1

Grace and mercy go together like peanut butter and jelly, fireworks and the Fourth of July. We've seen that grace is getting something wonderful we don't deserve, such things as God's forgiveness, provision, protection, guidance, and comfort. Complementing the blessing of God's grace is His *mercy*, which is not getting something we do deserve: instead of the punishment due because of our sins, God offers us forgiveness, and instead of separation from our holy God, He invites us into relationship.

Mercy and grace are life-giving blessings from God, and one way we show our gratitude for them is to extend mercy and grace to the people God allows to enter our lives. God wants us to bless others with the grace He has given us: give kindness they don't deserve, forgiveness when they let us down, and companionship when they are lonely. He wants us to do the same with mercy: choose not to retaliate when we are hurt, keep quiet rather than gossip, and offer compassion rather than judgment.

Our awareness of God's great mercy and His boundless grace can truly be fuel for our thankful hearts: God gives us what we don't deserve and mercifully doesn't give us what we do deserve.

Thank You, Lord God and the Giver of all good gifts, for blessing me richly with Your mercy and grace.

Seen and Loved

"Are not two sparrows sold for a copper coin? And not one of them falls to the ground apart from your Father's will. But the very hairs of your head are all numbered. Do not fear therefore; you are of more value than many sparrows."

—Matthew 10:29–31

Chances are you've been in situations where you felt invisible. Maybe you entered a room and no one welcomed you. Perhaps a conversation ended abruptly when that person everyone loves arrived and, walking right past you, came over and hugged the person you were talking to. Or maybe sometimes when you speak to a child or spouse and get no response, you feel unrecognized.

Look again at Jesus' words in Matthew 10. We can walk through our days thankful and secure in the truth that we are not—and never will be—invisible to our Creator God. In fact we are much loved and cherished, as He demonstrates by staying close to us all day. This same God of unchanging love for us knows the condition of our hearts, the concerns on our minds, and the hopes we are nurturing. We are always on His mind.

None of us likes to feel invisible, and we can be sure that our loving God, who designed us and pursued us for salvation, is walking with us every day.

Lord, I'm grateful for Your knowledge of me, presence with me, and love for me.

Just for You!

"I know the plans I have for you," declares the LORD, "plans to prosper you and not to harm you, plans to give you hope and a future."
—Jeremiah 29:11 NIV

The details were coming together. Chad figured a typical Saturday would be just right. He'd ride his bike to Chelsea's, and they'd pedal to their favorite coffee shop. There they'd list the errands they could do together by bike. He would suggest a spur-of-the-moment lunch at the beach with their favorite couple friends—one of whom would bring a camera. After lunch, he and Chelsea would walk a bit, followed discreetly by their camera-bearing friend. Then Chad would pop the question!

Like Chad, God makes individual plans for us. As we look closely at this reason to be thankful, consider how different plans grow from mere ideas. However good an idea is, it's nothing until it becomes a specific plan and someone executes it.

Consider too that the Designer of these personalized plans has perfect knowledge of each one of us, of our hearts, abilities, and dreams. Of course the plans will ultimately be a perfect fit.

Just as Chad tailored the proposal carefully and lovingly for Chelsea, our Father God fits His unique plans ideally to each of us. We can be thankful for life designs that God drafts specifically for us.

Thank You, Lord, for Your flawless plans for my life.

Seeking and Finding

*"You will seek me and find me when you seek me with all your heart.
I will be found by you," declares the LORD.*

—Jeremiah 29:13–14 NIV

In a world of *maybe* and *perhaps*, we can thank the Lord for His strong "you will" and "I will" in this passage. They offer a refreshing contrast to the fragile promises and commitments we find in this world.

Speaking to His people about the end of their seventy-year exile in Babylon, God wanted them to know that when they sought Him, they would find Him. What a promise for the holy and almighty One to make to His weak, wayward people! In case we aren't sure we heard Him right, God repeats the promise in a different way: "I will be found by you." In other words, He's not going to hide!

Being able to find God is a welcome promise in light of the fact that seeking God is part of the human condition. God created us with a desire for Him. As French philosopher and activist Simone Weil wrote, "At the centre of the human heart is the longing for an absolute good, a longing which is always there and is never appeased by any object in this world." Thankfully, when we recognize this desire for what it is, God not only gives us the ability to look for Him, He makes Himself available.

No maybes with this God. We have only to look, and we will find Him.

Lord, help me search wholeheartedly that I may find You.

God's Always-and-Forever Presence

"Surely I am with you always, to the very end of the age."

—Matthew 28:20 NIV

pparently the phrase was first used in the 1980s. Here is how UrbanDictionary.com defines *helicopter mom*:

> A hovering & controlling, but well-meaning, parent who gets way too involved in her child's life to the point of doing things that are completely inappropriate, such as personally attending all of little Sweetiepie's extracurricular activities, writing medium-sized Sweetiepie's school application essays, and submitting full-grown Sweetiepie's job applications.

A helicopter parent is much too present with his or her children, and that keeps them from essential tasks such as learning to think for themselves, failing, coping, or making decisions—and the list goes on. Many helicopter parents deserve a bad rap, but a *helicopter God* is a pretty wonderful reality.

Savor the truth that God is "with you always." And His presence means counsel, guidance, protection, peace, joy, hope, and the words you need in any situation. (The list goes on here too!)

Though *helicopter mom* is a contemporary term, the concept of a helicopter God is ageless. What a reason to give thanks!

Lord, help me be aware of Your presence so I can walk close to You.

The Yoke Jesus Offers

"Take My yoke upon you and learn from Me, for I am gentle and lowly in heart, and you will find rest for your souls. For My yoke is easy and My burden is light."

—Matthew 11:29–30

To nonfarmers, Jesus' invitation may not mean much. What is He asking us to do? A yoke is the crossbar that rests on the shoulders of two animals (oxen, for instance), connecting them so they work together on a given task (like plowing a field). The farmer is more productive with double the strength, and the oxen are less worn from sharing the load.

What does it mean to take on Jesus' yoke? What "work" must we do to find the rest Jesus offers? According to Jon Bloom's blog post, "Come, All Who Are Weary":

> Jesus answered this question in John 6:29: "This is the work of God, that you believe in him whom he has sent." And he answered it in John 15:4: "Abide in me" (like a branch in a vine). Believe and abide: that really is all the work God requires of us. Faith (believing and abiding) is resting on the hopeful promises of God. That is the yoke Jesus calls us to put on.

Are you weighed down by guilt, shame, anxiety, pain, indecision, or loneliness? Whatever your burden, Jesus invites, how about a yoke exchange?

Thank You, Jesus, for helping me with the burdens of this life.

Welcoming the Light

"The light has come into the world, and men loved darkness rather than light."

—John 3:19

What happens when you turn on a light in a cockroach-infested kitchen? The roaches that were on the linoleum flee, scrambling to hide under the refrigerator, stove, and cabinets. They love the darkness instead of the light just as we human beings love our dark deeds instead of the truth about them.

Perhaps at certain times in your life you struggled to be grateful for the light God shined on your behavior. Perhaps you're struggling today. We get comfortable with our poor choices. In fact, sometimes we are so comfortable with our sins that we don't even see them. Sometimes pride interferes, and we don't want to admit to God or even ourselves how we're blowing it. Maybe overcoming harmful habits would mean changing routines or relationships, and that sounds too difficult.

Now think of a time when you were extremely thankful that God showed you an error. Reflect on the freedom that resulted. Remember how that freedom made the repentance—turning away from sin—completely worthwhile?

If you are starting to feel as if you're racing away from the light, stop and consider what the Spirit is saying. We can be thankful that God does not leave us alone in our wrongdoing.

I don't like looking at my errors, but I'm grateful that You want me to be free of them.

God's Transformative Work

Whom He foreknew, He also predestined to be conformed to the image of His Son.

—Romans 8:29

It's a great comfort to know that God, by His Spirit, is at work in us. And He is working toward the specific goal of making us more like Jesus. Imagine being more prayerful, more aware of God's voice, more available to Him, more yielded to the Father's will.

Of course this process of God's making us more like His Son takes time, and during this process we will know pressure from culture, family, and friends. Pastor Rick Warren wrote in his blog post "Becoming Like Jesus Is a Slow Process":

> God is far more interested in who you are than in what you do. We are human beings, not human doings. . . .
>
> Jesus did not die on the cross just so we could live comfortable, well-adjusted lives. His purpose is far deeper: he wants to make us like himself before he takes us to heaven. This is our greatest privilege, our immediate responsibility, and our ultimate destiny. (pastorrick.com)

Since we can't remake ourselves, let's yield all we are to our good God to do the transformative work He wants to do.

Thank You, Father, that You are making me the person You—and I—want me to be: a person more like Jesus.

The Mystery of God

Can you fathom the mysteries of God? Can you probe the limits of the Almighty?

—Job 11:7 NIV

Do you enjoy a good mystery? There's something satisfying about puzzling out the who-done-it and why.

While that's fine with a book or a movie, too often we try to unravel the knot of God. We attempt to measure and predict Him, all in an attempt, admitted or not, of managing and containing Him. We want to figure out God so we can figure out our own future. But it doesn't work. God is too much the omnipotent, omniscient, almighty God to be figured out by us. Listen to these words from the book of Job: "Do you think you can explain the mystery of God? Do you think you can diagram God Almighty? God is far higher than you can imagine, far deeper than you can comprehend, stretching farther than earth's horizons, far wider than the endless ocean" (Job 11:7–9 *The Message*).

Even if you love a conundrum, instead of trying to puzzle out the mysteries of God, stop your wonderings and enjoy the wonder. Lose yourself in the joy of the Lord. Relax in knowing you don't have to understand in order to be blessed.

I don't understand You, Lord—You are simply too much for my mind to grasp. But I do believe You and will gratefully follow You always.

No What-Ifs

The LORD reigns; let the earth rejoice.

—Psalm 97:1

The psalmist summed it up: "The LORD reigns." Today we might say it this way: "God is sovereign over all." This truth gives us many reasons to be thankful.

God reigns: nothing is random in this world; no evil we witness is beyond His control or His redemption; He as King allows rulers of nations to assume those positions; He is writing His salvation story in the history of the human race, but He nevertheless calls us to pray and heeds our prayers.

We can also be thankful that God's sovereignty is a matter of black and white: there is no gray, or there would be no sovereignty. This means we can choose to trust Him rather than worry about what-ifs; we can find peace in the truth that our all-good, all-wise, all-powerful God is in charge of every situation that concerns us; and we can rest in the trust that things beyond our control (pretty much everything!) are well within His control.

Now consider the circumstances of your life, say aloud "The Lord reigns," and praise God.

I praise You, my King, and thank You for the peace that I experience because I know You are sovereign.

Entertaining Angels

Do not forget to entertain strangers, for by so doing some have unwittingly entertained angels.

—Hebrews 13:2 NKJV

Imagine Abraham is lounging in the shadows of his tent when he lifts up his gaze and sees three strangers drawing near. He springs up and invites them to rest in the cool shade. He sends for water to wash their dusty feet. And he arranges for bread and meat before joining his guests (Genesis 18:1–15).

You have to wonder: When did Abraham realize that the three strangers he entertained were no mere mortals, but rather angels—one of them the Lord Himself?

Though in the end Abraham knew to whom he spoke, when he first invited those strangers to be his guests, he unknowingly served angels. Yet he greeted them as honored guests.

Hebrews 13:2 urges us to welcome strangers, for we might—as Abraham did—unwittingly entertain angels. But perhaps the verse is less about angels and more about treating everyone—stranger or known, earthly or heavenly—as if they were the honored angels of God. For whether or not you accommodate one of heaven's host, you are always offering hospitality to one of God's beloved ones. Like Abraham, show this kind of deference to everyone you meet.

Teach me, Lord, to offer the same gracious hospitality to those who step into my life as You offer to me.

The Author of History

He who testifies to these things says, "Surely I am coming quickly."
Amen. Even so, come, Lord Jesus!

—Revelation 22:20

The Author of history, God Himself, is crafting His story well. Any skilled storyteller chooses carefully the setting for the tale, and the Lord chose the promised land and its vicinity for most of the action.

Of course characters determine the appeal of the story. We meet shepherds, kings, prophetesses, fishermen, queens, prostitutes, soldiers, apostles, and at least one doctor. We meet godly and evil, faithful and fickle, courageous and timid. We see that God's chosen people are relentlessly human.

The overriding conflict of the story is God versus Satan. It plays out as truth versus deception, life versus death, and darkness versus light, and it is evident in every key character's decision. The tension rises when Jesus is born, and the conflict reaches its climax in Jesus' death and its resolution in His resurrection.

Thankfully, in light of the chapter of God's story we are living in, we know the end: the resurrected King Jesus returns to earth to reign in a kingdom to which He has invited us. If a story is only as good as its teller, we're in the most fantastic plot ever written!

Thank You, Lord, for the ultimate happy ending! And thank You for making me an essential character in it all.

The Guidance of the Lord

Trust in the LORD with all your heart, and lean not on your own understanding; in all your ways acknowledge Him, and He shall direct your paths.

—Proverbs 3:5–6

When have you clearly experienced God's guidance and then thanked Him in the moment? We don't always recognize the Lord's guidance the second He's giving it, especially when it takes the form of a closed door or broken heart. But as we look back over our lives, God often helps us see how He has guided our steps.

That was Alicia's experience and, during a speech she gave when honored by a local ministry she contributed to, she acknowledged God's part in it all: "This opportunity changed my life. Honestly I thought my life was over the minute I lost my last job. I never knew how powerful an experience it would be to go in a new direction and work with this ministry. Here I've been able to give and see God bless my effort! Truthfully I don't feel I should be celebrated for doing this work! It was my privilege and such an amazing chance to see God at work." Alicia smiled. "But thank you—I will never forget this night! Or what the Lord has taught me."

Keep your eyes peeled for God's guidance so you can acknowledge Him as often as possible. If later is all you can manage, though, that works too!

Thank You, Lord, for directing my steps, building my faith, and blessing me.

Always Ready to Help

The LORD is my helper; I will not fear.

—Hebrews 13:6

George Müller lived in England in the nineteenth century and served as the director of the Ashley Down orphanage there. During his years of service, more than ten thousand children passed through his care. George is perhaps best known for his utter reliance on prayer. Countless times needed food and money came in at the last minute—without George asking anyone to help him except God. This is what he had to say about the help of the Lord: "We have a Father in Heaven Who is almighty, Who loves His children as He loves His only-begotten Son, and Whose very joy and delight it is to succor and help them at all times and under all circumstances."

The holy God who made sure George Müller and all those many orphans never went without what they needed is the same God who loves and cares for you today. He is *your* helper. When you are in need—whether for food or money, whether for encouragement or hope—call on Him. He is "always ready to help in times of trouble" (Psalm 46:1 NLT). Helping you is a joy and delight to Him because you are His child, and He loves you just as He loves His Son.

Thank You, Lord God, for always being ready to help. Use me to be the answer to someone else's prayer for help.

Being Aware of God's Presence

In Your presence is fullness of joy; at Your right hand are pleasures forevermore.

—Psalm 16:11

What does your day hold? Getting the kids to school, sweeping the front walkway, chatting with a neighbor . . . or rescheduling a meeting, confirming details about a business trip, checking in with the new hire. . . .

Whatever tasks fill your day, try doing them with an awareness of God's love for you and His presence with you. That awareness will transform your day-to-day, all-too-routine life, as a Carmelite monk in Paris learned almost four hundred years ago.

Brother Lawrence (1614–1691) shared his approach to life: "We can do little things for God; I turn the cake that is frying on the pan for love of him, and that done, if there is nothing else to call me, I prostrate myself in worship before him, who has given me grace to work; afterwards I rise happier than a king. It is enough for me to pick up but a straw from the ground for the love of God."

Like Brother Lawrence, we can learn to notice God's nearness in all we do—and then thank Him for His presence and for the joy it brings.

Thank You, Lord, that Your presence with me makes even the simplest, most routine actions significant occasions for joy.

From Wonder to Worship to Gratitude

"Can you bind the chains of the Pleiades? Can you loosen Orion's belt? . . . Do you send the lightning bolts on their way?"

—Job 38:31, 35 NIV

What sparks wonder in you? Every answer may be as unique as the answerer! Maybe the *big* things in the world prompt wonder. Does the vastness of the night sky, the constancy of the constellations, or the power of the lightning move you to amazement?

Maybe you're stunned by the *small*. You can't quite get your mind around the atom, the structure of an eye, or exactly how an acorn becomes an oak tree. Perhaps beauty prompts astonishment. When you study the face of a newborn or the petals of a rose, are you moved beyond words?

Consider this statement by Scottish philosopher and social commentator Thomas Carlyle (1795–1881): "Wonder is the basis of worship."

Let the things and people you admire lead you to the feet of almighty God, where you can worship the Creator of all. Let wonder prompt you first to worship and then move you from worship to gratitude!

The big, the small, the beauty, the love—much in Your world prompts wonder, worship, and gratitude. All praise to You!

Recognizing Our Dependence

For God so loved the world that He gave His only begotten Son, that whoever believes in Him should not perish but have everlasting life.
—John 3:16

Why do people hesitate to thank God or even other human beings? Billy Graham offered this insight: "When thanksgiving is filled with true meaning and is not just the formality of a polite 'thank you,' it is the recognition of dependence."

For some of us in the homeland of the Declaration of Independence, the idea of admitting one's dependence is as impossible as the idea of flying to the moon without a rocket. Admit we need something? Acknowledge that someone must do something for us because we can't do it ourselves?

Yet admitting one's dependence is key to accepting the gospel. We need to confess our need for a Savior. We need to acknowledge that Jesus took the punishment for our sins when He died on the cross, that only He could do that, and that He was victorious over death when He rose from the dead.

Our recognition of our need for forgiveness leads to the holy recognition of our dependence on God. Don't you think this should inspire a lifelong, wholehearted "Thank You"?

Lord, I want my words and actions every day to reflect Your love and my gratitude.

Grumbling or Grateful?

The Lord gives you meat to eat in the evening, and in the morning bread to the full.

—Exodus 16:8

As every parent of a toddler or two knows, hungry people tend to be cranky people. Imagine a chorus of hundreds of thousands of crabby complainers! Rather than a people grateful that they had been freed from Egyptian slavery, the Lord had people full of gripes. Doesn't that sound like us?

It probably had been a few weeks since the children of Israel had left Egypt, so the novelty of being free and traveling to a promised land was gone. New hardships appeared, and the people's words to Moses and Aaron were dramatic, accusatory, and ungrateful. The Israelites were hungry and cranky.

But as Moses explained, "Your complaints are not against us but against the Lord" (v. 8). Yet between the people's complaining and Moses' reprimand, the Lord made another promise to His faithless children: "I will rain bread from heaven for you" (v. 4).

You don't have to be a parent to understand the connection between hunger and complaining. When you hear yourself grumbling, stop that snowball of ingratitude from gaining size and speed. Take a deep breath, find three things to be grateful for, and thank God.

Forgive me for grumbling, Lord. Make me aware of when it starts so I can choose gratitude instead.

What a Privilege!

Because you are sons, God has sent forth the Spirit of His Son into your hearts, crying out, "Abba, Father!"

—Galatians 4:6

Just as we may not grasp the incredible awe the Jewish people felt toward Yahweh—so awed they hesitated to say His name—we may not grasp the amazing privilege it is to approach Him as "Abba" (Daddy) or "Father." This radical change is reason to be thankful indeed!

In the gospel of Luke, we read that the priest Zechariah had been chosen by lot to enter the Holy of Holies and burn incense to the Lord, and no priest took that assignment lightly. He had to carefully wash himself and then put on special clothes. He took with him into this holiest of places incense so smoke would cover his eyes and he couldn't actually see God.

Clearly this was a serious matter: the entrance was an act of awe and reverence. In fact, historians report that priests would have a rope tied on them in case they died in God's presence, so people could pull out the bodies without entering the room.

How things changed when Jesus shed His own blood for our sins! Awe and reverence are still appropriate when we approach God even though we are blessed to call Him "Abba."

May I always enter Your presence with reverence for Your holiness and with gratitude for the privilege of calling You Daddy.

Praise Without Ceasing

Pray without ceasing.

—1 Thessalonians 5:17

"Pray without ceasing" is the message of today's verse. The next verse says, "In everything give thanks." So perhaps another way of saying 1 Thessalonians 5:17 is "*Praise* without ceasing." And in the book of Psalms, the different writers showed us how to do just that.

Upon rising in the morning, David began each day with praise: "In the morning I will sing of your love" (Psalm 59:16 NIV). Why? Because "it is good to give thanks to the LORD . . . in the morning" (Psalm 92:1–2).

All through the day, more than "seven times a day I praise You," the writer declared (Psalm 119:164). And when the day drew to an end, the psalmist was found still praising the Lord: "I remember Your name in the night, O LORD" (Psalm 119:55).

In the best of times, David sang, "Great is the LORD, and greatly to be praised" (Psalm 145:3). In the most difficult of times, in the face of his own sins, David lifted his voice to say, "Be glad in the LORD and rejoice . . . shout for joy" (Psalm 32:11).

Will you do as David did and make "praise without ceasing" a way of life? Will you declare, "I will praise you every day; yes, I will praise you forever" (Psalm 145:2–3 NLT)?

Great are You, Lord! You are worthy of all my praise.

Even Then

We do not have a high priest who is unable to empathize with our weaknesses, but we have one who has been tempted in every way, just as we are—yet he did not sin.

—Hebrews 4:15 NIV

But you just don't understand!

How many times have you heard—or said—those words? Though the words may sound childish, often they are true. There are some things about us, about the lives we live and the things we face, that others simply cannot understand. Why? Because they haven't traveled the path we walk.

But there is One who always understands. In His all-knowing greatness, He knows us inside and out. Yes, but more than that, Jesus understands because He has traveled the very paths we walk.

Just like us, He was both loved and hated, honored and despised. He was offered the world and knew He had to refuse it. He dealt with tricky family situations. He worked until He was ready to drop and listened to those who still didn't appreciate all He did. He was misunderstood, misjudged, and betrayed; He was loved, honored, and cherished.

When you feel as if no one else could possibly understand, be grateful . . . because *even then* Jesus does.

Thank You, Lord Jesus. How wonderful to be so completely understood!

Getting It Right

"Do not worry about your life, what you will eat; nor about the body, what you will put on. Life is more than food, and the body is more than clothing."

—Luke 12:22–23

Successful as a writer of magazine articles, Landis was applying for a position as an editor. In fact, he was one of the final three candidates. At his final interview, Landis was told the decision would be made and everyone notified before the weekend. And he didn't hear anything.

On Sunday he lifted his prayers to the Lord. Anxious about his future, Landis asked the Lord to calm his heart and give him hope. Can you relate? We probably don't worry about everything we could worry about. Perhaps we are more in the category of "selective worriers." But anxiety is anxiety—and this is what pastor Tim Keller said about it in *Jesus the King*: worry is "rooted in an arrogance that assumes, *I know the way my life has to go, and God's not getting it right.*"

We worry about getting the new position and being able to pay for our kids' college and our own long-term health care. But we really don't know the best way for our lives to go, and we, along with Landis, can be thankful that we have every reason to think God will get it right!

Thank You for knowing the way my life should go. Thank You for designing Your best for me.

Jump In

As soon as Simon Peter heard him say, "It is the Lord," he wrapped his outer garment around him (for he had taken it off) and jumped into the water.

—John 21:7 NIV

Don't you just love Peter? He had a way of bounding into situations with his whole heart. When the events of John 21 unfold, the disciples, particularly Peter, had just been through a roller-coaster ride of emotions. The arrest, the crucifixion, the empty tomb, the resurrection: everything was chaos and wonder and confusion. So Peter and some of the other disciples slipped away for a bit of fishing—a bit of everyday, normal activity.

Though they had fished all night, they didn't catch a thing. Then a man appeared on the beach and said, "Throw your net on the right side of the boat" (v. 6 NIV). Soon they caught so many fish they couldn't even haul them in.

"It is the Lord!" John declared. And as soon as Peter heard those words, he jumped right in the water! Peter knew what it was to be separated from his Savior, so when given the chance, he couldn't get to Jesus fast enough. And the Lord welcomed him, sin-stained, dripping wet, and all.

Like Peter, when you have the chance to get closer to Jesus, jump in!

Thank You for being a Savior who calls to me. Help me to hear You—and to take the plunge!

Human Hearts Welcome

*If we confess our sins, He is faithful and just to forgive us our sins
and to cleanse us from all unrighteousness.*

—1 John 1:9

When you've been in a leadership position, have you ever found yourself thanking God that He can use us even when our heart motives for serving are not 100 percent pure? We find it nice to hear our colleagues express their appreciation. We like the identity that comes with having a significant role. We appreciate feeling as if we're contributing when the team enjoys a win. And we also like serving God.

It is good that God uses people whose hearts are human, that is, not entirely pure—because that's all of us! This impurity isn't permanent, though. God gives us very straightforward instructions in 1 John 3:9. That is good news!

Furthermore, confessing our sins—identifying and taking responsibility for them—can undoubtedly be a humbling exercise. When we realize how far short of God's standards we fall, our pride fades, our hearts soften, and we more willingly and genuinely serve those God calls us to serve.

In whatever ways you lead (or serve), thank the Lord that your heart, full of grand motives and maybe some others, is perfectly acceptable.

*Lord, thank You for helping me recognize my sin, cleansing my heart,
and using me in Your kingdom work.*

God's Great Goodness

The earth is full of the goodness of the LORD.

—Psalm 33:5

We serve a God whose goodness is the reason for everything that is good in this world. What good have you experienced? Your answers to that question may be quite unique and very personal. After all, all of us have witnessed and experienced different human interactions, are aware of sacrifices and pain others have not seen, and have been touched by people's kindness in ways that are meaningful only to us.

The friend sits through the night with the woman whose husband just lost his valiant battle against cancer.

A dad faithfully brings to the father-and-son group meetings the son of a single mom.

With their children older now and driving on their own, the couple give their minivan to a pastor and his family.

The neighbor faithfully guides a newly self-employed adult in how to complete income taxes.

When God's goodness rains down, whether we witness it or are blessed to be the beneficiaries, Anne Graham Lotz's thought should be true of us: "God's goodness should drive us to our knees in gratitude" (*The Vision of His Glory*).

Lord, thank You for people who have blessed me with goodness that reflects You. Please show me how I can bless others.

SEPTEMBER

The One Whom Jesus Loves

One of them, the disciple whom Jesus loved, was reclining next to him.

—John 13:23 NIV

Five different times in the book of John, the disciple John referred to himself as "the disciple whom Jesus loved." That phrase—does it strike you as just a bit . . . arrogant? Was John claiming that Jesus loved him more than He loved the other disciples? Who exactly did John think he was?

The answer to that question isn't in who John thought he was; it's in who he *knew* he was: "the disciple whom Jesus loved." Just as Jesus perfectly and completely loved Peter, Andrew, James, John, Martha, Mary, and all the rest, He loved John. Perhaps John's phrase was simply his way of reminding himself that he was wonderfully loved by the Son of God Himself. It was his way of hugging that knowledge to himself, of gratefully and joyfully wrapping himself up in the love of Jesus. When John audaciously recorded this fact about himself five times, he showed he wasn't afraid to claim the love of Christ as his own.

So don't you be either. Don't be afraid to claim His precious love for your own. Wrap yourself in the cloak of Christ's love; hug it tightly to yourself. Lean into its solid, immovable strength. Rest your head and heart in its certainty. You know who you are—the one whom Jesus loves.

Forever Your love is with me, Lord. And so I praise Your holy name!

Until He Finds

*"What man of you, having a hundred sheep, if he loses one of them,
does not leave the ninety-nine in the wilderness, and go after the one
which is lost until he finds it?"*

—Luke 15:4

Many of us grow up as one of the ninety-nine: those born into the sheepfold of God who never stray from His pasture or who find Him early and stay close. Then there are those of us who are the *one*. Whether we were born outside of the faith or we walked away from God's watchful care, we were lost and wandering over dangerous ground.

Does Christ leave us to wander? Does He whisper to the angels, "She should have known better" No, Jesus leaves the ninety-nine safely in their pasture and steps out into the wilderness of the world to look for the one who is lost. And He keeps looking until He finds her or him.

And when the one is found, does He criticize or condemn? No—and this is perhaps the most beautiful part: "When he finds it, he joyfully puts it on his shoulders and goes home" (Luke 15:5–6 NIV).

Hopefully, at one point in our lives or another, we will move from the one to joining the ninety-nine. How wonderful to have a Savior who seeks until He finds . . . and then joyfully carries us home.

Sweet Jesus, thank You for finding me and carrying me home.

Unfailing God, Unpredictable Me

He is the living God, and steadfast forever.

—Daniel 6:26

We've all had those days when we're not quite ourselves for whatever reason. Maybe we didn't sleep well. Perhaps we're preoccupied with work. A big decision looms, Dad's health is a concern, or we're not sure how to deal with a parenting issue at home. Various other issues may be on our minds.

Consequently we're not as patient or kind, not as compassionate or gentle as we want to be. Neither are we thinking clearly or very articulate with our ideas. We may find ourselves forging through life without a lot of forethought, prayer, or wisdom. The consequences of being off our game can be messy, and relationships are probably not improved.

In sharp contrast to us physiologically influenced and emotionally inconsistent (wishy-washy) human beings is God, the eternal and unchanging One. On those days when we're not ourselves, God is always Himself, He will always care about us, and He will always be good, faithful, wise, kind, and compassionate even when we are none of these things. Aren't you glad?

Thank You for being constant and unfailing even when I am as unpredictable as the weather.

An Experiment Worth Trying

Happy are the people whose God is the LORD!

—Psalm 144:15

Along the lines of the classic question "Which came first, the chicken or the egg?" is the question "Which comes first, happiness or gratitude?"

An anonymous wise person has come to this conclusion: "It is not happy people who are thankful. It is thankful people who are happy."

Perhaps you know happy people who depend on happenstance—on random chance—for life's good things: they may not know anyone (or Anyone) to thank and therefore aren't very thankful. But thankful people, those of us who thank God for all that puts a smile on our faces, will know the contentment that comes as we walk with Him.

So, not feeling especially happy? Start thanking God for something. As your list grows, you may find a taste of happiness. It's an experiment worth trying.

Lord, teach me to give thanks, even when I'm low—and then let me thank You for the happiness that follows.

The Way

Jesus said to him, "I am the way, the truth, and the life. No one comes to the Father except through Me."

—John 14:6

Jesus tells us that He is the way to heaven, the *only* way, as "no one comes to the Father except through [Him]." Yet there is more to the way of Jesus than His simply being the pathway to heaven; it's about more than an end destination. A life lived with the Savior is about the journey, each beautiful step of it. It's about living every moment with Him.

Jesus promises to be with us always—"Surely I am with you always, to the very end of the age" (Matthew 28:20 NIV). We often turn to that verse for comfort, as a source of courage and strength in the difficult times. But it is also a promise of guidance and wisdom in the daily journey of life. Acts 2:28 explains it this way: "You have made known to me the ways of life; You will make me full of joy in Your presence."

Jesus' promise to be our way to heaven is such an amazingly beautiful gift. But perhaps just as breathtaking is His promise to be our way through this life. His words, His example, and His Spirit teach us not only the way to live and to love, but also the way to peace, the way to joy, the way to God. Jesus does this with His continual presence in our lives, and that gives us reason to be "full of joy" . . . *always*.

You, Lord Jesus, are the way—the only way—and I'm so grateful for Your presence in my life.

It's Good for You!

Do all in the name of the Lord Jesus, giving thanks to God the Father through Him.

—Colossians 3:17

Giving thanks doesn't seem to have a downside. When we choose gratitude . . .

- our physical health improves. Grateful people generally feel healthy, tend to exercise more often, and are more likely to take care of their health than ungrateful people.
- our psychological health improves. Gratitude replaces such toxic emotions as regret, frustration, envy, resentment, and depression.
- we sleep better. This often happens when we spend a handful of minutes, right before we go to bed, writing down what we're grateful for. (psychologytoday.com)

Maybe you've experienced that being thankful can also help your mind-set, your expectations for the day, and your sense of God's presence. Think, too, about how you feel when you spend time with someone who clearly has a thankful heart: your thankful heart may be just the touch of winsomeness that will draw someone to Jesus.

Clearly, only good comes for us and for people around us when we choose to be thankful.

I want to be Your light by giving thanks and choosing gratitude.

Dance

David danced before the LORD with all his might.

—2 Samuel 6:14

Too often we are hesitant to dance, whether it's dancing in the literal or figurative sense of the word.

Perhaps that's because much of our society's dancing seeks to glorify the created rather than the One who created. But as Solomon so wisely said, while there is "a time to weep . . . and a time to mourn," there is also "a time to laugh . . . and a time to dance" (Ecclesiastes 3:4).

Life is not meant to be a solemn, morose affair. It is not meant to be endured. It is meant to be lived, which includes working, sleeping, eating, loving, hurting, weeping, laughing, and yes, dancing.

There will always be difficult times, but don't let them completely steal your joy and your desire to dance. Dare to delight in the God who loves you whatever the season you find yourself in: Twirl in the arms of a springtime rain. Shuffle along with the rustle of falling autumn leaves. Tap your toes in winter's first snow. Be led by the waltz of a summertime breeze.

Don't hesitate: dance for the sheer delight of being alive, of being loved by the One who will be your Partner through all eternity.

Lord God, I place my hand in Yours. Lead me through this life in Your beautiful dance.

Wooden's Wisdom

Incline your ear to wisdom, and apply your heart to understanding.
—Proverbs 2:2

We can be grateful for and benefit from wisdom, whatever its source. One rich source is legendary UCLA basketball coach John Wooden (1910–2010). Consider this sampling of insights from this Hall of Fame player and coach who led his Bruins to ten national championships and the NCAA men's basketball record of eighty-eight consecutive victories:

> Talent is God-given. Be humble.
> Fame is man-given. Be grateful.
> Conceit is self-given. Be careful.
> Things turn out best for the people who make the best of the way things turn out.
> You can't live a perfect day without doing something for someone who will never be able to repay you.

No wonder John Wooden was more than a coach to his players, and no wonder his legacy lives on. Basketball players and countless more nonplayers benefit from and are grateful for his wisdom years after he went home to his Lord.

Spirit, please help me recognize, and help me live by, wisdom that reflects Your values.

The Obedience of Christ

By one Man's obedience many will be made righteous.

—Romans 5:19

Of the many things we can be thankful for, American theologian John Gresham Machen (1881–1937) identified the paramount blessing: "I'm so thankful for the active obedience of Christ. No hope without it."

What if Jesus had accepted Satan's shortcuts to power and authority? Or what if, exercising His unlimited strength, He had refused to be arrested, He had spoken up to Pilate to defend His innocence, or He had stepped down from the cross? Asked differently, what if the sinless Lamb of God had not shed His sacrificial blood for the forgiveness of humanity's sins? What if Jesus had not chosen to submit to God's will and obey?

As Machen said, "No hope."

No hope for life on earth: no hope for guidance, strength, or wisdom, for peace that passes understanding, for a purpose to our time on this planet. Nor would we have hope for life eternal, no hope for a home in heaven or a new earth. Without the ultimate defeat of death, accomplished because Jesus yielded to God's will, we would not have hope for the glorious reign of Jesus.

Don't you agree? Of all we can thank God for, Jesus' obedience is the greatest!

Jesus, help me to live out an active obedience as You did.

It's Your Choice

"With God nothing will be impossible."

—Luke 1:37

Often people ask how I manage to be happy despite having no arms and no legs," said Nick Vujicic, who was born in 1982 inexplicably without limbs. "The quick answer is that I have a choice. I can be angry about not having limbs, or I can be thankful that I have a purpose. I chose gratitude."

Of course his growing-up years were difficult. Depressed and lonely, Nick couldn't figure out what he was supposed to do with his life. His faith in God saw him through his season of soul-searching and continues to sustain Nick today.

"What I have is true joy. It comes as a result of my faith and trust in God. . . . It's knowing that God is real and that He is in control of your circumstances, and that this life is not all there really is. God has so much more in store for those who have put their faith and trust in His Son Jesus Christ."

Want to be happy? Want wisdom and a reason for living? Use Nick's recipe: be thankful.

Lord God, thank You for Nick's testimony and example. Remind me to be thankful for all I have.

A Plotter or a Pantser?

"I will guide you along the best pathway for your life."

—Psalm 32:8 NLT

In the world of writing, there are said to be two kinds of writers: "plotters" and "pantsers." A plotter plans out each step of her story from beginning to turning point to end. The pantser, as the name suggests, flies by the seat of her pants, allowing the story to find its own way through the telling.

People live their lives in much the same way. After all, haven't you known those who have their entire lives mapped out from beginning to end? Then there are those who never seem to know where they're headed from one day to the next. While plotters may seem to have it all together, they don't usually allow for spontaneity, for the interruptions and opportunities of God. And though the pantser may seem delightfully free-spirited, she can find herself wandering aimlessly, without purpose or direction.

Whether you are a plotter or a pantser, or someone in between, the good news is this: God does not leave you to muddle through on your own. Instead He gives you this promise. Stay close to God, and He'll make sure your story is a beautiful one.

Open my ears, Lord, to hear Your advice, to listen as You guide me along the best pathway for my life.

Get Away with God

You are my hiding place; You shall preserve me from trouble; You shall surround me with songs of deliverance.

—Psalm 32:7

Do you ever long to hide away? When the little ones are scrambling over your feet, when the meetings are endless, when the tasks are tedious, do you ever long to simply slip away from the craziness?

While a trip to an island paradise probably isn't on your horizon, there is a place you can run away to, a place you can hide any time you choose. It's in the heart, in the arms, in the presence of God.

Close your eyes . . . for a heartbeat, for a moment, for more. Breathe in the sweet, steadying, ever-with-you presence of God. Allow Him to refresh you, to renew and strengthen you, to reset your priorities. Trust Him to keep the enemies at bay while He quiets your spirit and fills your soul with the joyful song of His love, His saving grace.

Too often God is painted as a taskmaster, always demanding more. But today, consider this image of God instead: "GOD's my island hideaway, keeps danger far from the shore, throws garlands of hosannas around my neck" (Psalm 32:7 *The Message*).

Seek out your very own tropical getaway. Get with God today . . . for a moment or maybe more.

Thank You, Lord, not only for understanding that sometimes I need to hide away, but also for being my hiding place.

An Amazing Invitation

Draw near to God and He will draw near to you.

—James 4:8

The Lord was sitting on His heavenly throne. Angels flew around Him, singing praise: "Holy, holy, holy is the LORD of hosts!" A powerful voice made the doors of the smoke-filled room shake—and seeing all this, the prophet Isaiah cried, "Woe is me, for I am undone!" (Isaiah 6:3, 5). This vision of God in all His holiness and glory made the prophet painfully aware of his utter sinfulness.

Yet this same God is the One to whom James called us to draw near. Forgiven and cleansed by Jesus' blood, we are invited to move up close to our holy God—and the promise is that God will lean down to us rather than pull away or hide.

The God who controls lightning, the God who sent down fire when Elijah asked and later took him to heaven in a chariot of fire, the God who used the great nations of Assyria and Babylon to bring the promised punishment to His rebellious people, and the God who manipulated the legislation of the Roman Empire and arranged the stars of heaven to signal the Messiah's birth: this same God is the One who, through James, beckons us to draw near.

The Lord is still sitting on His throne, but He invites us to share it with Him. Let's thank Him for His astonishing grace!

May I thank You for this amazing invitation, Lord, by accepting it and spending time with You.

A Wonderful Cycle

By faith [Moses] left Egypt, not fearing the king's anger; he persevered because he saw him who is invisible.

—Hebrews 11:27 NIV

Imagine being able to live life seeing "him who is invisible." The author of *Jesus Calling*, Sarah Young, shares a way to do that from the Lord's perspective: "Gratitude enables you to perceive Me more clearly." When we think about that, we can understand something about why it works that way.

For example, when Julie gets home from school, she loves the homemade chocolate chip cookies that welcome her. Yet Julie puts off the joy of that first bite and expresses her gratitude. Whenever we express our gratitude to God for the abundance of blessings He has given us, we are looking outward, away from ourselves, to the One we are thanking. The more consistently we give thanks to God, the more time we will spend looking toward Him. And the more we gaze upon Him, the closer we will be to seeing "him who is invisible."

What a wonderful cycle: we give thanks to God so we perceive Him more clearly; therefore we find more reasons to thank Him, so we do, and we perceive Him more clearly. . . . We do indeed live viewing Him who isn't visible to the naked eye. What a blessed design from our Father!

Gracious God, You deserve all our praise and thanks! Thank You for blessing us even for giving thanks.

Enough—and More

Oh, satisfy us early with Your mercy, that we may rejoice and be glad all our days!

—Psalm 90:14

Different perspectives on gratitude help us appreciate the value of that precious jewel.

From the other side of the world comes this Chinese proverb: "When eating bamboo sprouts, remember the man who planted them." As our sage pointed out, any blessing can prompt a backtracking of thanks for everyone involved in our enjoying it. Such backtracking, even if we don't go very far, is a good exercise in gratitude. As we "remember the man who planted," let's also remember—and praise and thank—God, the One who planted all we have.

Recall some moments of such gratitude in your life. When has your heartfelt gratitude for X overshadowed your desire for Y? And with your thoughts of Y banished, X may suddenly have been transformed into more than enough.

Our Xs and Ys will be unique and personal, but this experience is, thankfully, universal. Like the Chinese sage, let's be thankful for all that's involved in a gift, and let's make sure our thanks eclipse our wants; may our gratitude silence our envy.

Thank You, Lord, that I know all I have comes from You and that in You, all I have is more than enough.

Rejoice . . . Always?

Rejoice in the Lord always. Again I will say, rejoice!

—Philippians 4:4

Rejoice always! Not just on good days, not when everything is going our way, not even on alternating Thursdays of months that end in *y*. Rejoice *always*.

Really? But . . .

- I've so much to do and not nearly enough time to do it.
- there's this illness that's tearing my heart to pieces.
- my marriage isn't working as I'd thought it would.
- my job is demanding more and more.
- my children are driving me crazy.
- my tire is flat, and so is the spare.
- I'm so stressed, so exhausted, so lonely.

God's answer? "Always be glad because of the Lord!" (CEV). "Always be full of joy in the Lord" (NLT). "Celebrate God all day, every day" (*The Message*). Not because things are easy, not because it's all going your way, but because there is an all-powerful God who endlessly loves you. And because He assures us that we can do "all things through Christ who strengthens [us]" (Philippians 4:13)—including rejoice.

Teach me, Lord, to rejoice always . . . because each moment is one is spent with You.

Paying It Forward

"Whatever you want men to do to you, do also to them."

—Matthew 7:12

Carla remembered those initial days on campus. The university seemed huge, and she felt more than a little lost.

But Carla also remembered the difference Melody made. She was always available by text with answers to freshman questions and reassurance for freshman concerns. Melody had been a lifeline.

Carla resolved to do for a handful of freshmen each year what Melody had done for her. As she paid forward Melody's kindness, Carla was thankful for the opportunity to give, and the freshmen she came alongside were very grateful for her help.

Maybe the concept of paying it forward calls to mind Jesus' command that's come to be called the golden rule: "Whatever you want men to do to you, do also to them." Melody had done for Carla what Melody would have wanted done for her. Then Carla did the same, and who knows how many people paid it forward from there?

Whose uncomfortable first days—on campus, in the office, at the Bible study, with a newborn—could you make easier? The Bible simply says, *Treat others—including strangers—the way you want to be treated.* Take your favorite kindnesses and spread them around!

Thank You, Lord, for opportunities to love others with Your love.
Please help me shine Your light whenever You nudge me to pay it
forward.

Thankful for Little

There is one who makes himself rich, yet has nothing; and one who makes himself poor, yet has great riches.

—Proverbs 13:7

From time to time we hear about wealthy human beings who led lonely, difficult lives because the acquisition of money and possessions did not satisfy. They realized that the astounding bank statements and opulent homes had not fulfilled their souls. These people had invested their lives in their work, but at the end of the road, they had nothing.

In sharp contrast is the poor man who enjoys great riches despite a simple existence and few if any savings. The word "makes" in Proverbs 13:7 is key: Did the poor man make himself rich by sharing generously what God blessed him with? Doing so can mean soul-satisfying blessings. Jesus is the greatest example of someone making himself poor: "Though He was rich, yet for your sakes He became poor, that you through His poverty might become rich" (2 Corinthians 8:9).

Having little can indeed fuel gratitude for what we do have. We can find great joy in truly thanking God for what He has given us. Archbishop of Canterbury Thomas Secker underlined today's verse when he said, "He enjoys much who is thankful for little." We find much joy and enjoyment when we are truly grateful for whatever God blesses us with.

Lord, thank You for what You have given me. Help me find the riches that come with sharing it as You direct.

Divine Interruptions?

He was moved with compassion.

—Matthew 9:36

Do you enjoy interruptions? You're on the move and then . . . you're stopped, stalled, interrupted again. No, few of us enjoy it.

But just think of how often Jesus was interrupted. Martha demanded help from her sister. Jairus begged healing for his daughter. Pharisees tossed a woman onto the dirt at His feet. Physical pain, hungry bellies, selfish greed, and power-hungry ambition initiated so many interruptions.

And what did Jesus do? Did He roll His eyes heavenward and ask His Father, "Why?" Did He turn away with a wave of His hand, saying, "Not now"? Did He grumpily and begrudgingly take care of whatever the interrupter needed?

No. Jesus taught Martha that some things are more important than a spotless kitchen. He reassured a grieving father and lifted a little girl to life. He reminded ready-to-condemn Pharisees that even they had sinned, and He taught a fallen woman she could begin again. When Jesus was interrupted, He healed and fed, taught and touched.

In truth it wasn't people who interrupted Jesus; it was His own compassion. Will you, then, out of gratitude to Him, offer that same compassion to those who interrupt you?

Teach me to see interruptions as opportunities . . . to teach and to touch and to glorify You.

Friendship with God

"Come and pray to me, and I will listen to you."

—Jeremiah 29:12 NIV

Teresa of Avila reportedly said, "Prayer is nothing else than being on terms of friendship with God." And so it is. Consider first how you speak to a friend: not awkwardly, but comfortably, with love and a sense of security, knowing you are listened to and not merely judged. Next, consider what you tell a friend: the big, the little, and the everyday, the good, the bad, the confusing, and the clear. What do you, in turn, offer your friend? A listening ear, eagerness to hear what he or she has to say, readiness to soak in whatever bits of wisdom are offered.

Then think for a moment about those you consider worthy of your friendship, people who have earned your trust, your respect; people you know you can count on no matter what.

Because Jesus came, you can speak directly to God—not awkwardly, but as one who knows she is both welcomed and loved. You can tell Him everything, big and little and all things in between. And you can know He will answer in wisdom and grace.

No one is worthier of your friendship than God; no one is more reliable in sunshine or in rain. And prayer is the pathway to your friendship with Him.

Though I know it is true, it is still so amazing that You, Lord of all creation, wants to be a Friend to me.

Knowing Whom to Thank

O LORD my God, I will give thanks to You forever.

—Psalm 30:12

Think about the best present you ever got when you were growing up, how your heart was about to burst, and how good it felt to say "Thank you" to the giver. Think about the most precious gift you have ever received as an adult, how your heart overflowed with gratitude, and how frustrating but good it was to try to fully express your gratitude to the one who knew you so well and cared so much about you.

Also think about the last televised awards program you caught a few minutes of. What did every recipient do, although some were more polished than others? Yes, they thanked people who had contributed to their success, from parents to spouses to children, from managers to directors to makeup designers, from writers to photographers to viewers.

But what if, in such a moment of pure joy, we have no one to thank? English poet and painter Dante Gabriel Rossetti reportedly said this: "The worst moment for the atheist is when he is really thankful and has nobody to thank."

When you think back on your best presents so far in life, aren't you glad to know whom to thank, whether it's just the Lord or the Lord and a loved one?

Thank You, Lord, for blessings that make my heart overflow. Thank You for being the Source of every good thing.

Flickering Faith

Lord, I believe; help my unbelief!

—Mark 9:24

The father was living a nightmare. Ever since his son was young, an evil spirit would seize the beloved boy and throw him into fire or water. Desperate, the father begged Jesus, "If You can do anything, have compassion on us and help us" (Mark 9:22). When Jesus reassured the father that He could indeed heal the boy, the dad offered this prayer that has become a favorite, a rock of truth, for people experiencing the flames and floods.

When have you prayed for something and, perhaps after several years, found yourself utterly incapable of believing any longer? Theologian, philosopher, and mission doctor in equatorial Africa Albert Schweitzer recognized this common experience: "At times our own light goes out and is rekindled by a spark from another person. Each of us has cause to think with deep gratitude of those who have lighted the flame within us."

When has the light of your faith flickered or even gone out? God wants His people to rally around one another when someone's faith falters: we are to pray for and encourage one another when we're struggling to believe. Think of the nightmares to which you can bring needed light just by sharing your flame!

Thank You, Lord, for understanding a flickering faith and for using Your people to keep the light burning.

Sharing God's Words

The entrance of Your words gives light; it gives understanding to the simple.

—Psalm 119:130

Shannon had always appreciated the Bible, but, if she was honest, occasionally the words on the page seemed to fall rather flat. At youth group, though, Scripture was always alive. In fact, as she listened to the pastor's spot-on and helpful teachings, she realized that his words were God's words, spoken with gentle strength and of course genuine confidence.

Shannon had an idea: she would start reading Scripture aloud to herself. After all, the first Bible "readers" learned its rich truths by listening to it. When Shannon tried it, she heard God's truths in a new way, and she found herself able to weave those truths into everyday conversations.

As she told Joan, "When I try to make time with God my top priority, all these things that I've always worried about—getting good grades, dealing with my parents, having good friends—seem to fall into place" (Matthew 6:33). She said to Stan, "I know you're hurting, but I also know God has a plan for you, a plan for good things and not for only sadness and pain. I'm going to believe that for you" (Jeremiah 29:11).

Rather than falling flat, the words Shannon spoke from Scripture came to life for herself and her hearers.

Lord God, thank You for Your written Word—and for those people who have taught me the truth on its pages.

Coincidence or Provision?

"A priest happened to be going down the same road, and when he saw the man, he passed by on the other side."

—Luke 10:31 NIV

Someone coined the saying, "Coincidence is God's way of remaining anonymous." But is it really that God remains anonymous? Or is it simply that we don't give Him the credit He is due?

Consider this: God is so intimately involved in our lives that He directs our steps (Proverbs 16:9), numbers our days (Psalm 139:16), records our every tear (Psalm 56:8), and knows the number of every hair on our heads (Matthew 10:30). Surely such an all-knowing God is able to arrange for just the right person, just the right word, just the right help.

When God promises to supply our every need (Philippians 4:19), might not the "coincidences" of our lives be the very proof of His provision? After all, in Jesus' story of the good Samaritan, it was not only the priest who "happened to be going down the same road," it was also the Samaritan—exactly the person the injured man needed. Coincidence or provision?

So the next time an unexpected blessing comes your way, don't say, "What a coincidence!" Instead, give credit where it's due and praise the Lord who provides just what you need, just when you need it.

You have promised to meet all my needs—open my eyes to see the ways You do that, so that I can fully praise Your name.

From Sin-Sick to Healthy

"Those who are well have no need of a physician, but those who are sick."

—Mark 2:17

It's a funny thing. Sometimes we don't realize how sick we've been feeling until we're better! Until after we've seen a doctor, followed his orders, and gotten the rest we need. Not realizing how sick we are is one reason we may hesitate to make that appointment. Rather than acknowledging how lousy we're feeling, we tell ourselves, *Oh, it's nothing* or *I'll be okay in a few days!*

This same not acknowledging we're sick happens spiritually as well as physically. We may not realize how ill (sinful) we are until we're better—until after we've been nudged by the Spirit, followed His instruction to confess our sins, and asked for forgiveness as He prescribes. Yet not realizing how spiritually sick we are is one reason we may hesitate to spend time with the great Physician, with God Himself. Pastor and writer John Piper puts it this way: "He demands something great: that we admit we are not great."

Acknowledging our sins or sickness enables us to see how unwell we are, and once we've confessed and received God's forgiveness, we'll realize just how much we needed a doctor!

I am grateful, Lord, for both the diagnosis of my sin-sickness and the remedy—confessing my sins and receiving Your forgiveness.

The Perfect Poet

My heart bursts its banks, spilling beauty and goodness. I pour it out in a poem.

—Psalm 45:1 *The Message*

Robert Browning once said, "God is the perfect poet." And so He is. The Lord created not only a world of order and function, but a world so filled with beauty that it has inspired countless generations of poets to try to capture its rhythm and meter and grace.

Each morning He writes a sunrise upon the sky, unveiling the meter that will rule the day. Will it be peace or storms? Sunlight or rain? Snow or warming breezes?

Then, marching through the day, the Lord unleashes His creation to fill stanza after stanza with nature's own poetic songs— the rhythmic rocking of the ocean's waves, the melodies of the songbirds, the pentameter of our own beating hearts.

His poetry continues through the velvet black night with the soft tinkling, twinkling of stars and the lull of the wind in the trees—all under His watchful care.

But don't think God's perfect poetry is reserved for nature alone; you are the poem He is still writing, a poem full of beauty and rhythm and grace. Will you allow God to finish writing His sonnet of love upon your heart? Will you let your life be a poem of praise to Him?

Lord, write Your poetry upon my heart, so that I may be full of Your beauty, Your rhythm, and Your grace.

Our Redeemer

As for our Redeemer, the LORD of hosts is His name, the Holy One of Israel.

—Isaiah 47:4

According to the Old Testament, the primary role of the kinsman-redeemer (so named in the book of Ruth) was to buy back what was lost as well as to help those who couldn't help themselves. Those conditions certainly applied to Naomi and Ruth. Not only had Naomi lost her husband and sons, and Ruth her husband and homeland, but those losses had left them in poverty. They needed a redeemer.

They found him in Boaz, who was willing to buy back what was lost and to help Naomi and Ruth when they couldn't help themselves. Boaz took them into his family.

We too have lost something—it was lost long ago in the garden with a snake's temptation and a moment's weakness. But in truth we lose it ourselves again and again, day after day, "for all have sinned" (Romans 3:23). We, like Naomi and Ruth, need a Redeemer. We need Someone to buy back what we've lost and to help us do what we cannot do on our own: get back to God.

According to the Old Testament, Jesus came to be our Redeemer. When we, like Ruth, humbly lay our lives at His feet, Jesus takes us into His family. Thank You, Lord Jesus.

I lay my life at Your feet, Jesus, and surrender myself to Your will, trusting You to redeem me.

An Illusion of Growth

*The child [Jesus] grew and became strong; he was filled with
wisdom, and the grace of God was on him.*

—Luke 2:40 NIV

Growth rarely happens at the pace we'd like, but we are thankful when it does. We feel relief as our newborns grow to pediatricians' specs and time frames. We appreciate the character development that comes from learn-the-hard-way mistakes. Yet we do get impatient when seeds of Christlikeness don't grow quickly. We may see positive changes in external behaviors, but we don't want to see pretending. We want these actions to be evidence of genuine heart change overseen by the Holy Spirit.

Heart change takes time: seeds grow slowly. Pretending—and that preplanted and sprouted sod people use to create immediate lawns—offers instant change and the illusion of growth. Author of the best-selling *Love Does*, Bob Goff offered this metaphor: "Don't plant sod where God's planting seed. He's more interested in making us grow than having us look finished."

God patiently waits to see in us the kind of growth that He saw in His Son, Jesus: greater strength (spiritual and physical), more wisdom (the ability to make godly decisions), and trust in God (knowing He loves, protects, guides, and provides).

Let's be grateful for the possibility of becoming the people God wants us to be, even if it takes longer than we'd like.

*Lord God, thank You for the pace and plan You have for my growth
and the growth of those I love.*

What Are You Hearing?

"Blessed are your eyes for they see, and your ears for they hear."
—Matthew 13:16

If we were more aware of reasons to give thanks, wouldn't we do exactly that? It all depends on what is on our radar. This may be an urban legend, but its point is spot-on.

Visiting a friend in the Big Apple, a rancher from Montana was quite taken aback by the crowds, the noise, and the hustle and bustle of New York City. Business appointments, lunch dates, trains to catch—everyone was in a hurry. As the two friends walked down the street, the rancher couldn't believe the constant din of honking horns and shouting people.

Suddenly he put his hand on his friend's arm to stop him. The rancher had heard a sound of home. They were standing beside a large potted plant outside a hotel lobby. He pushed aside a branch and saw a cricket. Amazed, the New Yorker asked, "How did you hear that?"

In response the rancher dropped a handful of coins onto the crowded sidewalk. Despite the racket of the city, people near the coins recognized the sound, stopped, and turned. "You hear what you're listening for," the rancher said.

Let's look and listen a little harder to spot blessings as they rain down on us. Then gratitude will grow!

Lord, attune my heart to Your many blessings that I may live with a thankful awareness of Your goodness to me.

Don't Give Up!

Be of good courage, and He shall strengthen your heart, all you who hope in the LORD.

—Psalm 31:24

A new day has dawned. Will this be a day you sail easily through, in which every task is quickly accomplished, every challenge overcome, and every temptation turned away and sent packing? Or will this be one of those other days, when the tasks multiply too quickly, the challenges seem insurmountable, and the temptations are just so . . . *tempting*?

Whatever kind of day this morning brings you, don't give up. Run the race set before you (Hebrews 12:1), fight the good fight (2 Timothy 4:7), and keep the faith (2 Timothy 4:7)—so that you may win the "eternal prize" (1 Corinthians 9:25 NLT).

Yes, it will be a race. It will be a fight. And you must hold tight to your faith. So let the words of Psalm 31:24 inspire you: "Be brave. Be strong. Don't give up. Expect GOD to get here soon" (*The Message*).

On this new day, the fact is God is already here running the race by your side. He will strengthen you for the fight and even fight for you. And when you turn to Him in faith, just watch and see what He will do for you!

I praise You, Lord, for Your presence with me each day— strengthening, inspiring, and even fighting for me.

OCTOBER

Limitless

*No eye has seen, no ear has heard, and no mind has imagined what
God has prepared for those who love him.*

—1 Corinthians 2:9 NLT

Take a moment to read today's verse again and to really ponder
it. Not only has no one ever seen or heard the goodness God
has in store for His children, but "no mind has *imagined* what
God has prepared for those who love him" (emphasis added).

Our minds can imagine a lot of goodness and wonder—think
Disney World and blasting off to the moon. But those wonderful
things are earthly and finite. God's goodness is divine and everlasting, and it is for here and now, today.

Why is it, then, that when we face a situation that's just too
big for us to handle, we so often think it's too big for God? Why
do we forget that He is "able to do immeasurably more than all
we ask or imagine" (Ephesians 3:20 NIV)?

Why do we put God in a box when He invented the box—and
everything outside it?

Why do we put limitations on the One who is limitless?

Why do we set boundaries on Him who is boundless?

Open your eyes, your ears, your imagination to the wonders of God. Ask Him to show you what He can do—and then
sing His praises!

*Fill my eyes, my ears, my mind with the wonders of Your
imagination.*

Washing Dishes

Wash me, and I shall be whiter than snow.

—Psalm 51:7

Washing dishes: not the most enjoyable of tasks, but certainly a necessary one. It's not a difficult chore. Just a bit of water, a bit of soap, a bit of scrubbing—and the dish is done. Ready to be used again. It's an easy task for you, but not so easy for the dish. Regardless of how fancy the china, no dish has ever managed to clean itself.

Hmmm . . . sounds kind of like us, doesn't it? We all need a good cleansing from the daily messes we make, the sins and the mistakes of life that leave us feeling unworthy to be used by the One who so wants to use us. But that cleansing is no easy task. Because no matter how accomplished, how successful we may be, no person has ever managed the task of cleansing himself or herself. We need Someone to do it for us. That Someone is Jesus.

What is impossible for us is easy for Him—made easy by a not-so-easy journey to the cross. A bit of water, a bit of blood, a bit of placing ourselves in His hands—and the cleansing is done. Then . . . we're ready to be used by Him again.

It may not be enjoyable to get cleansed, but it is certainly wonderful to find oneself clean!

I am so grateful that You are willing to wash me, Lord, to make my sin-stained soul whiter than snow once again.

Giving and Receiving

Be clothed with humility.

—1 Peter 5:5

Motivational speaker and writer Brian Tracy offered this wise counsel: "Always give without remembering, and always receive without forgetting."

If we were to remember every time we gave someone something—anything from a smile to a ride to a meal to a place to stay, a job interview, a promotion, a prayer, a favor—we would have monstrous egos and an incredible amount of pride. Keeping track of what we have offered people—*remembering*—makes giving very much about us. In the moment, we may thank God for providing us with both something to give and the opportunity to do so, but after we give, let's let it go.

Part two of Mr. Tracy's advice is equally sound: "Always receive without forgetting." Imagine how our genuine gratitude for a smile, a ride, a meal, a place to stay, a job interview, a promotion, a prayer, or a favor would keep us humble as well as mindful of God's goodness to us through His people.

God prompts us to give to others just as He prompts others to give to us. Let's be humble and use our memories just for gratitude.

Lord, make me sensitive to Your prompts to give and able to express my gratitude when I receive.

Help and Hope

We put our hope in the LORD. He is our help and our shield.

—Psalm 33:20 NLT

*I*n some parts of the United States, the word *help* is pronounced *hope*. A simple twist of dialect perhaps, but like the definition of a parable—an earthly story with a heavenly meaning—this simple tangling of consonants and vowels also has a deeper meaning.

In the Bible, the word *hope* is not merely a wish or a dream. It's not like crossing your fingers or blowing out the candles on a birthday cake. Instead it is a promise. And because it is a promise from God, it is sure and certain, unbreakable, and to be fully relied upon. As David said, "God's promise is complete and unchanging; he will always help me and give me what I hope for" (2 Samuel 23:5 CEV).

Read those words once more and savor their sweet meaning. And every time you find yourself saying the word *help*—however you choose to pronounce it—remember the *hope* you have in God: the promise of His help.

I put my hope in You, Lord, and in the promise of Your help.

Bloom and Grow

Flowers appear on the earth; the season of singing has come.
—Song of Songs 2:12 NIV

Some flowers, like the wildflowers of the meadows, seem to flourish with no effort on our part, basking in the sun and soaking up the rain the Father provides for them. But others, like the rose, need our care and attention. They must be protected from the glare of the sun and the chill of the frost. They must be regularly watered and fed. Diseased leaves and branches must be pruned away. If untended, the rose's leaves will blacken and crumple, its blooms fade and then fall. But a rose, when well tended, is one of the most beautiful of all flowers.

Like the rose, our gratitude to God also blooms and grows when well tended. But it must be protected from the scorching words of the world and the frosty chill that denies His goodness. Our gratitude must be regularly watered with the memories of His past blessings and fed with the promises of His Word.

Gratitude will not flourish if we do not help it. If untended, thankfulness will blacken and crumple away; the bloom of our faith will fade and then fall. But if carefully minded, gratitude will bloom and grow into the most beautiful of hearts.

Teach me to nurture and nourish my gratitude to You, so that my faith may bloom and grow.

Giving God the Glory

You were bought at a price; therefore glorify God in your body.
—1 Corinthians 6:20

She has won gold, gives God the glory, and proudly proclaims her gratitude to Him. *She* is US artistic gymnast Gabby Douglas, and her gold medals are from the 2012 and 2016 Olympic Games as well as other international competitions through the years. Gabby thanks God for blessing her with awards and the opportunities these accomplishments give her to share her faith.

Talking to the *Christian Post*, Gabby explained, "It was definitely important for me to praise God because He's given me this God-given talent to go out there and represent Him and share my faith with everyone. I'm not going to hold it in because He's blessed me so much throughout my gymnastics career. . . . I love sharing about my faith."

Whatever our line of work—at home, in an office, at church, in the neighborhood or community—let's glorify God's name.

Thank You, Lord, for the encouragement of Your people who boldly proclaim their gratitude from whatever platform You give them.

When God's Love Becomes Real

Let us love one another, for love is of God.

Beth was overwhelmed with thanksgiving. People who had sent cards, texted birthday wishes, or posted on Beth's Facebook page could not have known how much their warm, kind words meant to her. The people—family members, prayer partners, women in her Bible study, and even people from church she didn't know well—were together holding up a mirror to her, and she liked the person they helped her see. And by God's grace Beth was even letting herself trust, at least a little, in the reflection she saw. She was loved!

For so long Beth's perceptions of herself kept her from seeing clearly, much less believing, the reflection. She might glance at it, but then she had to look away. Beth simply couldn't trust the love that painted the picture of her. It so contradicted what had been etched into her soul during her childhood.

This year's birthday was different. Somehow the birthday love seemed more than ever to be God's love, and He enabled Beth to receive and to know that love, healing, and peace. Beth was feeling that this "love is of God," and she was grateful.

Lord, use me to share love that is truly of You so others may know Your love, healing, and peace.

Beauty in the Darkness

Let the beauty of the LORD our God be upon us.

—Psalm 90:17

"Are we there yet?" No parent behind the wheel likes hearing that question from the backseat. But we adults understand that feeling when we go through a dark season of life: "Are we there yet, Lord? Haven't You challenged my trust and grown my faith enough?" We may be grateful for the work God does in the dark, but we're always eager to get back in the light.

Think about the darkest season in your life. What and who helped you while you were in that tunnel? We can thank God, even though He seemed absent in the darkness, for providing people, truth, hope, and peace during life's dark times. We can also thank God for enabling us to put one foot in front of the other as we walked through the darkness, not knowing how long the tunnel would be.

Then, at some point after the dark season passes, we are, by God's grace, able to thank Him for the good we experienced as a result of the difficulty. Oftentimes we are also able to see the beauty He wove throughout our lives during the dark season— and even because of it.

"Are we there yet?" When you finally arrive, be sure to thank God for delivering you safely.

Thank You, Lord, that You are with me even when I can't sense You, and You'll see me through every hardship.

This Day

This is the day the LORD has made; we will rejoice and be glad in it.
—Psalm 118:24

Today, October 9th: *this* is the day the Lord has made, the day the Lord has gifted to you. What will you do with it?

Will you dwell in frustration on every little thing that goes wrong? Or will you celebrate all the things that go right?

Will you hug your loved ones close and cherish another moment with them? Or lament the loads of laundry and dirty dishes they generate?

Will you make lemonade from life's lemons? Or root out lemons from the lemonade? Will you focus on the darkness of the clouds or the brilliance of their silver linings?

Because this day is here. You cannot exchange it for another. You cannot rewind and replay it over again. You've got one shot at this day, one shot at making it count . . . for yourself, for others, for God.

This day is the day the Lord has made. What will you make of it? Will you rejoice and be glad in it?

Thank You for the gift of this day. Help me live it so that it becomes my gift to You.

Trusting in God's Kindness

Praise the LORD. . . . For His merciful kindness is great toward us.
—Psalm 117:1–2

Our thankfulness declares that God is kind, no matter what happens. Take a few minutes right now to thank God for five times this past month when He blessed you with His kindness. Then, as a reflection of God's kindness, send an anonymous monetary gift to some newlyweds, bake cookies for the local fire station, buy doughnuts for the workers repaving your street, write a thank-you note to someone who is kind to you, and tell the manager that your cashier was great.

Now for what is probably the harder assignment. In what circumstances—in the past month or brewing right now—do you have an opportunity to declare that God is kind by expressing gratitude even if you don't feel thankful?

Realize that God's kindness is not always obvious to us (case in point: the cross on Good Friday), but we know from reading God's Word and walking with Him through life that He is indeed always gracious and kind. And we can be grateful!

You know my heart: I believe You are kind despite _____;
help my unbelief.

What Are You Known For?

My cup runneth over.

—Psalm 23:5 KJV

What first springs to mind when people hear your name? Is it your world-famous fudge pie or your flaming red hair? Perhaps it's your quick wit and easy laughter. Or maybe it's your pepper-hot temper, quirky wit, or deep compassion.

Each of us is known for something. As children of God, we should be known for our attitude of gratitude more than anything else. After all, do we not have so much to be grateful for? So much more than any others can claim?

Be honest with yourself: What's the status of your attitude of gratitude? Do you choose to take a "my cup runneth over" approach to life? Again and again we see Jesus giving His thanks to God. If the Son of God felt the need to publicly express His gratitude, how much more should we?

Cultivate an attitude of gratitude in your life today . . . let it be what you are known for.

May my words and my actions always express how very grateful I am for all Your blessings.

A God Who Listens

I am praying to you because I know you will answer, O God. Bend down and listen as I pray.

—Psalm 17:6 NLT

God listens. Whether it's in the early morning hours when the world is softly tinted by the rosy hues of the sun's first rays, in the deeply quiet stillness of the middle of the night, or in the midst of the rush and tumble of the day: when you stop to speak to God, He stops to listen.

Think for a moment about the sheer wonder of that fact. The God who created all things—who sent light soaring through the darkness, who spoke mountains into being, who carved out oceans with His words—this same God listens to you.

When you lift up your voice to the Lord in prayer, He bends down to listen. Like a father leaning down to his beloved child, so the Lord draws nearer to you.

But God does more than listen; He answers. For His way of listening is not merely the idle hearing of words; He listens with purpose and with intent so He might best answer. *He will answer,* in His own perfect time and way.

Take time to pray today, and as you do so, be grateful for a God who willingly bends down and draws near so that He might listen. Then remember to take time to listen to Him.

Your love and kindness never fail me, Lord. Thank You for listening to me.

Jesus Spurns None

"I tell you, her sins . . . have been forgiven, so she has shown me much love."

—Luke 7:47 NLT

The people who were at the Pharisee's house for dinner were startled to see the woman approach Jesus and wash His feet with her tears, her hair, and the fragrant oil she carried in an alabaster flask. But Jesus understood that hers were tears of gratitude.

Yes, the woman's gift of ointment was extravagant, but so is Jesus' purchased-on-the-cross forgiveness. Her action was radical, but so is Jesus' love. And her example continues to teach us the gospel today. According to Biblehub.com, it was said of the woman: "Thanks to thee, most blessed sinner: thou hast shown the world a safe enough place for sinners—the feet of Jesus, which spurn none, reject none, repel none, and receive and admit all."

Despite people who are puzzled by believers' worship of their Savior, let's make our thanks to God loud indeed. He has helped us recognize our sins, admit them, ask for His forgiveness, and then receive it. Our heartfelt gratitude for Jesus' forgiveness should rival that of this thankful woman.

Lord, please make me consistently grateful for the price You paid for my sins.

A Work in Progress

*I am certain that God, who began the good work within you, will
continue his work until it is finally finished on the day when Christ
Jesus returns.*

—Philippians 1:6 NLT

ou are a work in progress, which simply means that God is
not finished with you yet. So when you have one of *those* days—
when absolutely everything seems to go wrong—remember that
God is still working on you. And when you, like Paul, know the
right thing to do and want desperately to do it, but still somehow manage to do what is wrong, don't give up (Romans 7:15).

The day you decided to follow Him, God began a good work
in you: He washed away your sins and started to transform you
into His image. But it is not a quick process; it's a complete over-
haul, a lifetime of renovation, of adding on here and taking down
there. And it never ends . . . at least not this side of heaven.

But the other side? Oh, how amazing that will be. For when
Jesus returns, He will finish the work that He started on the
day you first believed. He will make you perfect, just the way He
created you to be before sins, before sorrows, before this world
left its mark on you.

Until that day, remember that God's not through with you
yet. You're His work in progress, His masterpiece in the making.

*Thank You, Lord, for working in my life; please show me how to be
the one You created me to be.*

Gratitude Can Snowball!

I will sing to the LORD, for He has triumphed gloriously! The horse and its rider He has thrown into the sea!

—Exodus 15:1

Exodus 15:1 is the opening of the amazing song of thanks and praise that Moses sang after the children of Israel had crossed the dry bed of the Red Sea—and watched the Lord draw the waters back over Pharaoh's fighting men, horses, and chariots.

The excited gratitude that Moses was feeling after God's great demonstration of His power and His protection is unmistakable. Moses continued exultantly: "The LORD is my strength and song, and He has become my salvation; He is my God, and I will praise Him; my father's God, and I will exalt Him" (v. 2).

In what ways can you make these words of gratitude your own? Consider when God has been your strength, and when Jesus has given you a song in your heart, if not on your lips. Reflect on the ramifications of the truth "He is my God." What reasons for gratitude are rooted in that truth?

If you take time to read through all of Moses' song, you will see how his gratitude snowballs, increasing in passion as he rehearses the details of God's great work in his life. Today do what Moses did: write a few lines thanking God for His work in your life—and then praise Him aloud!

Thank You, Lord, for Your victories in my life that I can celebrate just as Moses celebrated Your victories in his.

Prompt Praise

Let those who love Him be like the sun when it comes out in full strength.

—Judges 5:31

Expressions of gratitude to God can be as unique as the grateful people themselves. Judge Deborah, who wrote this song recorded in Judges 5, offered in her praise an overview of Israel's history. After opening with thanksgiving, Deborah mentioned the glorious scene in Sinai before she talked about the Israelites' apostasy and their punishment. She pointed out tribes that didn't participate in the battles, described the defeat of Canaan, and greatly praised Jael's courageous yet gruesome murder of the enemy general Sisera. She closed with verse 31.

But perhaps the most important takeaway is the timeliness of Deborah's song, as Matthew Henry pointed out: "No time should be lost in returning thanks to the Lord for his mercies; for our praises are most acceptable, pleasant, and profitable, when they flow from a full heart. . . . Whatever Deborah, Barak, or the army had done, the Lord must have all the praise. The will, the power, and the success were all from him."

May our unique praise to our God, who has no equal, and gratitude for His guidance and protection be our priority as it clearly was for Deborah!

Lord, help me be prompt with my praise.

What to Do with Glad News

I will praise You, O LORD, with my whole heart; I will tell of all Your marvelous works.

—Psalm 9:1

When good things happen to you—when you are thankful for news you've heard, something you've seen, an experience you've had—what do you do? Look at what these folks did:

- The shepherds heard the angelic proclamation, ran to see the babe, and "when they had seen Him, they made widely known the saying which was told them concerning this Child" (Luke 2:17).
- The Samaritan woman with whom Jesus spoke at the well recognized Him as the Messiah and testified to many in the city: "He told me all that I ever did." The result? "Many of the Samaritans of that city believed in Him" (John 4:39).
- The Gadarene man whom Jesus delivered from demons "proclaimed throughout the whole city what great things Jesus had done for him" (Luke 8:39).

The people in these three scenes took the good news they had received, and they passed it along. When you have glad news, tell it! You never know whom you may impact.

Lord, please give me courage to share with others the all the amazing things You do.

Grow in Grace

Grow in the grace and knowledge of our Lord and Savior Jesus Christ.

—2 Peter 3:18

Our life with Christ is not meant to be a stale or passive one. We should always be growing, learning more about who He is and how He wants us to be. Part of that learning includes understanding and accepting His grace for us—and then learning to give that grace to those around us.

The grace of God *is* promised to us: "If we confess our sins, He is faithful and just to forgive us our sins and to cleanse us from all unrighteousness" (1 John 1:9). But with that promise comes an obligation: "Forgive one another. . . . Forgive as the Lord forgave you" (Colossians 3:13 NIV). Don't be so busy picking a speck out of your brother or sister's eye that you ignore the plank in your own (Matthew 7:3)!

When you *do* get around to addressing that plank in your own eye, remember God's grace then too. He asks you to give it to others, but don't forget to give it to yourself. Yes, acknowledge the wrong, turn away from it, and try to make it right. But don't beat yourself up or get mired down in guilt. Let God's grace grow in your heart and cover you.

Thank You, Lord, for the gift of Your grace. Teach me to accept it and give it—both to others and to myself.

Written by Hand

See with what large letters I have written to you with my own hand!
—Galatians 6:11

When was the last time you were surprised by a handwritten note that came by snail mail? Maybe someone sent a thank-you note, so unexpected in our day of communicating via text or email. You were grateful to receive it.

Maybe it was a thinking-of-you card, and the timing seemed choreographed by God. It couldn't have arrived on a better day. You thanked both God and the sender. Or perhaps you received a birthday card from someone you never expected to hear from.

We all like to know someone appreciates or is thinking of us, and to see it in *handwritten* black and white is extra-meaningful. That snail-mail delivery is an occasion to thank God.

Early churches thanked God when they received a letter from Paul, John, Peter, or James. Whether the letters taught and encouraged or exhorted and corrected, they were welcome and important. In his letter to the church at Galatia, we read that Paul wrote it himself instead of dictating it. A letter Paul himself scrawled out would have been extra-exciting.

Let the memory of an especially significant snail-mail note inspire you to send a handwritten note to someone today. Chances are you'll be sparking that person's thankful heart.

Thank You, Lord, for this simple gesture that I know from experience can make a person so grateful.

The Crown

*I have fought the good fight, I have finished the race, and I have
remained faithful. And now the prize awaits me—the crown of
righteousness, which the Lord, the righteous Judge, will give me on
the day of his return.*

—2 Timothy 4:7–8 NLT

In our world, crowns are usually reserved for the royal. It
is much the same in the kingdom of God but for one very
important difference: you can *choose* to be a chosen one. How?

Fight the good fight, doing what is right when everyone else
is choosing wrong. Finish the race by not giving up, and continue to follow the course God has laid out for you—even when
it's difficult and lonely. Remain faithful; trust that God will
keep every promise, that He will do everything He has said He
will do.

When you live that kind of a life for God, a prize is waiting
for you: the crown of righteousness. It marks you as belonging
to the royal family of God, one of the elite, one of the chosen
ones (1 Peter 2:9).

And unlike the crowns of earthly royalty, which can tarnish
or be dented or even stolen, the crown of righteousness that
God places upon your head will last forever. Praise the Lord for
such an honor!

*Because You are with me, I can finish this race and claim my
promised crown. Thank You, Lord Jesus.*

Praiseworthy Paradoxes

"I am the resurrection and the life. . . . Whoever lives and believes in Me shall never die."

—John 11:25–26

Some of the richest truths of our Christian faith are presented as paradoxes. For example, when Jesus talked to Martha a few days after her brother's death, He said, "I am the resurrection and the life. He who believes in Me, though he may die, he shall live. And whoever lives and believes in Me shall never die" (John 11:25–26). For followers of Jesus, the end of one's earthly life opens the door to eternal life in heaven.

In that same vein, Jesus said, "He who is greatest among you shall be your servant. And whoever exalts himself will be humbled, and he who humbles himself will be exalted" (Matthew 23:11–12). Again, we may be surprised by whom God exalts and doesn't exalt!

Take time to ponder these two paradoxes—and one more. Pastor and writer A. W. Tozer made this statement: "Gratitude is an offering precious in the sight of God, and it is one that the poorest of us can make and be not poorer but richer for having made it."

The paradoxes of our faith make it exciting, unpredictable, and hope-filled. Things are often not what they seem. Aren't you thankful?

Lord, thank You for working out Your wondrous will even though I can't always see it.

"Such Great Love"

I . . . beseech you to walk worthy of the calling with which you were called.

—Ephesians 4:1

Faithful Jews in the Old Testament knew that their sins were forgiven when flawless animals were sacrificed and their blood shed. Jews understood that only priests from the designated tribe of Levi could enter the inner sanctum of the temple and only after much ceremonial washing. These Jews memorized the Torah and anticipated a messiah who would liberate them from oppressive Roman control.

Living after Jesus' resurrection, we know that He was the flawless, sinless Lamb of God. His blood was shed as He died, and the moment He did, the veil in the temple was torn from top to bottom, opening the way for laypeople to enter God's holy presence. Jesus perfectly obeyed the law and showed that the laws were more matters of the heart than behavior. And Messiah Jesus liberated people from the power of death.

Now that Jesus' blood has done its work, we thank God for His love by living in a way that truly honors Him.

Please help me live out my gratitude to You by living worthy of Your amazing love for me!

Under the Bed

I will sing aloud of Your mercy in the morning; for You have been my defense.

—Psalm 59:16

not everyone is a morning person, but whenever our day starts, there is no better way to begin it than with a prayer of gratitude and praise.

David acknowledged the practice of first-thing praise in Psalm 59, specifically thanksgiving for God's protection. He wrote this psalm when King Saul's men were plotting to kill him. With enemy soldiers intent on keeping him from the throne of Israel, David understandably praised God when he awakened to a new day: God had protected him through the night.

We would do well to start our days with a prayer of gratitude for God's faithfulness through the night that just ended and the day that is just beginning. In addition we can ask for His help.

Joyce Meyer wrote, "I encourage you to spend time each morning focusing on the good things God has done in your life. Think about the . . . ways He's healed you and changed you, and how good it is to know He cares for you and hears your prayers."

Whether your day starts at dawn or much later, use it as a cue to thank God and enlist His help in loving others.

Lord God, help me learn to walk through each day mindful of Your presence and protection!

A Challenge and a Promise

Love never fails.

—1 Corinthians 13:8 NIV

The timeless words of 1 Corinthians 13 describe the very nature of love: "Love is patient, love is kind. It does not envy, it does not boast, it is not proud. It does not dishonor others, it is not self-seeking, it is not easily angered, it keeps no record of wrongs. . . . It always protects, always trusts, always hopes, always perseveres. Love never fails" (vv. 4–8 NIV).

In this passage, we see a love without demands or conditions. This passage describes no ordinary, earthly love that ebbs and flows depending upon how well you please another. This is true, godly, agape love.

The words of these verses can be seen as both a challenge and a promise. For the challenge, replace "love" in the passage with your own name. Are you patient? Are you kind? Do you protect, hope, and persevere? Or do you fail those who count on you? Do you fail God's expectations of you?

But for the promise—God's promise to you—replace "love" in the passage with His name. God is patient, He is kind. He always protects, hopes, and perseveres. God never fails.

Today, challenge yourself to love with a 1 Corinthians 13 kind of love—and be grateful for a God who so promises to love you.

Thank You, Lord my God, for loving me with a love that never fails.

Measuring Up

"My grace is sufficient for you, for my power is made perfect in weakness."

—2 Corinthians 12:9 NIV

If you've done much bread baking, you know that it is a precise and measured science. In regular cooking you might wing it with a sautéed dish or a casserole or soup, tossing in ingredients with abandon. But when it comes to baking, you've got to get it exactly right. Too much flour and you'll be left with a dry-as-dust texture. Too little yeast and your lovely loaf will be flat upon arrival.

Baking ingredients must be added in precisely the right amounts in order to help dough rise. But God does not require precision or perfection from us in order to help us rise. Because Jesus came, we are not "measured."

Instead, God's grace fills in wherever we are found wanting. So when you mess up and your mercy is running low, God gives you His. When you leave out the leavening of love, God adds His. And when your faith is feeling flat, God's grace takes care of it.

When you bake bread, measure carefully. Then thank God that for all the times you don't quite measure up, He still chooses to help you rise.

Lord, thank You for the grace that fills in and smooths over the lumpy parts of my life and helps me rise up to You.

Bad Fortune, Good Fruit

Count it all joy when you fall into various trials, knowing that the testing of your faith produces patience.

—James 1:2–3

oy comes easily, even automatically, when all is well, when we have no complaints, when the sun is shining. But God calls us to consider life's trials as joy. Perhaps that's easier to do when we take the long view, when we hold on to the hope that joy will come later after the storm of life has calmed down.

Have you ever noticed that seeds for good are often sown in life's tough times? As with any seed, that good fruit takes a while to appear. After all, maturing has to happen. But the promised fruit is worth the wait.

Among the possible fruit that results from life's rough patches are humility and patience: it's always humbling when life events remind us that we are not in charge and then invite us to be patient as those events play out.

And on a very practical note, during hard times we are becoming "able to comfort those who are in any trouble, with the comfort with which we ourselves are comforted by God" (2 Corinthians 1:4).

Humility, patience, heart transformation, the ability to comfort others: by God's grace, even bad fortune yields good. That's cause for joy.

Thank You for the hope I can have when trials come because Your goodness is more powerful than the world's bad fortune.

Who God Sees

You are altogether beautiful.

—Song of Songs 4:7 NIV

How do you see yourself? What labels do you choose to define who you are? What about the world—who does it say you are?

The truth is that we can be a bit hard on ourselves. And the world certainly isn't interested in giving us an accurate picture; it's more interested in selling us the latest cream, potion, or phony fast fix.

Rather than relying on these skewed and faulty definitions, allow the Word of God to tell you who you are in His eyes:

- You are completely lovely to Him (Song of Songs 4:7).
- You are His delight (Psalm 18:19).
- You are His own beloved child (1 John 3:1).

No, this does not mean you are perfect, but you are perfectly loved. And God sees in you the person you can become.

Be the person God sees. Show the whole world how "altogether beautiful" you are . . . and show the one staring back at you in the mirror as well. Choose some new labels, and be lovely, be delightful, because you are His own child.

Thank You, Lord, for the way You see me . . . Your beloved and beautiful child!

Humility and Honor

A man's pride will bring him low, but the humble in spirit will retain honor.

—Proverbs 29:23

*H*onor may be one of those words we think we understand until we try to define it for someone. And what does it have to do with gratitude? We'll get some help from a dictionary as well as Proverbs 29:23.

Baker's Evangelical Dictionary of Biblical Theology says honor is "an internal attitude of respect, courtesy, and reverence" that results in "appropriate attention or even obedience. Honor without such action is incomplete; it is lip service."

Who, then, merits honor? The *Evangelical Dictionary* continues, "A person grants honor most frequently on the basis of position, status, or wealth, but it can and should also be granted on the basis of character." Honor based on character is the link to Proverbs 29:23, which reminds us that "the humble in spirit" earn esteem. In contrast to the proud, modest folk recognize their imperfection, incompleteness, and need. The humble therefore can receive help. The unpretentious also know how to say, "Thank you."

The humble in spirit are readily grateful and therefore doubly worthy of people's honor. And honor isn't so hard to define after all, is it?

Please develop humility in me so I can earn and bring honor to You.

Doing What Is Good

Let's not get tired of doing what is good. At just the right time we will reap a harvest of blessing if we don't give up.

—Galatians 6:9 NLT

Jesus went around doing good everywhere He went (Acts 10:38). That sounds so wonderful—*is* so wonderful. But it is not easy.

People don't always appreciate the good work you do. Sometimes it's because they think they can do it better. Sometimes it's because they think you didn't do enough, and then, ironically, sometimes they think it's because you did too much. Even (and sometimes especially) the work you do for God and for His people can come under fire.

When that happens, don't give up. Don't let some armchair quarterback put you out of the game. Don't "get tired of doing what is good." Jesus Himself often endured criticism from people who did not accept the good He did.

God's Word promises that "nothing you do for the Lord is ever useless," ever in vain (1 Corinthians 15:58 NLT). Though you may not see the results of your efforts, you are both planting seeds for God's kingdom and adding up treasures in heaven.

God will bless you for that . . . and you can thank Him for His blessings by doing good everywhere, weary or not.

When my efforts aren't appreciated, Lord, help me remember that You are the One I'm longing to please.

The Things That Don't Cost Us a Thing

For you know the grace of our Lord Jesus Christ, that though He was rich, yet for your sakes He became poor, that you through His poverty might become rich.

—2 Corinthians 8:9

So much of our worth, at least in the eyes of our society, is defined by our wealth. Rich is good; poor is not. And while many a poor person would happily trade places with someone who is rich, the reverse is practically never true. After all, who would leave a mansion to live in a slum?

Well . . . ask that question a different way: Who would leave the wonders of heaven for a humble carpenter's home? Who would give up streets of gold for streets of dust? Who would exchange the power, glory, and honor of God to be born a helpless baby, to endure ridicule and pain and shame?

We know the answer: Jesus. He did all those things, and He did them for us. He became poor so that we might become truly rich. In doing so, He redefined what it means to be rich and to be poor. It's not the earthly riches that matter—they so quickly fade away. It's the things that don't cost us a thing that are truly important—things like unconditional love, mercy, and grace. They are our wealth, whether society agrees or not.

I am most thankful for the things that don't cost me a thing—for the things You purchased for me.

Tangibles and Intangibles

Not unto us, O Lord, not unto us, but to Your name give glory.

—Psalm 115:1

It makes sense that when we thank God, we often start with the tangibles. And we are absolutely right to acknowledge that family, friends, home, food, and clothing are gifts from God. He is also the One, however, who guides our steps and opens doors so that we can earn a paycheck and therefore fill the refrigerator, buy clothes to wear, and pay the rent or mortgage.

Consider how God has shepherded you, guided your steps, and opened doors that led to blessings. In addition to providing a job or guiding a career path, God has given you opportunities for relationships, education, ministry, and community work as well as the skills and abilities you need to be effective and to flourish in those choices.

We can thank God for the talents and passions He has woven into us, for guiding us to places and people who can benefit from what He has entrusted to our care, and for using those connections with people to bring us satisfaction, fulfillment, and joy. Let's not forget these intangibles as we praise God and give Him the glory.

I feel both humbled and loved, Lord God: everything I have truly is from You. I praise and glorify You!

NOVEMBER

The Eeyore Within

Now may the God of hope fill you with all joy and peace in believing,
that you may abound in hope by the power of the Holy Spirit.

—Romans 15:13

ood morning, Pooh Bear," Eeyore said to Pooh. "If it is a good morning," he said. "Which I doubt."

This simple exchange in a children's book between a stuffed bear and a stuffed donkey reveals much about this extremely gloomy yet enormously lovable character. Of all of A. A. Milne's memorable creatures dwelling in the Hundred Acre Wood, Pooh's friend Eeyore has become many people's favorite.

In another exchange with Pooh, Eeyore notes, "It's snowing still."

"So it is," Pooh answers.

"*And* freezing," Eeyore adds. "However, we haven't had an earthquake lately."

Most everyone identifies with Eeyore to one degree or another. Are you a bit like this character, bound to see the bad in every event? If so, ask God to help you immediately recognize and stop the negative thinking and to fill you with His hope and joy. Then every day can begin as a "good morning."

Thank You, Lord, for loving me and filling me with Your joy when
I—like Eeyore—struggle to see the good.

God Sings over You

The LORD your God is with you, the Mighty Warrior who saves. He will take great delight in you; in his love he will no longer rebuke you, but will rejoice over you with singing.

—Zephaniah 3:17 NIV

Have you ever had such a great day that you just had to sing? Have you ever been with a person who made you so happy that you wanted to sing? When your heart was simply too happy to be silent?

That's the way God feels about . . . *you!* You give God joy—so much that He "rejoice[s] over you with singing."

Notice the rest of today's verse: God is with you. He is your mighty Warrior who comes alongside to save you. He delights in you. And because of His great love for you, He gives you a way to be forgiven.

So this morning—and every morning—as you rise up to meet the day, ask yourself: *How can I make God sing today? What words can I offer, what things can I do that will so please God that He simply has to sing?*

The next time someone makes you feel as if you're not good enough, the next time you begin to question if you really matter, hum a few notes of a favorite hymn and let gratitude fill your heart as you remember this truth: you are God's beloved child, and you make Him sing.

May the words of my mouth and the meditations of my heart make You sing with delight!

God Sings to You

You shall go out with joy, and be led out with peace; the mountains and the hills shall break forth into singing before you, and all the trees of the field shall clap their hands.

—Isaiah 55:12

Just as God Himself sings with delight *over* you, His creation sings *to* you—reminding you of His power and presence, majesty and might. Reminding you to praise Him.

Turn off all the noise in your life for just a few moments and listen as all the earth sings its praises to God (Psalm 66:4). From the softly babbling brook to "the meadows . . . covered with flocks and the valleys . . . mantled with grain; they shout for joy and sing" (Psalm 65:13 NIV). The mountains and the hills "sing out their songs of joy" (Psalm 98:8 NLT). "The rivers clap their hands in glee" before the Lord who crafted and created them (Psalm 98:8 NLT). And to Jesus the Lamb, "every creature in heaven and on earth and under the earth and in the sea" sings its praises (Revelation 5:13 NLT).

Creation was created to praise. *You* were created to praise. Join hills and the mountains in their songs. Clap along with the praises of the rivers of trees. "Sing and make music from your heart to the Lord, always giving thanks to God" (Ephesians 5:19–20 NIV).

Teach me, Lord, to hear the songs of Your creation and to join them in their praise of You.

Close to His Heart

*He tends his flock like a shepherd: he gathers the lambs in his arms
and carries them close to his heart.*

—Isaiah 40:11 NIV

Take a moment to read today's verse once again. Now, close your eyes and imagine the scene. *You* are that lamb. And your *Abba*, your Father God, is the One who watches over—the Shepherd tending His flock.

When you are hurt, when you are worried, when you are scared, when you simply need a moment of respite and rest, God gathers you into His arms and carries you close to His heart. Notice the word "carries." This is not a quick hug. This is not a pat-on-the-head-and-off-you-go moment. God *carries* you close to His heart, until you are ready to walk once again.

No matter what kind of day, week, or month you are having—truly great or truly awful—God is with you. He's not a phone call away. He's not even a prayer away. God is right there with you, holding you close, His heart touching yours.

How do you say "Thank You" for that kind of love? Begin by doing as Jesus asked Peter to do: as a lamb, feed other lambs (John 21:15). Wherever you go, in whatever you do, nourish His lost and hurting sheep with His words, with His kindness. There is no better way to thank the God who carries you so close.

*For this moment, Lord, I will rest here with You, in Your arms, with
my heart upon Your heart.*

Promise Made, Promise Kept

Let us hold fast the confession of our hope without wavering, for He who promised is faithful.

—Hebrews 10:23

There's nothing like an election cycle to bring out our inner skeptic. When, if ever, have you gone to the polls confident that a candidate you vote for will keep all his or her campaign promises? Maybe never, and one reason elected officials don't keep their promises is because they soon realize just how difficult their promised changes are to make.

God, however, possesses complete power to fulfill whatever promise He makes. God cannot lie. When He says He will do something, He will. He will keep every promise He makes. Oh, He may not keep it in the way we expect. But we can be sure He will indeed fulfill all He guarantees He'll do.

What particular God-promises offer you comfort? Hope? Peace? "I will never leave you nor forsake you" (Hebrews 13:5). "Those who wait on the LORD shall renew their strength . . . they shall run and not be weary, they shall walk and not faint" (Isaiah 40:31). And those are just some of Jesus' greatest hits!

If the latest election left you skeptical and disappointed, remember the One who always does exactly what He says He will. And thank Him.

Thank You, almighty and faithful God, for keeping every promise You make!

Truly Awesome

Let all the earth fear the LORD; let all the inhabitants of the world stand in awe of Him.

—Psalm 33:8

We hear the word *awesome* a lot, but it has gone the way of the word *love*. We love pizza, our children, Sunday naps, swimming, and God. Good news is awesome, as are surfable waves, the latest *New York Times* best seller, the restaurant that just opened, and God.

Having watered down the meaning of *awesome*, we need to recapture the reason we can stand in awe of God, and many—if not all—of those reasons will elicit our gratitude.

Said English writer G. K. Chesterton about such a response, "I would maintain that thanks are the highest form of thought; and that gratitude is happiness doubled by wonder." As we stand in awe of God, praising Him for who He is and thanking Him for all He's done, there really could be no greater subject to contemplate! These Father-focused thoughts lift our eyes to God and our minds above our everyday concerns and duties.

And Mr. Chesterton was right: gratitude is indeed a result of happiness—but of happiness "doubled by wonder." Isn't it *awesome* to realize that our infinite God is touching very-limited us with His goodness and grace?

Awe, wonder, thanks, gratitude—how else could I respond to Your immeasurable goodness, grace, and love, my God and King!

Glimpses of God

"Anyone who has seen me has seen the Father."

—John 14:9 NIV

Jesus came to give us a glimpse of God: The words He spoke were the words of God. The works He did were the works of God. We can know God because we know the Son (John 14:10–11). We glimpse His face in . . .

- His compassion as He touched the lepers, the lame, and the blind.
- His mercy when He offered forgiveness instead of condemnation to the woman thrown into the dirt.
- His sorrow as He wept for His friend.
- His grace on the beach over a breakfast of fish with a fisherman named Peter.
- His power by the empty tomb.

Jesus touched the untouchable, reached the unreachable, and loved the unlovable. Jesus showed us who our Lord is—a God of love and mercy and grace. And for all the times when we ourselves are untouchable, unreachable, and unlovable, aren't we so very grateful that He did?

Thank Jesus for the glimpses of God He gives you.

Please give me a heart like Yours, Lord Jesus, to touch, to teach, to reach, and to love others for You.

Beginning and End

*"I am the Alpha and the Omega, the Beginning and the End," says
the Lord, "who is and who was and who is to come, the Almighty."*
—Revelation 1:8

The Lord God is the Alpha and the Omega, the beginning
and end of all things. There is no place He has never been.
There is no time—past, present, or future—He has never been.

That means the Lord also knows *your* beginning and end,
and every moment in between. So when He says in Jeremiah
29:11, "I know the plans I have for you, . . . plans to prosper
you and not to harm you, plans to give you hope and a future"
(NIV)—God knows *exactly* what He's talking about. Every last
detail of every single moment.

Yesterday may have been troubled, today may be overwhelming, and tomorrow may not even bear thinking about, but trust
that God is present in each of those moments. Know that He is
working in them.

James Wells perfectly captured this truth in the words of his
familiar hymn: "I care not today what the morrow may bring, if
shadow or sunshine or rain. The Lord I know ruleth o'er everything, and all of my worries are vain."

There is no need to worry, no need to fear. Believe and be
grateful for a God who is the beginning and the end.

*Father, I submit my vain worries to You and ask for Your peace in
their place.*

Faithful with Our Thanks

He knelt down on his knees three times that day, and prayed and gave thanks before his God, as was his custom since early days.

—Daniel 6:10

The jealous governors under King Darius had set a legislative trap in hopes of sending Daniel, follower of the one true God, to the den of lions so they could be rid of their rival forever. These rulers compelled Darius to forbid prayer unless it was directed to the king himself.

Yet Daniel prayed as he had always done. The Scripture tells us that Daniel "gave thanks before his God."

Think about a time in your life when you found it difficult to give thanks to God. What kept you from praying? Or what enabled you to pray despite the circumstances?

It was Daniel's custom to pray, but we don't get the impression that he was merely going through the motions that day after prayer had been banned. After all, his life was at stake. Would he take that risk for a mere charade? In a government hostile to worshipers of God, Daniel let nothing shake his loyalty or silence his thanks.

"Jealous governors" or other enemies may try to halt our prayers. Let's make sure our gratitude is as firmly rooted in our hearts as it was in Daniel's.

Lord God, You are worthy of our prayers. Thank You for Your faithfulness.

More Precious Than Rubies

Wisdom is more precious than rubies, and nothing you desire can compare with her.

—Proverbs 8:11 NIV

Merriam-Webster.com defines wisdom as the "ability to discern" or "good sense." It is compared to insight and discernment. And according to God, it is more precious than rubies.

Wisdom allows you to discern truth from lies, right from wrong. It helps you make better decisions. With wisdom, you are better able to understand others, blessing you with richer, stronger relationships. "[Wisdom] will protect you; love her, and she will watch over you"—that is the promise of Proverbs 4:6 (NIV). Therefore, the verse warns, "don't turn your back on wisdom" (NLT)!

But how do you go about acquiring this precious gem? Does it require great money or sacrifice? No. It simply requires asking God.

God will not shun you or scold or scoff at you because you don't know the right thing to do, the right choice to make. No! God is eager to guide you, to help you, to show you the way. When you find yourself lacking wisdom, ask God, "who gives generously to all without finding fault" (James 1:5 NIV).

You can have the precious gifts of discernment, common sense, and insight—all for the asking.

Lord, I praise You not only for Your wisdom, but for Your generosity in giving it to me.

Real People Like Me

Here am I! Send me.

—Isaiah 6:8

ou may have heard Hebrews 11 referred to as the Hall of Faith. Many of the home-run kings and all-star favorites are listed there, and we can be grateful for the examples of people such as Noah, Abraham, and Moses. Also listed there, however, are certain people who didn't get as much ink in the sports sections or as many people buying their jerseys—and we can be encouraged by their presence because they're a lot more like us.

Sarah appears. The Sarah who laughed—in disbelief rather than joy—when, at the age of ninety, she learned she was going to have the son God had promised to Abraham. Also in the Hall of Faith is Rahab, the harlot of Jericho who lied to protect Israel's spies hidden on her roof. We encounter Barak, who lacked courage to go into battle without Judge Deborah at his side, and Samson, whose weakness for women blinded him to conniving Delilah's purpose.

We see in Hebrews 11 people who lacked unwavering faith or pristine moral records. We see people without courage and discernment. And not only did God use them for His good purposes, He included them in the Hall of Faith. If God can use such fallible and human heroes, maybe He can use us!

Lord, I am thankful for the Bible's pictures of real people who stumble like me but whom You love and use nevertheless.

All-Sufficient and Supreme

He who dwells in the secret place of the Most High shall abide under the shadow of the Almighty.

—Psalm 91:1

It makes sense that our infinite God would have many names. Learning about these Hebrew names and their literal meanings can help us know our God better and appreciate Him more.

El Shaddai is translated "God Almighty" but means, more literally, the All-Sufficient One. Looking at the Hebrew fleshes out its meaning: *El Shaddai* suggests that God is "the One who mightily nourishes, satisfies, protects, and supplies His people." According to MyRedeemerLives.com, "El Shaddai is our All-Sufficient Sustainer. . . . It is God as 'Shaddai' who abundantly blesses." We can be thankful for each of these wonderful traits of our God.

El Elyon is translated "Most High God" or "God Most High" and emphasizes God's absolute supremacy. The name communicates that no being exceeds Him in majesty or power. God's people are wise to recognize Him as "the Most High God their Redeemer" (Psalm 78:35).

Understanding even just these two of God's many names prompts rich worship and deep thanksgiving.

I am grateful to be Your child, my all-sufficient God, unsurpassed in glory and honor.

"Welcome!"

"Truly I tell you, whatever you did for one of the least of these brothers and sisters of mine, you did for me."

—Matthew 25:40 NIV

Jesus lived a life that said, "Welcome!" Though He was tired and longed for a few moments of solitude, He welcomed the masses: "The crowds . . . followed him. He welcomed them and spoke to them about the kingdom of God, and healed those who needed healing" (Luke 9:11 NIV).

And though some disparaged and criticized Him, Jesus welcomed the lost: "The Pharisees and the teachers of the law muttered, 'This man welcomes sinners and eats with them'" (Luke 15:2 NIV).

We are blessed with a Savior who welcomes. We all, at one point or another, are lost and wandering, seeking a Savior. We all need the welcome He so lovingly gives. In return, He asks that we live lives of welcome too.

Give food to the hungry, water to the thirsty. Invite the stranger in. Clothe the poor, tend the sick, minister to those in prison. Because whatever you do "for one of the least of these," you do for Jesus (Matthew 25:35–40 NIV). By welcoming those around you, you welcome Him.

Lord, open my heart to those around me—just as You have opened Your heart to me.

The Light

You, LORD, keep my lamp burning; my God turns my darkness into light.

—Psalm 18:28 NIV

The light of the sun does two things: it chases away the darkness, and it makes things grow. The light of God's Word does those same two things: it chases away the darkness of evil, and it makes *you* grow.

It is sunlight that signals a plant to start growing. It shows the plant which way is up through the darkness of the soil. In much the same way, God's Word shows you which way to escape the darkness of this world: "Your word is a lamp to my feet and a light to my path" (Psalm 119:105). When we turn to the light of His Word, He rescues us from our wanderings and chases the darkness away.

But think about this: How often do plants need light? Every day. So how often do you think we need the light of God's Word?

Yes, sometimes it's hard to carve out that time for God. Some days are easier. On those days, dig a little deeper, read a little more. And on the days that aren't so easy, at least slip in a verse, just a little light to help you remember which way to go and which way to grow.

Spend time in God's Word today. Let its light chase away any darkness and help you grow.

I praise You, Lord, for the light of Your Word that shows me which way to go.

Wait

Our soul waits for the LORD; He is our help and our shield.

—Psalm 33:20

W*ait*. In its original Hebrew form, it means to "look eagerly for." But its connotations are that of enduring and being strong. It means to "bind together to make stronger," like a "twisted rope" (Biblehub.com).

This is not the kind of waiting we do when we're standing in line; it's waiting for God to keep His promises. It's holding on to the rope of faith and knowing He won't let go.

When we wait for the Lord, He is our help and our shield. Couldn't we all use a little help? Couldn't we all use a shield? Especially, it sometimes seems, in the everyday battles of life.

Yes, there are big battles we all have to fight, but it's those everyday battles that can slip in, catch us unawares, and really do some damage. Like that battle to do the right thing, even when no one else is looking. Or to live right in a world that glorifies wrong. Or to return a harsh word with a kind one. Maybe it's struggles with money, work, or health issues, wayward children, aging parents, or difficult relationships. Or perhaps it's simply the battle to bat away all the temptations and distractions, to remember that God really is Lord of all.

Take a moment now to breathe, to wait on the Lord. And then thank Him for being your help and your shield.

Thank You, Lord, for Your promises. I hold tight to them today.

Growing in Gratitude

Shout joyfully to the LORD, all the earth; break forth in song, rejoice, and sing praises.

—Psalm 98:4

*I*n this world of both instant communication and Instant Pots, it's important to remember that some important things come slowly. Hear the wisdom of radio host and author Nancy Leigh DeMoss: "The grateful heart that springs forth in joy is not acquired in a moment; it is the fruit of a thousand choices" (*Choosing Joy*).

As much as we may want to live with a heart rooted in gratitude, we can't flip a switch or push a button to make that happen. Arriving at the point is a process, and by definition a process takes time.

Every new day gives us countless opportunities to develop gratitude. Think of it: with everything we see, hear, taste, touch, think, and experience, we can choose to be grateful. Review your day so far. Identify a handful of moments when you expressed thankfulness—and another handful when you could have, and be grateful now!

Many things develop and improve over time. Today let's be encouraged that we are more thankful today than we were yesterday—and that we can choose to be even more thankful tomorrow.

Lord, give me a keener awareness and appreciation of Your goodness every day.

A God So Big

Who else has held the oceans in his hand? Who has measured off the heavens with his fingers? Who else knows the weight of the earth or has weighed the mountains and hills on a scale?

—Isaiah 40:12 NLT

Our God is so big that He holds the oceans in His hand and measures the heavens with His fingers. He is so strong that He shaped the mountains and dug out the deepest recesses of the seas with just the strength of His words (Genesis 1:9–10). And He is so mighty that He gives orders to the morning and shows the dawn its place in the sky (Job 38:12).

God can do anything. Just ask Abraham bouncing that baby on his one-hundred-year-old knee. Ask Joseph as he stared out from the palace window to the prison he once called home. Ask Moses as he stood on dry ground in the middle of the Red Sea. Or how about Mary as she held the tiny hand of her own Lord? Or the lame man who leaped to his feet, or the blind man who watched a sunset for the very first time? Ask that soldier who stood at the foot of the cross and knew that he had seen God. Ask Peter as he stared into an empty tomb.

The God who holds "the oceans in his hand" is big enough to handle your biggest troubles. Rejoice—because God can do anything!

As I think of all the wonders You have done, I praise You, Lord of my life.

Someone to Watch over You

He will not let your foot slip—he who watches over you will not slumber; indeed, he who watches over Israel will neither slumber nor sleep.

—Psalm 121:3–4 NIV

Sleep is such a blessing. To drift off into that velvety soft darkness, where stresses are soothed away, where mind and body and spirit are renewed and restored.

Yes, sleep is a wonderful thing . . . until it won't come. Until the fears that whisper their worst in the darkness leave you tossing and turning, your mind spinning and churning, and you're unable to still yourself enough to sleep.

Psalm 121 assures us that God never sleeps nor slumbers. When you feel stretched to your limits, remember the One who has no limits; find rest in the One who is inexhaustible. Before you turn back the covers for the night, spend a few moments kneeling before the "everlasting God" who "neither faints nor is weary" (Isaiah 40:28). Turn over all your cares to Him. Trust Him to do what is best for you. Then quietly slip into bed and drift into blessed sleep.

Fill my sleep with Your sweet rest and peace as I trust all my times to You.

Don't Forget Thanksgiving

Let us come before His presence with thanksgiving; let us shout joyfully to Him.

—Psalm 95:2

Have you ever noticed how after Halloween, many stores immediately bring out their prelit trees, ornaments, Christmas wreaths, and candy canes? The weeks between Halloween and Christmas are often a blur of colored leaves and turkey, prepping for gift shopping, and holiday parties.

In the frenzy of holiday preparations and Black Friday deals, it can be all too easy for us to skim over Thanksgiving. Sure, we serve the turkey and gravy, and mention what we're grateful for, but do we linger on giving thanks? Or once the Black Friday and Cyber Monday deals come out, do we immediately focus on all the *things* we want and all the savings we could have? Are we more excited about counting the gifts than we are about counting our blessings?

When the retail world becomes loud, ask the Lord to speak louder. When your eyes become focused on the newest, shiniest gadgets, ask Jesus to fix your eyes on Him and His gifts—and on the greatest gift of salvation.

Don't let autumn and its season of gratitude get lost in the blur of Christmas fanfare. Let Thanksgiving have its day—and its attitude—in your heart.

Father, I'm so grateful for an annual reminder to give You thanks. Keep me focused on all I have, not on all I want.

Being in God's Presence

You will make me full of joy in Your presence.

—Acts 2:28

Imagine coming before almighty God. Imagine standing at His feet as you behold His glory. In such a moment we would be mindful of His power and His holiness, His majesty and His splendor. But wouldn't we also sense His welcoming love?

We might not even notice as songs of praise fill the heavens because we are so intently listening for His voice, waiting for Him to say our names. As real and as thrilling as being at God's throne is, we might not be able to keep ourselves from reflecting on our lives and marveling at His great faithfulness.

But then being in God's presence becomes more personal. We notice His eyes of kindness, compassion, and love. We see the glimmer of pleasure and even joy. We are home. We are where God created us to be: we are in relationship, in unhindered fellowship with the King of kings, the Author of history, and the Sustainer of the universe.

Imagine coming before God. How could we not be thankful in God's presence? How could we not shout joyfully?

Lord, I am filled with awe as I picture Your throne, Your glory, and Your eyes of love. Thank You.

Thanks Throughout the Day

It is good to give thanks to the LORD, and to sing praises to Your name, O Most High.

—Psalm 92:1

Agreeing that it is indeed "good to give thanks to the LORD," let's imagine together what moments of gratitude throughout your day might look like.

Waking up: We thank God for the day ahead—and we ask His guidance. What does He want us to do with this gift of life?

The routine: The routine can bring frustration and impatience, flat tires and bad traffic, and yes, worries. We can always thank God for His presence, whatever the circumstances that invite discontent rather than gratitude.

Evening crunch time: This could mean prayers for patience with an oldest child's homework issue, for wisdom with a middle child's life question, for insight into a youngest child's mood, and for selfless love for a weary spouse. But if we can only muster a couple syllables, "Thank You" counts!

It's never too late to say "Thank You" to God. As the psalmist said, "It is good to give thanks to the LORD!"

Lord, please teach me to give You thanks throughout the day. That would truly be good!

Making a List

Oh, give thanks to the God of heaven!

—Psalm 136:26

Have you ever made the time to put in writing some of the things you are thankful for? Why not try it? You have nothing to lose—and much to gain. Consider jotting down three things you're thankful for right before you crawl into bed. Think back over your day and note where God showed up!

Or keep a running list of what you're grateful for. Add two things to your list each morning as you drink a cup of coffee. Keep your list on your phone, or go retro and use paper.

Maybe you like to journal, and the idea of a gratitude journal is appealing. Giving yourself time to look at what you're thankful for and why may radically increase your thankful quotient.

And chances are good that you will also experience a lighter heart, a more optimistic attitude, a sharper awareness of God's work in your life, and a greater sense of His presence with you.

So go ahead! Grab your phone or a piece of paper—and give thanks to the God of heaven!

Please, Lord, help me see the many reasons I have to be thankful every waking hour, every day of the year!

Inside the Twenty-Third Psalm

The LORD is my shepherd.

—Psalm 23:1

The Twenty-third Psalm is a beloved source of comfort and beautiful promises of who God is:

- He is our Provider. "I shall not want" (v. 1).
- He leads us to rest. "He makes me to lie down in green pastures; He leads me beside the still waters" (v. 2).
- He is our salvation. "He restores my soul; He leads me in the paths of righteousness for His name's sake" (v. 3).
- He is our Protector. "Though I walk through the valley of the shadow of death, I will fear no evil; for You are with me; Your rod and Your staff, they comfort me" (v. 4).
- He is our victory. "You prepare a table before me in the presence of my enemies; You anoint my head with oil" (v. 5).
- He blesses us fully. "My cup runs over" (v. 5).
- He is ever faithful. "Surely goodness and mercy shall follow me all the days of my life" (v. 6).
- He is our true home. "I will dwell in the house of the LORD forever" (v. 6).

No wonder Psalm 23 is a favorite the world over: it announces so many facets of God's goodness to us!

For all You have done and all You do for me, I praise Your holy name!

The President's Proclamation

*Oh, that men would give thanks to the LORD for His goodness, and
for His wonderful works to the children of men!*

—Psalm 107:8

Our nation's presidents have often appreciated the value of gratitude to God. Every president since George Washington has issued a proclamation of thanksgiving. The actual proclamation to observe a day of Thanksgiving came from Abraham Lincoln, who said:

> It has seemed to me fit and proper that [the gracious gifts of the Most High God] should be solemnly, reverently and gratefully acknowledged as with one heart and one voice by the whole American People. I do therefore invite my fellow citizens in every part of the United States, and also those who are at sea and those who are sojourning in foreign lands, to set apart and observe the last Thursday of November next, as a day of Thanksgiving and Praise to our beneficent Father who dwelleth in the Heavens.

And so each president since has re-declared a day of giving thanks to God. Isn't it good that our presidents value offering gratitude to the Lord?

Thank You, Jesus, that I live in a nation where I can worship You freely and give thanks to You openly.

Only One Thing

One thing I ask from the LORD, this only do I seek: that I may dwell in the house of the LORD all the days of my life.

—Psalm 27:4 NIV

David was a mighty and powerful man. There were many things he could ask of his people and of God. But what did he want most? To live with the Lord in His temple forever.

This was no small thing David asked. In Psalm 15, he described the life of the person who would dwell with the Lord:

> The one whose walk is blameless, who does what is righteous, who speaks the truth from their heart; whose tongue utters no slander, who does no wrong to a neighbor, and casts no slur on others; who despises a vile person but honors those who fear the LORD; who keeps an oath even when it hurts, and does not change their mind; who lends money to the poor without interest; who does not accept a bribe against the innocent. (vv. 2–5 NIV)

It's an impossible list to follow perfectly, but David's request is our future reality: "In My Father's house are many mansions; if it were not so, I would have told you. I go to prepare a place for you" (John 14:2). Thank You, Lord Jesus.

Lord, like David, I ask this thing of You—to let me live with You forever.

Are You a Good Sheep?

"I am the good shepherd. The good shepherd gives His life for the sheep."

—John 10:11

Much has been said about Jesus as the Good Shepherd. But have you ever stopped to ask yourself if you are a good sheep? In John 10, Jesus described the relationship He wants to have with His followers:

- "I know My sheep, and am known by My own" (v. 14). How well do you know Jesus? Are you the closest of friends, or just passing acquaintances?
- "I lay down My life for the sheep" (v. 15). Are you willing to lay down your life—or your ball game, your social media, your smartphone—for Jesus?
- "My sheep hear My voice" (v. 27). Do you spend time in His Word getting to know His voice so you will recognize Him when He calls to you?
- "Follow Me" (v. 27). Do you follow Jesus all the time or only when it's convenient?

You are blessed with the Good Shepherd, who loves, protects, and provides for you. What can you do today to thank Him for His care and to make His job a little easier?

Thank You for being such a Good Shepherd; please help me learn to be a good sheep.

Willing and Able

Behold, You have made the heavens and the earth by Your great power and outstretched arm. There is nothing too hard for You.

—Jeremiah 32:17

We serve a God who has done extraordinary things to save His people. He shut the mouths of lions, knocked down walls, and stopped the sun in its trek across the sky. The God who created all the heavens and the earth and everything in them proclaimed, "I am the LORD, the God of all mankind. Is anything too hard for me?" (Jeremiah 32:27 NIV).

In fact, there is no question that God is able. But perhaps even more important, we serve a God who is not only able but *willing* to do exceptional things to save His people. He sent His own Son to show us how to live and love. He allowed that Son to be slain to wash away our sins. Then He resurrected His Son to defeat death and open the gates to heaven to all who would follow Him.

Our God has done marvelous things to save us. He has allowed no boundary to bar us from His heaven. Why? Simply because He loves us: "For God so loved the world that He gave His only begotten Son, that whoever believes in Him should not perish but have everlasting life" (John 3:16). Love is what makes God willing.

I am so grateful, Lord, for Your saving love.

Armor for the Battle

*Be strong in the Lord and in the power of His might. Put on the
whole armor of God.*

—Ephesians 6:10–11

According to God's Word, we are fighting "spiritual hosts
of wickedness in the heavenly places" (Ephesians 6:12), so
let's be grateful for the spiritual armor God provides. Paul's
descriptions of the various pieces suggest the protective gear
worn by the Roman soldiers of his day.

According to Compellingtruth.org, the Roman soldier's
belt was crucial because it held in place the rest of his armor.
Similarly, the Christian soldier's *belt of truth*—our knowledge of
God's truth—is essential in our battle with Satan. He would
make us doubt God's love. We gird ourselves with this belt so we
can sort out truth from lies from the evil one.

Next, Paul referred to the Roman soldier's breastplate. As
soldiers in God's army, we initially put on our *breastplate of righteousness* when we confessed our sins and received God's forgiveness.
This piece of armor protects our most essential organs.

Soldiers in God's army have also "shod [their] feet with the
preparation of the gospel of peace" (Ephesians 6:15). We are
therefore ready to march in obedience.

In our battle against spiritual enemies, we show wisdom as
well as gratitude when we put on the armor God provides.

*Lord, thank You for the glorious protection Your armor provides me
from the evil one.*

Standing Strong
Against the Enemy

*Take up the whole armor of God, that you may be able to withstand
in the evil day, and having done all, to stand.*

—Ephesians 6:13

In addition to His truth, righteousness, and gospel, the parts
of spiritual armor we examined yesterday, God provides us
with faith, salvation, and the sword of the Spirit for the battle.

Faithhub.net tells us a Roman soldier's curved shield provided safety when the soldier crouched behind it. Likewise, our
faith in God's power is a *shield*. Even greater strength comes in
community as we believers stand side by side.

Next, just as a Roman soldier's helmet protected his head,
our *helmet of salvation* protects us from corruptive thoughts.

Members of God's army wield the *sword of the Spirit*, the Word of
God. The written Word gives us the truth we need to stand strong
against the enemy. God's Word-come-to-life (Jesus) and spoken
word (the Holy Spirit inside us) further empower us for battle.

Finally comes the vital weapon of *prayer*. Through prayer, we
find God's strength, hear His direction, and gain the ability to
use effectively the rest of our armor.

To be effective soldiers, we wisely and gratefully put on the
armor of God.

*Thank You, Lord, that my faith, my salvation, Your Word, and
prayer equip me for battle.*

Remembering the Right Things

"This cup is the new covenant in My blood. This do, as often as you drink it, in remembrance of Me."

—1 Corinthians 11:25

A contributing factor to our sometimes poor performance in the gratitude department just may be a poor memory. Scripture suggests that we aren't the first of God's people to struggle to remember the most important truths and realities we know.

In the Old Testament we read of the spectacular and devastating plagues that God rained down on the Egyptians who were holding His people captive. After the firstborn in every Egyptian household died, Pharaoh sent the people of Israel out of the land, and Moses was soon saying to the people, "Remember this day in which you went out of Egypt, out of the house of bondage; for by strength of hand the Lord brought you out of this place" (Exodus 13:3). Don't you wonder how they could ever forget?

In the New Testament, Paul wrote to the church of Corinth about an even more remarkable work of God in history: the apostle called people to observe the Lord's Supper and remember Jesus' death on the cross. How could they—how could we—ever forget? Let's keep a sharp memory of all the times God's delivered us.

Lord, teach me to remember Your deliverance more than I remember my trials.

DECEMBER

In His Image

So God created mankind in his own image, in the image of God he created them; male and female he created them.

—Genesis 1:27 NIV

What does it mean to be created in the image of God? It means that we look like Him—not physically, but spiritually. Of course, we don't look exactly like Him; after all, He's still working on us. But to be created in the image of God means that everything good within us—any speck of kindness, any joy, any moment of selfless love—is a reflection of Him. After all, "every good action and every perfect gift is from God" (James 1:17 NCV).

We shouldn't settle for looking just a little bit like God. We spend so much time and money and effort on our outward appearance, which so quickly fades. Shouldn't we be even more committed to making ourselves a beautiful reflection of God? How about primping our prayer lives, styling our Bible study, and polishing our praises?

Take a look in the mirror of His Word today. How much of His image do you see? Are you patient and kind? Are you good to others and faithful? Are you gentle and joyful? Are your words filled with peace and love? A life that reflects the image of God is a life that praises Him.

When the world looks at me, Lord, let them see You.

Subtle Ingratitude

"A good man out of the good treasure of his heart brings forth good. . . . For out of the abundance of the heart his mouth speaks."
—Luke 6:45

We can occasionally gain significant insight into something by considering its opposite. We better appreciate, for instance, silence after noise, and success after we have failed. Let's look at three comments that offer a glimpse of gratitude's opposite.

- "Unexpressed gratitude feels like ingratitude to the ones for whom you are grateful."—Andy Stanley
- "A proud man is seldom a grateful man, for he never thinks he gets as much as he deserves."—Henry Ward Beecher, pastor and abolitionist
- "Most human beings have an almost infinite capacity for taking things for granted."—Aldous Huxley

What unspoken gratitude is it time for you to speak? In what area of your life do you feel as if you deserve more? And what aspects of your life do you take for granted?

Ingratitude is not a fruit of the Spirit, who wants us to live from hearts filled with abundant thanks. He can help us see each other as we are, answer these questions, and change ourselves.

Thank You, Lord, for showing me the subtler forms of ingratitude and helping me get rid of them.

Giving Thanks in the Moment

Blessing and glory and wisdom, thanksgiving and honor and power and might, be to our God forever and ever.

—Revelation 7:12

D o you find it a struggle to live in the moment? Our minds easily stray to the past or the future. Whether to good memories or regrets, whether to dreams or fears, our thoughts often go far afield, don't they? When this happens, we may miss what is happening now and the blessings right at hand.

Have you ever longed deeply for something, finally received it—then quickly moved on to your next want or need? That activity reveals an aspect of ingratitude. Once we have what we had hoped for, the sparkle of that item, opportunity, or relationship tends to fade quickly. The remarkable is less fascinating, and the special seems mundane.

Struggling to live in the moment, we don't always give God the thanks we want to give. Why not make that a goal? Start working toward it right now by considering what longed-for thing, opportunity, or relationship you can thank God for today—and thank Him!

Jesus, thank You for continuing to work out Your will and purposes in me, for growing in me a thankful heart.

The Wonders of God

Stand still and consider the wondrous works of God.

—Job 37:14

𝓘f you ever doubt the power, the might, the loving care of God, just "ask the animals, and they will teach you, or the birds in the sky, and they will tell you; or speak to the earth, and it will teach you, or let the fish in the sea inform you" (Job 12:7–8 NIV). Picture these: Sunlight streaming through the clouds, like the fingertips of the Father. A hawk soaring, gliding on the winds. A soft breeze lifting autumn's flurry of leaves. A falling star streaking across the nighttime sky. The flash of lightning and rumble of a summer thunderstorm. The gentle hush of falling snow.

Creation is not God, but it is *of* God. It tells us that He is a God of order, a God of care, and a God of wonders.

For it is God who made the clouds to wrap like a garment around the earth (Job 38:9). He alone gives the hawk the wisdom to fly (39:26). He is the One who scatters the winds (38:24) and orders the stars (v. 31). Only the Lord knows "the way to the place where the lightning is dispersed" (v. 24 NIV), and only God holds the key to "the treasury of snow" (v. 22).

When you doubt the Lord's power and love, consider the wonders that the hand of the Lord has created.

With my whole heart, I will praise You—I will tell the world of all the amazing things You have done!

Work Made Holy

Whatever you do, work at it with all your heart, as working for the Lord.

—Colossians 3:23 NIV

A new day has begun, and there is much to be done. Whether you're off to the boardroom, the eight-to-five job, or tending home and little ones all day, you always have so many things to accomplish. Is there a way to make all you do . . . *holy*?

Today, approach every task as if you're doing it for Jesus Himself. That floor to clean? Scrub it as if your Savior were the next One to walk across it. Groceries to bag? Imagine you're handing them to Christ. Meetings to take? Meet your Lord there.

Praise the Lord with your work. Let your efforts so glorify Him that people *see* Him in your work. *Why?* you ask. Not because you are trying to earn His love. That is His gift, not something you can earn.

No, in this new day let the work of your hands glorify God because "you know that you will receive an inheritance from the Lord as a reward" . . . because, in whatever you do, it truly "is the Lord Christ you are serving" (Colossians 3:24 NIV).

Lord, please bless the work of my hands this day, as I strive to give honor to You.

Gratitude Recalibrated

Why are you cast down, O my soul? . . . Hope in God.

—Psalm 42:11

Among its many calls to give thanks, the Bible recognizes the reality of despair, of a soul "cast down." Aren't you glad God acknowledges the pain and darkness we sometimes face?

In some cases, the darkness simply cannot be ignored. Holocaust survivor Elie Wiesel experienced evil of historical proportions during his time in a Nazi concentration camp. Mindful of that backdrop, consider his words: "No one is as capable of gratitude as one who has escaped from the kingdom of night. We know that every moment is a moment of grace, every hour an offering."

Your "kingdom of night" may be personal pain from an experience that seems like nothing next to other people's stories. But pain is pain, it is not a competition, and there is no need for comparison: God comforts *all* the hurting.

When despair is your companion, consider the words of poet Henry Wadsworth Longfellow: "It has done me good to be somewhat parched by the heat and drenched by the rain of life." Ask God to help you endure and to keep giving thanks.

Merciful God, when my soul is cast down, help me choose to hope in You. Help me to know Your comfort.

Chosen

You are a chosen generation, a royal priesthood, a holy nation, His own special people, that you may proclaim the praises of Him who called you out of darkness into His marvelous light.

—1 Peter 2:9

*C*hosen is a big word in our culture: *chosen* for the promotion, for the team, to be a friend. To be chosen—or not to be—is a significant thing. It can determine your wealth, your status, your "pecking order" within a group of peers.

But whether or not you are chosen by the boss, the coach, the lunch-table crowd—it doesn't matter. You have been chosen by the only One who truly matters: the Lord God Himself.

He called you out of the darkness of your own sins and wayward ways. He called you to live a holy life. And it was not because of anything you did—so you don't have to worry about being *un*chosen.

God has a purpose for you in His kingdom, a place for you to fill. And His grace? It comes from a love for you so great that He wants you by His side for all time.

So if you're ever passed over—by the boss, by the team, by the would-be friend—don't let it upset you too much. Instead, give thanks to the God of all creation, who has chosen you for His own.

You choose me, Lord, and that's so incredible to me. Help me each day to choose You too. Thank You!

The Lights of Christmas

Shine among them like stars in the sky.

—Philippians 2:15 NIV

There's something almost magical about Christmas lights. You can take a simple tree, a humble mailbox, even the most neglected of homes and drape it in sparkling, twinkling Christmas lights and *voilà!* They are transformed from the ordinary into the extraordinary.

God works a bit like those Christmas lights. He takes a simple shepherd, a humble fisherman, even the most neglected of sinners and drapes them in healing mercies and unconditional love and *voilà!* They are transformed from the ordinary into the extraordinary. His light shines through them to chase away the darkness, to lead His people from slavery to freedom, to teach them to become fishers of men, to help them sparkle like stars in the nighttime sky.

If you think about the heroes of the Bible, there were no superheroes, no men or women in tights and capes. There were only ordinary people, just like you. But they were loved by and allowed themselves to be used by an extraordinary God. And He made them extraordinary too. Won't you follow their example and let yourself be transformed? You too will shine like the stars, like magical Christmas lights.

Shine through me, Lord, so that I may show the world how wonderfully extraordinary You are!

Like His Father

"The water I give will be an artesian spring within, gushing fountains of endless life."

—John 4:14 *The Message*

When Jesus encountered the Samaritan woman at the well, He didn't hesitate to engage her in conversation. Like His Father, Jesus didn't look at the outward appearance. As the Lord Himself told Samuel the prophet, "GOD judges persons differently than humans do. Men and women look at the face; GOD looks into the heart" (I Samuel 16:7 *The Message*). Thus Jesus did not judge her as others did; He saw her as a person rather than as a societal outcast, a dreaded Samaritan, a rejected sinner.

Like His Father, Jesus looked inside. What did He find? He saw a heart following the wrong path and open to a new way; a soul that was seeking—even if she didn't quite know how or whom to seek; a thirsty woman ready for living water.

Like His Father, Jesus looks at the heart.

Aren't we all grateful that He does? Aren't we thankful that Jesus doesn't see only our outward mishaps, mistakes, and outright sins? As He peered into the Samaritan woman's heart, He looks into ours and offers us the same living water, so we also can be made whole in Him.

Lord Jesus, thank You for looking past all my sins to see my parched soul longing for Your "artesian spring."

Gratitude for What We Give

"Freely you have received, freely give."

—Matthew 10:8

*G*od richly blesses us with time, treasure, and talents. We show our gratitude to Him as well as our faith in His faithfulness when we share, and share lavishly, what He has entrusted to our care.

The instructions in Matthew 10 are words Jesus spoke to His disciples when He sent them out to preach to "the lost sheep of the house of Israel" and to "heal the sick, cleanse the lepers, raise the dead, cast out demons" (vv. 6, 8). "Freely you have received, freely give" follows next.

Like the disciples, we have been entrusted with the gift of the gospel that we too are to generously share. In addition we have been entrusted with possessions and money, which we are also to freely share.

Think for a minute about the best gift you ever received—and the gratitude you felt. Now think about the best gift you ever gave—and the gratitude you felt then. We are blessed with what God has given us. We are also blessed when we share—freely and generously—all that He has given us.

Lord God, thank You for the joy of giving and how it can be richer than the joy of receiving.

Anyway

"He who dipped his hand with Me in the dish will betray Me."
—Matthew 26:23

Moments before Jesus told His disciples that one of them would betray Him, He washed their feet. Yes, even the feet of the one whom He knew would turn Him over to the authorities; even the feet of one who would deny Him; even the feet of all the disciples who would later run away from Him as fast as those same feet could carry them. Jesus washed their feet anyway.

You might say that the word *anyway* provides a sort of one-word summary of Jesus' approach to His ministry. Though Jesus knew the Pharisees would never accept Him, He sowed the seeds of His Word anyway. And though Jesus knew the cross lay ahead, He went to Jerusalem anyway.

Our Savior knows we will let Him down. He knows we will do the exact thing He has asked us not to do. We will wander and lose our way. Yet He chooses to love us, care for us, serve us, provide for us, protect us, even die for us . . . anyway.

Jesus washed the feet of His sometimes faithless followers. Like Him, when your efforts appear to be pointless and wasted on those who don't care, serve anyway, give anyway, love anyway. Thank Jesus for all His *anyways* with your own.

Thank You, Lord, for all the times You've chosen to love, to bless, to forgive me anyway.

Because We Love Jesus

"If you love Me, keep My commandments."

—John 14:15

The rules—the commandments—do not save us. Christ with His love, His mercy, His grace, and His blood saves us. So why do we bother with the rules? Because we love Him. Think of it this way:

A young boy, Gabe absolutely loves sports, especially baseball. He relishes the game of it, the strategy of it, and, yes, even the rules of it. When he first became interested in baseball, his mother knew nothing whatsoever about the game. But she set out to learn. She watched the games, she learned the strategies, and now in the backyard one-on-ones she tries her best to obey the rules. Because she loves the game? No. Because she loves the boy, and it is important to him.

Jesus really gives us just two rules to follow, though, those two commandments—to love God and our neighbors as ourselves— touch every area of our lives. Though the rules do not save us, we do our best to learn and to follow them because we love Him—and because they are important to Him.

Help me, Lord Jesus, as I try to show how much I love You by keeping Your commandments.

Ask, Seek, Knock

"Ask, and it will be given to you; seek, and you will find; knock, and it will be opened to you."

—Luke 11:9

It is surely intentional that today's verse on asking, seeking, and knocking follows so closely Jesus' instructions on how to pray. And while the Lord's Prayer teaches us how to pray, the verse after that tells us how God responds to our prayers: "For everyone who asks receives, and he who seeks finds, and to him who knocks it will be opened" (Luke 11:10).

If you ask, you will receive. God *will* answer your prayers. Does that mean you'll receive the bright red convertible you sent up that hopeful, heavenward wish for? No. Does that mean the illness will be healed, the relationship mended, or the job found? Not necessarily. What it does mean is that God will answer—with the answer that is best for you. After all, "if you . . . know how to give good gifts to your children, how much more will your heavenly Father give good gifts to those who ask him" (Matthew 7:11 NLT). When you offer your prayers, you can trust Him to give you a good answer.

When you seek God in prayer, He promises to be found. And when you knock, He will open up the door of heaven to you. Ask, seek, and knock, because your Lord will respond.

To know that You hear and answer my every prayer is so comforting to me—and I am so thankful to You.

Savoring Gifts

I will give thanks to you, LORD, with all my heart.

—Psalm 9:1 NIV

There's nothing like Christmas morning for children. They wriggle through breakfast, stealing glances at the bright packages underneath the tree. Their anticipation is contagious.

When you hand children gifts, they eagerly tear off the wrapping paper, throwing it aside. Are the gifts what they were hoping for? Squeals of excitement soon pierce your ears as they jump up and down! But then most children do something adults are guilty of too—they quickly move on to the next gift. Sure, they begged all year for the gift, but they're distracted by the promise of more.

When it comes to prayer and gratitude, does this sound familiar? We may beg God for something—and when we receive it, we're as ecstatic as children on Christmas morning. But our attention almost immediately shifts to something else. We barely give ourselves time to bask in the joy of answered prayer.

When "Christmas morning" finally comes and you receive from the Lord what you long sought, what distracts you from giving the Lord praise for answered prayers? Let's give ourselves permission to really savor every gift God gives.

Father, thank You for always answering my prayers. Remind me to relish the moments of deliverance and give You the thanks You deserve.

Patience, Kindness, Goodness

The fruit of the Spirit is . . . longsuffering, kindness, goodness.

—Galatians 5:22

L et's look at three qualities the Spirit develops in us as we follow Jesus.

First, the Holy Spirit grants us the ability to be *longsuffering* or *patient* with enemies as well as loved ones, despite present evils and current frustrations. Patience is evident when, by God's grace, we are slow to anger and quick to forgive. Spirit-fueled patience also enables us to wait on God's timing for His perfect plans.

Calling *kindness* "a virtue of grace," Bible teacher R. C. Sproul said it "involves a willingness to keep one's power and authority in check. It does not crush the weak. It is thoughtful . . . tempering justice with mercy."

Goodness is basic integrity reflected in choices we make. As the Spirit makes us more like Jesus, He leads us to do good to others.

We show our gratitude to the Spirit by yielding to His work in our hearts and developing His qualities.

Father, longsuffering, kindness, and goodness do not come easily.
Thank You for working to make them real in my life.

Be Who God Made You to Be

Each person is given something to do that shows who God is.
—1 Corinthians 12:7 The Message

God created you with a plan and a purpose in mind: "Before I shaped you in the womb, I knew all about you. Before you saw the light of day, I had holy plans for you" (Jeremiah 1:5 *The Message*).

You were made to be somebody special to God—and *for* God. Your challenge in this life, then, is to discover the somebody He created you to be. Thankfully you're not left on your own to do that. The Lord will not only guide you in His plans for you, He will also "bless you abundantly, so that in all things at all times, having all that you need, you will abound in every good work" (2 Corinthians 9:8 NIV).

The trouble is that it's so easy to be distracted from the somebody God created you to be by the somebody the world says you should be—or the nobody some people would reduce you to.

Dear one, don't worry about who the world says you are or says your plans should be. If God made you to be a teacher, then teach. If an encourager, then encourage. If a writer, then write. Whatever you do, do it in such a way that shows the Lord's heart.

Be who God created you to be—the amazing child of His heart (Psalm 139:14).

Thank You, Lord, for making me amazing—help me fulfill the plans You have for me.

Cheerfully Receive

Give thanks to the Lord for His goodness, and for His wonderful works to the children of men!

—Psalm 107:8

God loves a cheerful giver (2 Corinthians 9:7). Such a person gives gladly and with joy in her heart; knows that the more she gives, the more she will be given; understands she can never outgive the greatest of Givers.

But have you ever wondered how God would like us to *receive* His gifts? After all, He blesses us so richly—with both gifts of the Spirit and gifts of this earth. Should we accept them reluctantly, as if they weren't really meant for us? Should we be solemn and silent about our blessings? Wouldn't it be bragging to tell the world about what God has given to us?

The psalmist who wrote today's verse said we shouldn't keep silent about the good things God has done for and given to us. And it was declared again in Psalm 150:2: "Praise Him for His mighty acts; praise Him according to His excellent greatness!"

Be a delighted giver, and bless the Lord also by being a grateful and joyful receiver.

Your generosity astounds me, Lord! Thank You for all You've gifted to me.

An Instinct to Praise

And Mary said: "My soul magnifies the Lord, and my spirit has rejoiced in God my Savior."

—Luke 1:46–47

When the angel Gabriel appeared to Mary in Galilee, he gave her life-altering news: she was going to birth the Savior of the world. Then the angel delivered more astonishing news: her cousin Elizabeth, he said, "has also conceived a son in her old age" (v. 36). Not only was Mary going to give birth; Elizabeth, who was older and barren, was also going to be a mother. Gabriel stated, "For with God nothing will be impossible" (v. 37).

Imagine what Mary and Elizabeth must have felt: shocked, afraid, maybe a little dazed. Mary's reaction was to thank the Lord. She didn't understand, and it didn't seem physically possible—but she said, "My soul magnifies the Lord, and my spirit has rejoiced in God my Savior." Later in her prayer, Mary recounted God's faithfulness and ended with praise for who God is and what He had done throughout the generations.

When Gabriel delivered his glorious yet puzzling message, Mary's instinct was grateful praise. She knew and trusted the faithfulness of God, and because of that, she praised Him. With the Lord, the impossible is always possible.

With Your help, Lord, my reach is endless. Thank You for all the possibilities You pour into my life!

Unimaginable Plans

The angel said to her, "Rejoice, highly favored one, the Lord is with you; blessed are you among women!"

—Luke 1:28

We don't know much about Mary, but the culture of the day suggests that this resident of the small town of Nazareth was young, and her offering of pigeons when Jesus was dedicated at the temple implies that she was probably poor. We can imagine that Mary was thankful for her husband-to-be, a hardworking and respectable man of God named Joseph. Maybe her thoughts and prayers were of grateful anticipation of all that awaited her as a wife and mother.

Yet the God who knows hearts had bigger plans for Mary: He chose her to be the mother of His Son. He knew that she would yield her life to His plan—as we see in her song of praise (Luke 1:46–55). God knew Mary would raise Jesus with wisdom and grace and teach Him all she knew about the one true God and Scripture. Such traits meant much more to God than Mary's age, social status, or financial situation. All that mattered to Him was her heart. Thankfully, God's priorities haven't changed.

Remember with gratitude that God knows your heart for Him as He knew Mary's, and He plans amazing things for you as well.

Thank You, Lord, for stepping into our ordinary days and surprising us with unimaginable plans!

Trusting and Yielded

My soul magnifies the Lord. . . . For He who is mighty has done
great things for me, and holy is His name.

—Luke 1:46, 49

When newly pregnant Mary entered Elizabeth's house, this older mother-to-be eloquently spoke of her humble joy that "the mother of my Lord should come to me" and then affirmed Mary: "Blessed is she who believed" (Luke 1:43, 45).

As Mary's song of praise, the Magnificat, shows, Mary did believe. Her praise for God's mercy, faithfulness, and strength reveals not only her knowledge of Israel's history but her genuine experience with her God. She praised Him for exalting the lowly and providing for the hungry. With gratitude and joy, Mary praised God who "regarded the lowly state of His maidservant; for behold, henceforth all generations will call me blessed" (v. 48).

When Mary entered her cousin's home, Elizabeth affirmed her as a blessed believer in God. Let's strive to be like Mary, who yielded to His will and the angel's outrageous promise. May her grateful and trusting words be ours as well: "Let it be to me according to your word" (v. 38).

Thank You, Lord, that Mary humbly submitted to Your radical plan
for her life—and please help me do the same.

Swaddled in God's Love

She brought forth her firstborn Son, and wrapped Him in swaddling cloths, and laid Him in a manger.

—Luke 2:7

We never outgrow our need for spiritual, psychological, emotional, and physical security, do we? Consider a newborn. In Jesus' day, parents used swaddling cloths to wrap rather tightly around their newborns to help ease the little ones' transition from the snuggly womb to the world outside. Today, when newborns emerge from the womb, parents use soft blankets to tightly swaddle their babies. Swaddling keeps babies warm and helps them sleep because the restrictiveness is a familiar sensation. (Swaddling also keeps them from scratching themselves with their sharp baby nails!) Bundled and in parents' arms, babies often relax, and crying usually stops. This cozy cuddling offers womblike safety and security that enables newborn babies to rest peacefully.

Your heavenly Father wants you to know safety and security; He wants you to sleep peacefully. That's one reason He has given His children His written Word. There, in black and white, are warm and comforting words about His love. They can remind us of God's power, goodness, faithfulness, and protection. And those truths about who our loving God is can wrap around us in safety and help us sleep.

I am grateful for Your love and Your words and for the security they give me. Thank You, Father.

Joseph's Courage and Sacrifices

An angel of the Lord appeared to him in a dream and said, "Joseph son of David, do not be afraid to take Mary home as your wife, because what is conceived in her is from the Holy Spirit."

—Matthew 1:20 NIV

It's easy to overlook people who, by choice or assignment, stay in the background even as they commit amazing acts of faith. Consider Joseph the carpenter, whose wedding plans changed with the angel's announcement. "Faithful to the law," Joseph "did not want to expose her to public disgrace," so he planned to privately divorce his suddenly pregnant fiancée (Matthew 1:19 NIV).

In Joseph's day, a betrothed woman who was pregnant could be married, divorced, or stoned to death. The decision was Joseph's. Consider this man, who could lose his standing in the Jewish community and who may have been overwhelmed by hurt, disappointment, anger, disbelief, sadness, and embarrassment. But God sent an angel who commanded Joseph to "take Mary home as your wife." We can only imagine Joseph's anguish.

Whatever his human concerns and whatever this decision would cost him, he married the beloved young woman whose tale mystified him. Let's be thankful today and notice role models like Joseph, who obey God and serve Him at great cost and without fanfare or concern for self.

Thank You, Lord, for people like Joseph who serve quietly without demanding acknowledgment.

373

Choreographed by God

It came to pass in those days that a decree went out from Caesar Augustus that all the world should be registered.

—Luke 2:1

Do you get excited when you recognize God's fingerprints on a specific event? Jesus' birth was one such event.

The following conditions did not merely happen, as "It came to pass" may imply. God choreographed much in order to have the Son of David born in the City of David. Consider that when Mary became pregnant, Judea was now a province of Rome and subject to the government census. Consider also that the prophet Micah had said, "Bethlehem . . . out of you shall come . . . the One to be Ruler in Israel" (Micah 5:2). Mary lived in the wrong town, and as her time to give birth drew near, she needed to get to Bethlehem in order to fulfill the prophecy. This occurred because Caesar Augustus commanded a census, and Mary and her betrothed, Joseph, needed to travel to that very town.

The birth of Jesus came to pass as prophesied long before: Almighty God worked through the powerful Roman government and perfectly timed the birth of a baby to a young virgin. We can spot His fingerprints in these "happenings." Joy to the world!

Thank You, Lord, for fulfilling prophecies, steering governments, and involving Yourself in the details of life so Your perfect plan unfolds.

News Too Good Not to Share

After seeing him, the shepherds told everyone what had happened
and what the angel had said to them about this child.

—Luke 2:17 NLT

xciting news—your daughter-in-law is pregnant, your sister is getting married, your husband got the promotion— prompts joyful gratitude to the God who answered your prayers. He has ended your period of waiting for Him to act. And being chosen as the first to know makes you feel honored.

It was an honor the shepherds never would have expected. "Living out in the fields, keeping watch over their flock by night," the shepherds were the first to hear, "There is born to you this day in the city of David a Savior, who is Christ the Lord" (Luke 2:8, 11).

After the "multitude of the heavenly host" finished praising God (v. 13), the dirty, smelly shepherds rushed to see the baby. Just as the angel said, they found the child lying in a manger as an undoubtedly exhausted Mary and Joseph looked in awe at the miracle baby.

The exciting news was too good for the shepherds to keep to themselves. They "told everyone" the angel's message. This exciting news is too wonderful to keep to yourself! This Christmas season, with whom will you joyfully and gratefully share the message that Jesus Christ is born?

Thank You for giving us, like the shepherds, opportunities to tell
others about Jesus our Savior.

O Come, Let Us Adore Him

In him was life, and that life was the light of all mankind.

—John 1:4 NIV

Pause for a moment, and thank God for the miracle of the incarnation, of our infinite and eternal God taking on a human body to become the "light of all mankind."

Jesus stepped out of heaven and came "in the likeness of men" (Philippians 2:7). We can't begin to comprehend all that this voluntary demotion involved when the infinite God chose to be confined to a human body. It's like a human choosing to become an ant.

Furthermore, Jesus chose to enter the human race as a helpless infant. The all-powerful God teethed, ran a fever, and learned to walk. Then, thirty-three years later, this all-powerful God submitted to death. Charles Wesley penned the Christmas hymn that summarizes Jesus' journey this way:

> Christ, by highest heaven adored; Christ, the everlasting
>   Lord:
> Late in time behold Him come, offspring of a virgin's womb.
> Veiled in flesh the Godhead see, hail th' incarnate Deity!
> Pleased as man with men t'appear, Jesus our Immanuel here.
> Hark! the herald angels sing, "Glory to the newborn king."
> Hallelujah! Celebrate God incarnate with joy and
>   gratitude!

O come, let us adore Him, Christ the Lord. We praise You, Jesus.

A God You Can Count On

I am the LORD, and I do not change.

—Malachi 3:6 NLT

Does it ever seem as if nothing in this world stays the same? You finally get things figured out—how to successfully negotiate with your boss, what foods the kids will eat, where the bread aisle is in the grocery store—and then suddenly everything changes. Your boss gets a new job and you're back to square one with someone new. Your kids suddenly hate spaghetti, which they absolutely loved last week. And the grocery store decided to remodel, and you have no idea where the bread is anymore.

Isn't it nice to know that in a world that is ever-changing, there is One who is never-changing: God?

God never changes His mind or tells a lie. He always does what He says He will do. And He keeps every promise that He makes (Numbers 23:19). He does not waver the way shadows shift (James 1:17). Our God is the same today as He was yesterday, which is the same as He will be tomorrow (Hebrews 13:8).

In this world of constant movement, when God says He loves you, you can believe it. When He says you're His beloved child, know it. And when He promises you salvation, build your life on it. And then thank Him for being a God who never changes.

With everything around me changing so quickly, thank You, God, for staying the same—wonderfully faithful and true!

Understanding Optional

"For My thoughts are not your thoughts, nor are your ways My ways," says the Lord.

—Isaiah 55:8

If each of us made a list of all the things we don't understand, each person's list would be different. Some don't understand the appeal of politics, the offside rule in soccer, or Euclidean geometry. Others don't understand how salt makes chocolate sweeter, why sentences shouldn't end in *to*, or how finding the value of *x* in algebra serves any purpose at all.

While many things on our lists would be different, some things would be the same—especially when it comes to understanding God. Because that's something none of us can do. We don't understand why sunshine and rain fall on both the good and the evil. We don't understand earthquakes, tornadoes, and floods. We don't understand why some prayers are answered yes and some are answered no. The fact is this: we simply don't *get* God.

But that's okay.

Among so many things we don't understand, in God's case we don't *have* to understand. We can trust Him even if we can't comprehend Him. We can trust and thank Him for the care we know is coming our way. Understanding is optional.

Thank You, Lord, for being a faithful God whom I can trust, especially when I don't understand.

"I Will Be with You"

"When you pass through the waters, I will be with you; and through the rivers, they shall not overflow you. . . . For I am the LORD your God . . . your Savior."

—Isaiah 43:2–3

When the inevitable storms of life hit, what do you find most reassuring? Often the most helpful resource is someone whose presence alone can calm our fears. Isn't it amazing that God Himself promises to be near when we need Him most?

Now consider who is saying, "I will be with you." Making this promise is almighty God, the Creator of everything. Imagine what you might do if you were mindful 24/7 of His presence with you.

After all, having someone nearby—whether cleaning up the kitchen after a dinner party, facing the precarious financial threat that blindsided us, or dealing with the pressures of life that threaten to crush us—enables us to do things we simply might not do or even consider doing on our own.

Did you notice how personal God's promise is: "I am the LORD *your* God . . . *your* Savior" (emphasis added)? When tough times come, remember that you have more than helpful Scripture and other tools—you have the Lord Almighty.

Thank You, good and gracious God, that You are close even when I can't sense Your presence. Make me aware of You today.

What's in a Name?

"To the one who is victorious, I will give . . . that person a white stone with a new name written on it."

—Revelation 2:17 NIV

In *Romeo and Juliet*, William Shakespeare wrote: "What's in a name? That which we call a rose by any other name would smell as sweet."

Perhaps . . . but if the rose had a heart of its own, it might not *feel* as sweet if it was called, say, *spiderwort* or *skunk cabbage*. There is power in the names we are called, power to lift up and encourage and to belittle and tear down. In Scripture we see the Lord used names to heal, to forgive, and to restore.

Remember the bleeding woman who dared to touch the hem of Jesus' robe, the one who'd been ostracized for years? Jesus called her "Daughter" (Mark 5:34). On another occasion, Jesus told His disciples they were no longer to be called His servants; instead, He named them His friends (John 15:15). And what does God call you, the one who chooses to love and follow Him? With a love so lavish He sacrificed His own Son, God names you His very own child (1 John 3:1). And when your day in heaven comes, He will even give you a new name written on a white stone.

What's in a name? All the love of the Lord.

The names You give to me, Lord, are the ones that make me whole—daughter, friend, child of God.

Do Not Be Afraid

"Don't be frightened."

—Matthew 28:10 *The Message*

How many times did the Lord or one of His angels offer these words to His people? Here are three examples.

1. To the terrified disciples huddled in their storm-tossed boat (Mark 6:50).
2. To Jairus when he heard the news that his beloved daughter was dead (Mark 5:36).
3. To the women who sought their Savior at an empty tomb (Matthew 28:5).

When the Lord or one of His angels appeared to His people, the words "Do not be afraid" were heard (Matthew 28:10). Perhaps it is because the glory of the Lord and His heavenly host were just too majestic for human eyes to behold without fear.

But notice what the Lord did with those words: He comforted, He strengthened, He reassured, and He rescued. He gave life to the lifeless and hope to the hopeless. We can see by the numerous accounts that our Savior does not want us to be afraid. Just as He helped the disciples and all the rest, He helps us—He comforts, strengthens, reassures, and rescues.

I am so grateful for Your presence. Because You are with me, Lord Jesus, I will not be afraid.

Character Matters

Oh, give thanks to the LORD, for He is good!

—1 Chronicles 16:34

With the help of Dr. Charles Stanley, let's reconsider some benefits of being thankful:

- Gratitude keeps us continually aware that the Lord is close by.
- It motivates us to look for His purpose in our circumstance.
- Thanksgiving helps bring our wills into submission to God.
- It reminds us of our continual dependence upon the Lord.
- Thankfulness is an essential ingredient for joy.
- A grateful attitude strengthens our witness to unbelievers.
- Thanking God focuses our attention on Him rather than on our circumstances.
- Gratitude gives us eternal perspective.
- When we're wearied by our circumstances, thanksgiving energizes us.
- Gratitude transforms anxiety into peace, which passes all understanding. (Vertical Living Ministries)

Good always flows from gratitude! So let's pursue a steadfast heart full of thanks.

Lord, whatever life's circumstances, help me keep my eyes on You and choose gratitude.